# AIDS IN PRISON

# AIDS in Prison

Edited by
PHILIP A. THOMAS
and
MARTIN MOERINGS

## Dartmouth

Aldershot • Brookfield USA • Singapore • Sydney

Published by
Dartmouth Publishing Company Limited
Gower House
Croft Road
Aldershot
Hants GU11 3HR
England

Dartmouth Publishing Company
Old Post Road
Brookfield
Vermont 05036
USA

**British Library Cataloguing in Publication Data**
AIDS in Prison
    I. Thomas, Philip A.  II. Moerings, Martin
    365.66

**Library of Congress Cataloging-in-Publication Data**
AIDS in prison / edited by Philip A. Thomas and Martin Moerings.
        p.      cm.
    "Socio-legal studies".
    ISBN 1-85521-297-8
    1. AIDS (Disease)–Epidemiology. 2. Prisoners–Diseases.
3. Correctional institutions. I. Thomas, Philip A. (Philip
Aneurin) II. Moerings, Martin.
    RA644.A25A363584    1994
    614.5'993–dc20
                                                                94-19949
                                                                CIP

ISBN 1 85521 297 8

# CONTENTS

# PREFACE

We wish to recognise and thank certain institutions and individuals for support during the preparation of this collection of essays. The Cardiff Law School, University College of Wales at Cardiff and the Pompe Institute, University of Utrecht were generous in their financial support. In addition, the International Institute for the Sociology of Law, Onàti, Spain, provided financial assistance and a forum in the summer of 1992 which allowed several contributors to meet and discuss the content of the book. Three people, in particular, gave generously of their time. Penny Smith, Sue Campbell and Zafar Khan, of the Cardiff Law School, provided, in their separate ways, skills which improved the quality of the book. Remaining deficiencies must be laid at the doors of the editors.

Philip A. Thomas
Martin Moerings

September 1993

# INTRODUCTION

Since 1981 more than two and a half million cases of AIDS have been registered worldwide. The disease is predicted to claim a further six million lives by the end of the century. A further 13 million adults and adolescents and one million infants are seropositive. The World Health Organisation (WHO) predicts that the total figure of 14 million cumulative infections could almost triple by the end of this decade. Sexual transmission accounts for around 75 per cent of the spread of the disease with heterosexual transmission continuing to rise. Five out of every 11 adults being infected are women and by 1995 the number of new infections will be spread equally between the sexes. It is predicted that one million women were infected in 1993 and by the year 2000, over 13 million women will have been infected, and about four million of them will have died.[1] Even if all new infections were stopped in their tracks now, total AIDS cases would still quadruple by the end of the century. AIDS and HIV infection have reached pandemic proportions in Africa and south east Asia. In seven cities in the USA, including New York and San Francisco, AIDS is now the leading cause of death among men and women between the ages of 25 and 44. Scientists continue to doubt whether an effective vaccine will be available within several years.

The scourge of this disease continues unabated although there are indications that it is suffering from 'news fatigue'. But the horrors pile upon each other and statistics such as those listed above bring home the enormous challenge posed. A major difficulty is convincing the Western public that 'nice' people are at risk. For too long it was portrayed as a disease of the underclasses and deviant groups. Rather like sexual diseases it was seen as involving a degree of negligence, personal responsibility and moral culpability. The idea that 'it could never happen to me' has reduced its impact on society at large. Indeed, it has been argued that the problem will not be allocated its true weight for so long as it is defined as being located within minority groups.[2]

HIV and AIDS make clear, as few medical problems can, the complex interrelationship between political, social, cultural, economic and biological forces. They do not simply represent physical conditions to be dealt with by the health care

---

1 *The Guardian*, 8 September 1993.

2 *E. Carter and S. Watney*, Taking Liberties: AIDS and Cultural Politics (1989) and R. Shilts, *And The Band Played On* (1988).

1

agencies which in turn place certain calls upon state resources. They open a Pandora's box of prejudice, homophobia, racism and xenophobia. We are brought up starkly to confront our own mortality. Our understanding of sexuality, fidelity, normality and morality are challenged. Illnesses, associated with ageing, have been joined by a problem which is found predominately amongst the young and sexually active. Our increasingly science-orientated society faces a virus, which currently defies a galaxy of scientists, searching for answers to the virus and associated illnesses.

HIV and AIDS are often, and incorrectly, located exclusively within 'risk groups'. These marginalised classes include drug users, prostitutes, gay men and the subjects of this book, prisoners. These groups, on the fringe of 'acceptable' Western society, are commonly held responsible for the spread of the virus and for this a heavy price must be paid by the perpetrators. Nevertheless, it must be constantly repeated that the virus is not spread per se by homosexual behaviour nor by drug users. Infection occurs as a consequence of risky practices such as sharing amongst drug users and by indulging in anal or vaginal sexual intercourse without the use of condoms. Thus, it is the practice and not the person which must be examined.

Prisons and their inmates have a special status in the examination of the HIV/AIDS phenomenon. The prison population already has a disproportionately high number of drug users. Whilst incarcerated in single sex institutions prisoners who are overwhelmingly young and sexually active are denied their usual sexual relationships and partners. Even those jurisdictions which allow prison conjugal visits can hardly be described as fulfilling the sexual drive of prisoners in anything other than in its most basic form. Thus, we argue, not only are prisons disproportionately filled by people with special needs in terms of drugs but also the institutions themselves create problems by the rules that apply therein. We argue that the chance of enhanced risk practices is exaggerated by the very fact of being inside a prison. If this is true then we also argue that there rests with those responsible for prison management a duty to ensure that prisoners are kept within a safe environment. This is particularly important as prisoners experience a period of reduced rights and legal capacity whilst in custody. Therefore as their rights are reduced by law so should the legal duties of their custodians in relation to them be commensurately increased.

We offer the following explanation of prison life based on import and deprivation variables. The import model was developed to explain the absence of subcultures in prison. This model relates to traits which have been imported from civil society. Thus, for example, the relative absence of such in Scandinavian prisons was explained by the solitary lives of Scandinavians whereas, in comparison, the existence of subcultures in the US prisons is explained by the corporate lives of Americans. Whilst recognising this analysis as questionable it nevertheless has parallel value for the purposes of this book. Namely, how far can HIV and AIDS inside the prison wall be explained exclusively as a problem created within prison as opposed to societal features being imported into the prison environment?

DRUG ABUSE

We consider two examples of the import model. The first is the issue of drug users which indicates that users are in prison because they committed illegal acts such as theft and robbery in order to sustain their drug requirements. They may be inept criminals because of their drug habits and therefore end in prison. They also become recidivists because of the financial demands associated with drug dependence. In addition, the prison is an alienating institution within which close personal relationships are difficult to forge and maintain. The stripping away of self esteem and autonomy by the prison regime may encourage the use of drugs as a form of mental escapism. What we see is the collection of drug users and pushers who constitute a collection of experience, sources and need within one alienating institution. A criminal dragnet trawls civil society and the catch is landed in prison. Therefore, it is unsurprising that the percentage of seropositive drug users who enter the prison system is relatively high and that there is a continuation of behaviour practiced outside the walls.

## SEX BETWEEN MEN

The second example is sexual activity within prisons and in particular homosexual behaviour. In some countries, including the United Kingdom, the age of consent between men is higher than that between men and women. In addition, indecent behaviour in public focuses, in police practice, on activities between men thereby resulting in selective law enforcement. For example, in the United Kingdom gay men seeking sexual contacts in parks or public lavatories are more likely to be arrested than heterosexuals or lesbians acting in a similar fashion. Thus the social values of society are reflected in the prison population. Given that the virus has appeared disproportionately among the gay community the targeting of gay men by the police will again increase the number of homosexuals in prison. Alongside the regular homosexuals are those prisoners who cross over for the period of their incarceration. The circumstances of the prison regime are such that the single sex institution encourages some men to seek sexual satisfaction, and sometimes comfort, from other men.

The process of selective law enforcement, as illustrated by our two examples, has a bearing on our subject matter. Prisons are disproportionately filled by ethnic minorities, the unemployed, the undereducated and the young. Those 'criminals' who damage the social environment, commit fraud and white collar crime, or bribe civil servants seldom enter prison. Thus, as Michel Foucault has stated, prisons have the function of focusing attention on the crimes of the lower classes thereby redirecting attention from the activities of the powerful in society. Prisoners are negative role models who must be despised and rejected. The prison constitutes a wedge between the classes.

The deprivation model offers an alternative explanation to that of the import model. It resolves patterns of prison behaviour by stating that they are a consequence of the prison itself and in particular arise out of the deprivation which accompanies imprisonment. The most striking description is that provided by Ervin Goffman in his book *Total Institutions*. In prison the person looses his or her identity which is replaced by a prison number. Personal choice is severely restricted. Freedom of movement is closely controlled. Personal space virtually disappears as it is compressed by the institution and invaded by strangers. Clothes are removed and replaced by a common uniform. The social roles of father, mother, son, daughter, lover, friend, sportsperson are removed and replaced by the role of inmate. The individual disappears as the prisoner is created by the prison. For this new person the externally created legal rules have less importance than the internally constructed social norms which dictate the operation of daily routines and life within the prison. Legal rights enforceable through the courts have less practical value than the discretion exercised by the prison officers in their routine management of the system.

Both the examples of drugs and homosexual practice indicate that we should be seeking an explanation which neither depends exclusively on the import nor the deprivation model. To do so would fail to recognise that our examples are a product of both civil and institutional life. The institutional nature of prison creates special pressures and thereby special needs for the inmates whilst civil activity produces a selective prison population which falls into the high risk practice category when considering HIV and AIDS. Nevertheless, if the rationale of imprisonment is to protect civil society from the dangerous classes then the role is simply to incarcerate through selective incapacitation. This results in targetted groups of anti-social people being locked away to reduce the risk to society. Within such a strategy health, rehabilitation and resocialisation have little or no place and, in particular, the physical and moral welfare of prisoners, locked away in dangerous places, may also be ignored.

## DRUGS INSIDE AND OUTSIDE PRISONS

The legal and social responses to drug usage in civil society are reflected in the prison regime. This suggests that the import model has an impact on prison behaviour. If needle exchange programmes and methadone-buses operate in the city then it is likely that the prison environment is more liberal and responsive to the problems faced by drug users. For example, in the Netherlands there is official tolerance concerning drug issues which is carried forward into the prisons where there are drug-free units and active methadone programmes. Thus, the more aware and tolerant is civil society the more likely it is that the prison will operate complementary policies.

## INFORMATION AND PROBLEMS

Before a problem can be analysed and solved it must first be identified as a problem. For example, the surgeon does not remove an appendix simply because it is there but because, as a result of clinical diagnosis, it has been identified as problematic. Evidence is required and not simply hunches, prejudice, rumours or phobias. Anything less than hard evidence may be dismissed, ignored or paid scant attention.

The recognition of a problem occurs within a political context. As Bulmer has argued social problems are not objective givens, the existence of which cannot be questioned.[3] Rather, the definition of the social problem arises out of a political process which is affected but not dominated by objective reality. The transformation of the occurrence into a public issue and the conflict between interested parties in the definitional process can produce different effects on participants and policy. We suggest that, according to available but disparate evidence, there is a serious health risk in prisons but official, political recognition has yet to be granted in similar terms.

---

3 H. Bulmer, 'Social problems as collective behaviour' 18 (1971) *Social Behaviour* 298.

In addition, we argue that public debate about the causes of the problem has been stifled and misdirected by the lack of official data. The government departments responsible for prison management and policy are the custodians of official reality and also the gatekeepers to effective research and data gathering. Without the willingness of the gatekeepers to open the prison gates to researchers then information will of necessity remain schematic, incomplete, anecdotal, personal and impressionistic. The authors have, where possible, referred to alternative realities as supplied by unofficial sources and in particular to the prisoners themselves. Although the voices of the underclasses are weak and tainted by criminality they are voices which should be heard. Thus, we are faced with competing realities representing competing truths reflecting different political agendas. The contributors to this book have, where ever possible, acted to make audible the voices of those who have little or no political muscle or public credibility: the prisoners.

## INTERNATIONAL STANDARDS

Individuals are committed to prison as punishment and not for punishment. It is the deprivation of liberty which acts as the formal punishment, and, apart from this, prisoners should retain as many civil rights as possible. This view was promoted in the Golder case at the European Court of Human Rights.[4] The judgment explicitly rejected the theory that a prison sentence in itself involves a number of obvious limitations which exceed the mere physical deprivation of liberty. Moreover, this is the starting point for many regulations which deal with prisoners' rights. Thus, in principle, prisoners' rights to privacy and to their physical integrity should be respected. This also includes the right to health care at a standard offered within civil society. This 'equivalence principle' applied to health care has been developed by Harding[5] and is embodied, inter alia, in the European Prison Rules, the WHO Guidelines 1993,[6] and adopted domestically, for example, by the British Medical Association and the General Medical Council. Furthermore, in 1990 the 8th United Nations Congress on the Prevention of Crime and the Treatment of Offenders recommended to member states that they implement the WHO's AIDS strategy in their national prison systems.

However, we consider that prisoners are not simply entitled to equivalent care: their status requires it. The prison environment, with a primary purpose of control and containment, represents a tangible threat to the physical, mental and emotional well-being of inmates. All prisoners are susceptible to HIV infection by virtue of their particular environment. It is of even greater relevance to prisoners who are already confirmed as HIV positive or who have AIDS.[7]

---

4 Golder v. United Kingdom (1975) 1 EHRR 524.

5 T. Harding, *Health in Prisons* in 10 Council of Europe Prison Information Bulletin (1987), 9.

6 Section 1 'All prisoners have the right to receive health care, including preventative measures, equivalent to that available in the community without discrimination, in particular in respect to their legal status or nationality.' *WHO Guidelines on HIV Infection and AIDS in Prisons*, WHO, (March 1993).

7 P.A. Thomas and R. Costigan, *Health Care or Punishment?: Prisoners with HIV/AIDS* 31 (1992), The Howard Journal of Criminal Justice, 321.

## CONCLUSION

The contributors to this book have brought together both the theory and the actual operational practices affecting prisons in a number of jurisdictions. It is perhaps surprising to read how a virus which respects no political boundaries has produced such different responses. We hope that the provision of basic information from several Western-style countries provides a contribution to the development of best practices in managing the control of HIV and AIDS. We are anxious that within this process of better management the actual inhabitants of prison, the prisoners themselves, are given a say, their views respected and thereafter acted upon. In addition, we see in this collection of national responses broader views on how prison management and prisoners are perceived and treated. The HIV virus, in this sense, becomes a test case for the manner in which prisons are perceived, organised and operated both within the bureaucratic structures and also within the wider society.

# AIDS IN PRISONS IN NORWAY

LILL SCHERDIN
*Department of Criminology,*
*University of Oslo*

The Norwegian population has not been as severely affected by AIDS as has been the case in many other countries. In 1991 some 1,120 people were known to be HIV positive and 252 had been diagnosed with AIDS. 170 were already dead. The increase in the infection rate over recent years appears to be stable. In the first six months of 1992 new HIV positives registered numbered 56 compared with 62 in the same period of 1991. Among drug users the earlier exponential increase curve has flattened out. The increase in HIV diagnosed persons is no longer increasing and the numbers of infected drug users has decreased slightly. In 1989 they numbered 24 and in 1990 dropped to 18 and in 1991 some 13 new cases of infection among drug users were reported.[1]

Nevertheless, the arrival of AIDS in Norway shocked the nation. The unpredictability of life and security, especially for the young and the middle classes well used to high-prediction success, was disturbing. The security of society was damaged but it was felt that order symbolised, for example, by the prison system would prevail. But not even the penal institutions were immune and were in turn affected and changed by the virus.

## PRISONS AND PRISONERS

Historically, a feature of Norwegian prison policy has been the low rate of incarceration coupled with the relatively short sentences imposed. In 1991 Norway had 56 prisoners per 100,000 inhabitants, a figure approached only by a few countries such as Japan, Iceland and the Netherlands. But like other European countries and the USA the figure is rising.

Norway's population is around four million. In absolute terms this also means that the number of prisoners is low and the prison system is small. In 1990 there was an average of 2,379 prisoners in prison. This represents a highpoint in the graphical prison population curve when drawn from 1970 to 1990. In 1970 prisoners numbered below 1,700, including 30 per cent in custody. After a temporary rise in the early 1970s the prison population stabilized between 1,700 and 1,800. In the early 1980s the

---

1 National Institute of Public Health, SIFF, 1992.

numbers again began to rise. Four per cent of the prison population in 1990 was female and approximately 25 per cent of all prisoners were on remand.[2]

Prison sentences are relatively short with 57 per cent being three months or less. For murder, serious drug offences and rape the average sentences are seven years and three months, three years and three months and three years and two months. Although the increase in the average number of prisoners since 1970 is reflected in a greater number of shorter terms of imprisonment[3] the number of new prison sentences has actually decreased, at an even rate, from 1974 to 1989. This means the trend to give longer sentences is the reason for the growing prison population. This trend reflects the punitive AIDS in Prisons in Norway concern over drugs and reflects the priority given by the police to these issues.[4] The situation in 1990 was that the proportion of sanctions connected with theft (previously the most frequent offence) has diminished considerably since 1970. In total, 65 per cent and 57 per cent of the cases in 1970 and 1980, respectively, were concerned with theft, as compared with 36 per cent in 1990. Over the same period the proportion of drug cases has displayed a corresponding increase.[5] Cases involving drugs constituted 3 per cent, 6.5 per cent and 20 per cent of all offences respectively in 1970, 1980 and 1990. In turn, the prison population increasingly reflects these growing drug charges and research indicates that those charged are often themselves drug users. Thus, with more drug users going into prison for longer sentences the stage is set for an HIV 'problem' in Norwegian prisons.

On average, 1,500 prisoners are detained in closed, national prisons while those serving six months or less serve the time in local, smaller prisons. This chapter concentrates on three main national prisons: Ullersmo, Ila Landsfengel and Bredveit Kvinnefengsel, as well as the largest local prison, Oslo Kretsfengsel, which houses a disproportionate number of people on drugs related offences.[6]

All closed prisons are subject to the national Prison Regulations prepared by the Prison Board in the Ministry of Justice. In practice, however, there are differences between these four prisons.[7] The similarities, as well as the differences, between these prisons are important. They are the disciplinary trendsetters for the smaller, local prisons as they are able to influence the Ministry of Justice and its national prison policy.

---

2 Norwegian Crime Statistics, 1990. All data hereafter comes from this report unless otherwise stated.

3 These are mostly up to three months for sentences concerning theft and drunk driving.

4 Norway outstrips other Scandinavian countries in the length of sentences imposed for drugs offences.

5 A criminal found guilty of several crimes is recorded under the most serious of them. Thus it does not necessarily follow there is less theft as the drug conviction may mask lesser offences such as theft.

6 Most drug users live in the Oslo area and a sentence of six months or less will ensure incarceration in Oslo Kretsfengsel.

7 These prisons have 'contract wards' that are designed 'to give prisoners, under certain conditions, the opportunity to serve their sentence in a drug-free environment with a greater freedom than is available to other prisoners.' On average around 143 prisoners were in these 'wards' in 1990.

PRISON REGIMES BEFORE AIDS AND PRE-1989

Prison regimes frame and influence the form and content of human relationships within, and even outside, the prison walls. I now consider who could meet with whom and in what circumstances at the time of the recognition of AIDS.

The prison regime is one where each night a prisoner has his or her own cell. During the daytime prisoners may work, study or associate with each other. The origins of the present programme are found in the earlier scheme where prisoners were not separated, followed by a scheme, which was never fully implemented, wherein prisoners were segregated for 24 hours. Thus, the present scheme mixes both programmes. Without personal contact with others the term 'privacy', itself a strange term within a prison environment, changes to isolation with associated negative consequences. On the other hand, without privacy at night prisoners are more liable to bullying and domination practices.

Although the Prison Act 1958 provides access to collective prison life as a fundamental right for prisoners it has not, in practice, been interpreted as such. The regulations offer a number of opportunities for prisoners to be isolated: 'Where the collective treatment cannot be used or is not found to be suitable, the prisoners will receive single room treatment.'[8] Other regulations allow prisoners to seek isolation and it may also occur as punishment. At Ullersmo research shows that the largest group of isolated prisoners were there for 'prison reasons' such as narcotics use and possession, attempted escapes, failure to return from home leave and disciplinary issues.[9] The average isolation period was one month. However, Oslo Kretsfengsel which was built in the heyday of single cell thinking still has restricted possibilities for collective life. The consequence is that the single cell nocturnal system limits the time and space available for co-operation around drug usage as well as homosexual practices and sex between men.[10] These limitations also affect involuntary sexual activity such as male rape.

THE PRISON REGIME: PRISONERS AND CIVIL SOCIETY

The issues of privacy and collectivity within prison are also affected by the relationships that prisoners have with those located outside the institution. Home and prison visits, telephone conversations and correspondence have a bearing on the individual's planning for the future. Here, special attention is placed on the issue of prison leaves (or 'fremstilleinger' which means accompanied by prison officers or the police) and also includes medical visits. Some of the visits include the possibility of sexual relationships and thereby the transfer of HIV. On the other hand, these visits are important to the psychological well being of prisoners who may be under reduced pressure to seek sexual encounters with other prisoners.

Prior to 1989 the rules were interpreted to allow prisoners visits from 'people close to them' and 'people it would be important for them to have contact with' for at

---

8 Prison Act 1958.

9 Prisoner Research I and II, 1983 in Eskeland, 1988.

10 The term 'sex between men' is used to avoid drawing a distinction between those who would be leading a heterosexual life outside prison and those who would lead a homosexual life in civil society.

least an hour a week.[11] However, visits could be refused if 'there were special reasons to believe that the visit could involve irregular behaviour'. This meant that the visit could not be controlled in an acceptable form. The unacceptable behaviour was associated with prior incidents and related to specific individuals. No groups of people were considered, *a priori*, ineligible to visit.

## VISITS AND LEAVES

The Prison Law 1958 does not forbid conjugal visits. In practice, Ullersmo, Bredtveit and Ila have suites for such visits. However, these rooms are not totally private as officers may look in from time to time. The situation, limited time, tension and uninviting accommodation often result in the room being used as an opportunity solely to talk. This is particularly true amongst the women imprisoned at Bredtveit but less common amongst the men at Ullersmo where the visits are less controlled and a curtain may be used by the prisoner for increased privacy. Consequently, in theory, homosexual partners may also use this suite for sexual contact.

Leave is granted from prison after one third of the sentence is completed. This is a discretionary process exercised by prison authorities. However, within the regulations there is an assumption that reasons must be given if leave is denied. The maximum period is 18 days a year and 24 days for those on contract wards. The maximum block of leave is five days which is normally unsupervised. 'Welfare leaves' are also allowed for special occasions such as weddings and funerals. In addition, leave is granted for educational programmes unavailable within the prison.

Leave for medical treatment is based on the right to receive such treatment as if prisoners were members of the public. If the prison medical service is unable to provide treatment then the prisoner may be given leave. However, this relies heavily upon the diagnostic skills of prison medical staff as well as the ability and willingness to seek and arrange alternative treatment.

Prison regulations permit prisoners both to receive visits and enjoy leave. Indeed, it might be argued that the rules provided a status of granting limited rights for facilities to maintain relationships within and outside the prison walls. However, with the coming of AIDS how were these regulations interpreted and practiced?

## PRISON AUTHORITY-RELATIONSHIPS IN THE SHADOW OF DISCRETION

The operation of discretion in closed spaces, where power is unequally distributed, is particularly subject to abuse. Whether the question is collectivity or isolation, visits with or without sex, the granting of provisional leave or medical care, the prison authorities make decisions within wide limits of discretion. It may be exercised arbitrarily or systematically as a control mechanism for prisoners labelled as 'difficult'. Eskeland's study of the operation of prison rules in Norway shows that the rule of law was tortuous to follow because of the intervention of wide ranging discretion. The study shows that the discretionary power exists as a continuous dark

---

11 Normally the prison practice was not to interpret the rules narrowly in terms of time, numbers of visitors nor 'importance' of the visitors. (Eskeland, 1988, NOU *The New Prison Law*, 1988. Some prisoners tell contradictory stories.

backdrop responding to the prisoners' stories of isolation, loneliness, anger and despair. However, it is in the area of the right to health care that the law is clearest. The rules state that the prison authorities shall provide adequate medical care. Nevertheless, even this right has been subject to deviation and by 1980 the authorities were obliged to address the issue.

## TWO AUTHORITIES, TWO DISCRETIONARY PROCESSES

There were two problems to be addressed within the prison system. The first was the improper exercise of discretion by prison authorities on health issues and, secondly, there was an inadequate provision of health care. It was argued that the medical staff should no longer be employed by the Ministry of Justice but should become part of the civilian health employment programme. Prison health programmes should become part of the national health structure in order to achieve parity in patient service. In 1980 agreement was reached between the Ministry of Health and Social Affairs and the Ministry of Justice.

The change took several years and, inter alia, produced a different outlook and spirit. A new authority was introduced to prison life. Given the relevance of medicine to issues of isolation, hygiene, overcrowding and the effects of punishment its impact was widespread. There emerged the dynamic of two independent authorities with different methods of exercising discretion according to different criteria and priorities. The issue of AIDS occurred during this period. Many asked what better flagship could the health authorities require in the battle for change than the principle of saving lives from the AIDS epidemic? Sailing in on the wave of AIDS prevention should, it was felt, provide support for major change.

## DATA GATHERING: A PREVENTION POLICY EMERGES

As the AIDS issue was being identified between 1984 and 1985 many prisoners were found to be HIV positive after taking voluntary tests. Of 70 men tested at Oslo Kretsfengsel 10 per cent were found to be seropositive. As these were prototests the results were watched closely by various authorities and agencies. The period between 1985 and 1987 was formative in terms of national prevention policy. Conservative forces demanded obligatory testing on the grounds that a complete view was required to establish a prevention policy. Their policy required far reaching legal involvement permitting the use of force in the name of treatment or punishment. The most extreme proposals demanded in the press were the isolation of infected people for an indeterminate time, tattooing sexual organs or banishment to isolated areas. Others supported voluntary testing in order not to drive infected people underground. It was argued that this test would provide a clearer view of infection and risk rates. In turn, the chances of reaching at risk and infected people were greater through this approach. Official policy was based on this methodology.

## DATA GATHERING

Although the voluntary approach was successful in civil society a similar struggle occurred within prison which, for example, split officers and inmates at Oslo

Kretsfengsel. Members of both sections were concerned given that 44 per cent of prisoners admitted to drug usage. The conservative approach recommended isolation in special HIV wards and indentifying those who were seropositive. In Oslo Kretsfengsel, for a short period in 1985, the prisoners demanded this form of isolation and were in a special section of ward B - 'Bayern'. However, education and awareness reduced the alarm of prisoners and the demand for isolation was withdrawn.[12] Oslo Kretsfengsel, with an average of 350 prisoners and a large throughput of prisoners, 1,900 every year, was the most turbulent prison. The situation in Bredtveit, Ullersmo and Ila Landsfengel, was more settled although somewhat different.[13]

In 1986 it was officially accepted that drug use occurred within prisons and this affected the discussions over AIDS. This issue was openly debated in the press, the Ministry of Justice and also within the prisons. Research in 1987 headed by Liv Finstad confirmed that drug usage occurred in prisons with the lowest proportion of drug users: Ila Landsfengel. Prisoners and those released stated that drugs were used and prison statistics for punishments and discoveries of drugs provided additional evidence. Sex between men was also acknowledged as a possibility although research findings were unavailable on this matter. After an initiative of the Ministry of Health and Social Affairs, the Prison Board stated in 1986 that 'the principles guiding the treatment of, and attitude towards, HIV infected people in society generally should, as far as possible, be valid also within the prison society'.[14]

In Norway homosexual organisations have profiled themselves as experts in matters of prevention and have been leaders in these activities. In addition, the Ministry of Health and Social Affairs has supported them, both financially and professionally, through the 'Directorate of Health'. From saunas to clubs, from toilets to parks, the gay community has been active in its educational function. Support groups have been formed which adopted such activities as role playing in risk situations. The aim was to develop common viewpoints and a common language to express these experiences. It was further hoped for change in collective and cultural patterns of action as' well as changes to individual behaviour. These activities have impacted on prisons through 'The Prison Project'.

The Prison Project, which lasted from August 1987 to August 1989, was financed for one year by the Ministry of Justice and thereafter by the Ministry of Health and Social Affairs. The Project took as its starting point the main principles guiding the general AIDS prevention campaign in Norway. It was devised to address prisoners generally, drug users specifically and those who worked within prisons. The aim was to educate, support and care for those in need. Another purpose was to encourage people to take the test thereby having a better epidemiological understanding. Such knowledge would allow for better strategic planning.

The Project concentrated on the same prisons as mentioned previously in this chapter. Independent experts, unconnected with the prison system, worked with

---

12 Summary and Evaluation of the Prison Project, May 1989. The following data comes from this source unless otherwise stated.

13 Ila had, by far, the fewest HIV positive prisoners and Bredtveit had the largest proportion. This was probably a result of the female prisoners themselves either being drug users, having had lovers who were drug users or having taken part in sex work, or a combination of these factors.

14 The Prison Board, 12 December 1986.

prisoners on preventative and psycho-social matters. It was considered important to work with prisoners as it was realised that some would revert to previous habits on release.

Building on the prevention model designed by the Association of Homosexuals against AIDS it was decided to co-operate with a project for former drug users called UNIK. The intention was to employ former drug users as co-leaders of the support groups amongst the HIV positive prisoners. Their personal knowledge and credibility amongst prisoners gave them enhanced status and thereby effectiveness. It would also enhance the feeling of self determination for prisoners. Change became their own responsibility and their own individual and collective victory.

## PRISON PROJECT RESULTS

The entire population in the national prisons, Ullersmo, Bredtveit and Ila were tested, during the years 1985 to 1989. The tests were voluntary. In 1985/86 nine new cases of HIV positive prisoners were found in Bredtveit, one in Ila and four at Ullersmo. Between 1987/89 only one new seropositive was found at each of the prisons. Oslo Kretsfengsel was especially important because of the high turnover of prisoners. This was thought likely to provide information that could be applied to the general society. There were problems with the provision of the test but about a third of drug users were tested. Sixty-five per cent of those tested admitted to using drugs. All the HIV positives were found in this latter group. A minimum prevalence of 10 per cent was found among the drug users. At this time the official estimate was that 70-80 per cent of drug users outside prison had been tested and the prevalence in the entire group was estimated at around 7 per cent. The higher percentage in prison accorded with the belief that the hardest, most active users with the longest user careers were in prison. A research project in Oslo police jail established that 13 per cent of the users there were seropositive.[15] No one who tested negative and thereafter was retested in prison converted to seropositive. This evidence, together with the follow-up test one year after the project, indicates that the rate of prison infection might be no higher than that outside. However, it is beyond dispute that prisoners have been infected through needle sharing.

## PRISON RISK BEHAVIOUR

The Project established that in prison there are a few syringes shared by many users. There appeared to be some effort to ensure that those who were seropositive only shared with infected prisoners but this was not always possible. In addition, the users were not sure about their health status.

There is virtually no data about sex between men in prison. There was only one homosexual HIV positive prisoner. No instances of rape have been reported through official or unofficial channels. This is no guarantee that such happenings have not occurred although the single cell at night system supports the belief that rape is not widespread.

---

15 Skog og Skretting, 1987.

Risk behaviour could also occur during conjugal visits. Prisoners felt that talk of condoms and infection could exacerbate feelings of estrangement and humiliation between partners. Females who were prostitutes felt the use of condoms with their lovers weakened the emotional bond as these were reserved for customers.

In meetings with officers they expressed concern about open wounds, whether obtained through illness, accidents or fighting, as this increased the risk of infection.

There seems to be agreement, inside certain limits, on the risk behaviour within prison although the level is questionable. The uncertainty as to the amount however has not been used to advocate a different official prevention policy.

## PRISON PROJECT PREVENTION STRATEGIES

The first prevention rule was that everyone in prison was to be treated as if they were infected. This rule included the officers. This had important consequences for hygiene and safety precautions through accidents, fights or in general daily activity. It meant that bleach should be generally available for the immediate cleaning of all kinds of bloodstains or body liquid spillage. It was also to be available for cleaning cells. It meant that bleach was available to clean the syringes in an unproblematic manner. Although clean needles were advocated the Prison Board had indicated in 1986 that this was unacceptable.

The assumption was that sex between men occurred in prison as it did outside prison. Therefore, condoms should be available both in the visiting rooms and in the cells.

Two prisoners from Berg - a local prison - had been employed by the Health Authorities to make an educational video film entitled 'HIV in Prison'. It gave clear, practical advice on cleaning needles and using condoms. It was to be generally available in all prisons.

## TREATMENT

Health officials were to provide immediate support and counselling after a prisoner had been identified as seropositive. Prison support groups were to be continued. Each HIV prisoner should have an independent medical contact outside the prison that has regular contact and acts as a hospital link person. This person was to work with the prison medical staff. Extra help, such as sheets for night sweats, were to be available and, finally, special rules covering pardon for people with HIV/ARC and AIDS were proposed.

In 1990 the Prison Board issued new instructions which adopted many of the recommendations laid out in the Prison Project. Each prison was instructed to make concrete regulations concerning hygiene. Every person was to be treated as if HIV positive and chlorine or bleach was to be available to prisoners for purposes of disinfection.[16] It was stated that condoms should be available in the cells as well as the visiting rooms and the educational video should be available. Each prisoner should receive information on HIV and AIDS on reception to prison. People with AIDS should not be detained in prison. HIV positives should be given priority for transport

---

16 The Prison Board, Rundskriv 8/90.

to hospitals and should receive such additional bedding and clothing requirements as necessary.

## PRISON PRACTICE AND THE PRISON PROJECT

At the time of writing almost three years has passed since the Prison Project was ended and exactly two years since the Prison Board sent the new instructions listed above. The policy has remained unchanged. I now examine the current prison situation as experienced by prisoners.

## PRISON INTERVIEWS

I interviewed seven prisoners, all of whom had received information about HIV/AIDS. Only two stated they had seen the educational video despite the fact that it had received special mention in 1990 by the Prison Board.

Their experiences on the confidentiality of blood tests varied. There had been complaints concerning breach of confidentiality although these have been challenged by other prisoners and medical staff.[17] It was suggested that some prisoners had leaked the information of their health status but in addition the positive differential treatment, such as extra bedding, food and counselling, identified HIV positive prisoners. Some prisoners felt that information was spread on a need to know basis through the staff while other prisoners had total trust in the medical staff's commitment to confidentiality. Health personnel denied any breaches of confidentiality.

The prisoners indicated that in the matter of blood spillage none of the prisons mentioned in this chapter had introduced new rules governing hygiene and no reasons had been offered. Despite the self interest of the officers new routines were not explicitly created although a model regulation was made at one of the smaller, local prisons and attached to the Instructions of 1990 as an illustration of how it might be achieved. However, arrangements in the different prisons were not fully in accordance with the model regulations and prisoners were not included in any explicit, collective action scheme in case of blood spillage as was stated in the model regulation.

I questioned prisoners about availability of condoms and chlorine. Although not available discreetly at the place of use condoms were generally obtainable. In some prisons the inmates had to request sheets and condoms from an officer outside the visiting room. This proved to be too embarrassing for some prisoners and their partners.[18]

No prisoner indicated that chlorine was easily or widely available although access to it was possible through the prisoner in charge of cleaning. Each prisoner thought that there would be no difficulty in obtaining bleach though none had tried.

Prisons had different local policies on bleach. At Bredtveit female prison the officers state that if the prisoners mixed too much cholrine with water a chemical reaction would occur thereby making it a dangerous substance. Toilets and wash basins became very dirty and the female prisoners collectively requested bleach. This

---

17 See, the Prisoners' Union Journal, *Kretslopet*, No. 3, October 1990.

18 Only male prisoners are allowed condoms in their cells.

was denied. It was later claimed that giving access to bleach would be signalling 'the wrong thing'. It might be interpreted as supporting the use of drugs in prison rather than promoting the health of the prisoners. This dichotomy has been played out in civil society. Similar issues have been debated which include, for instance, the responsibility for others as well as one's own welfare.[19] Such considerations underpinned the recommendations of the Prison Project that led, in turn, to the instruction of the Prison Board. This was not, however, how some of the prisons interpreted the instructions of the Prison Board in 1990.

In Ullersmo officials stated that chlorine could be used as a weapon against inmates and officers. It was therefore seen as a security risk. Once again, security and order were used as the justification for the exercise of discretionary judgements. In Oslo Kretsfengsel, one of the departments argued that if chlorine was mixed with the urine test the results would be worthless. Thus, it could be used to sabotage testing and therefore should be forbidden.

## URINE TESTING AND CONTROLLING PRISONERS

Concern over drug usage within prisons in Norway has risen dramatically and has reached a point where prison management revolves around controlling the taking of drugs. Drug use, since 1988, is checked on a systematic, regular but unannounced basis. Urine tests are taken by all prisoners. A negative test is the necessary licence for meetings with other prisoners. Enjoyment of prison community life is based upon the finding of non use of drugs. This control includes prison visiting and recreational opportunities. There are prisoners who have 'contracted' to take regular drug tests and those who refuse are kept in isolation. Drug control within prison management has the same high status as security and prison order. All other concerns are considered secondary. One prisoner informed the author: 'It is piss that decides' and another stated: 'I thought all the time that blood was going to be the thing but this whole merry go round turns on piss.'

Prisoners could not understand how bleach could affect urine tests given the stringent controls exercised over the testing process. Prisoners are removed from the cells and given the equipment by the officers who are present throughout the test. 'Bleach, being in liquid form, cannot even be transported under a finger nail as they claim some detergents have in the past. But, the system is such the officers have no real duty to counter our arguments or even to listen to them. They just say whatever comes into their heads at that moment and that is the end of it.'[20]

The urine test was not part of the stricter regulations launched as the new prison policy package in 1989 and confirmed as a total revision of Prison Regulations in 1992. But the urine tests were included in the evaluation research of the new restrictions, because the reactions to the urine test system were strong amongst prisoners. They felt it seriously affected their general living conditions. One said: 'I am not taking a urine test. This is a conscious choice. I am not a whore selling my soul. Is it really possible to use the collective life of prisoners as a weapon against

---

19 A. Prieur, 2 *Love between men in the time of AIDS* Pax, Oslo, 1988. L. Scherdin, *Sproyten som sprak* (The message of the syringe, or the syringe speaks) 1990.
20 Communication of prisoner to author, 1992.

drugs? Is this human? I have never used drugs but to give urine to be able to talk with people, no thank you! Because I refuse to give urine I am isolated 23 hours a day. This is crazy if you ask me.'[21] Another prisoner said 'It feels awfully difficult to stand in front of the officer to give urine but I am forced to go through with it in order to be allowed to associate with other prisoners. When I think I can be called down at any time to take a urine test ... it is constantly in the back of my mind. I don't use any form of drugs so I am not afraid that the test will be positive.'[22] Some prisoners indicated that they suffered from a psychological block which resulted in an inability to urinate in front of the officers.

Similar reactions were experienced as a result of the new strip search procedures. These are undertaken on a random but regular basis after visits. One prisoner said: 'It's unbelievably humiliating to strip after the visit. It is difficult for me to stand naked in front of adults. It influences the whole atmosphere of the visit. I cannot relax because I know I will have to undress.' Another one said: 'I feel disgusted by the fact that I have to strip after the visit. It is extremely humiliating.' Another prisoner said: 'Sometimes I feel like a prostitute when I have to undress before grown men.' One sixth of the interviewed group had refused visits because they refused to strip in these circumstances.

The subject of prisoners' visits and leave illustrates how changes are occurring in every aspect of prison life. There is now a category of people considered ineligible, under the new rules, to enter the prison as visitors. This category includes former prisoners and those who are thought to have connections with narcotics. The result is that some prisoners are denied contact with close friends, lovers or family, although in the latter category special permission may be granted. One result is that bureaucratic procedures have been extended in the length of time they are effective and also in their invasiveness of the prisoners' limited privacy. All visits are, in principle, controlled, resulting in sexual encounters, during supposedly uncontrolled visits, becoming less attractive. In practice, even under the new system, uncontrolled visits are supposed to occur after a given time based upon the assessed risk element of each prisoner. But this turns the former system on its head as prior to 1985 explicit reasons were to be given by staff if the visits were to be controlled and that no visit was to be controlled beyond a level proven to be necessary. One sixth of the prisoners interviewed no longer accepted visits subject to these controls and one sixth of family and friends stated their reluctance to visit because of the degradation to which they were subjected. The quality of the meetings had suffered as they are routinely monitored. In turn, telephone calls and letters are also regulated. The prisoners indicated that these controls restrict the expression of their feelings. Talks and letters were much more guarded in the awareness of 'the third ear or eye'. The level of satisfaction and intensity of meetings, already conducted in difficult circumstances, was greatly reduced by this surveillance.

In addition, prison leave has also been limited. One prisoner stated: 'I simply cannot understand that they have cut back on the number of leaves. The leave was my only chance to be in physical contact with my cohabitant and now my chance to see

---

21 Innsattes evalueringsgruppe, 1990. The following data comes from this research unless otherwise stated.
22 Ibid.

her is reduced to an absolute minimum. I cannot see this as in any way constructive. The leave was the only real chance of preparing for release, for a place to live, for work, etc. Now they have cut down on the only real rehabilitative possibility that existed.' Another inmate said: 'Do they really intend to isolate us completely? I am afraid life outside will be utterly strange to me when I come out.' Another said: 'It was the intention that leaves should function as bridges to life outside the walls - shall they burn the bridges down?'

As I have stated earlier in this chapter, privacy and togetherness give meaning to each other both within and outside prison. Self image is affected by this dualism. Prisoners are thereby concerned about the quality of their meetings with people from the outside. If the situation is damaged so is the quality of their dignity and ability to step back into society upon release. The sense of loss amongst the prisoners is clear. In reply they display anger and despair but in private they shed tears.

## AIDS, HIV AND TEARS

I discussed the importance of creating good habits through personal control of the intake of drugs or regulating one's sex life. Self control develops self reliance, self respect and dignity, both individually and collectively. The opposite is to create or endorse bad habits. If the above possibilities are denied to prisoners it may produce carelessness and denials of responsibility. Having been careless with the use of a syringe makes one feel that it is less meaningful to be careful during sex and vice versa. The present life, that is prison life, takes on greater importance as the vision of a future life, outside prison, is clouded by increased official control. With the disappearance of the future, current risk taking activities become increasingly acceptable to inmates.

The general character of the closed prison might already enhance these circles of powerlessness and the specific developments outlined in this chapter might support these 'evil circles'. Compared with prisons in other countries, where conditions are much worse, the description of the Norwegian prisoners' strong reactions to comparatively small changes also tells us about the humiliating and identity-altering experiences prisoners in general are undergoing.

## CONCLUSION

Prison life in Norway has changed in recent years. Paradoxically, as AIDS prevention activities have opened up prisons to external pressures there has been a dark undercurrent running in the opposite direction.

Finally, I address two issues both of which are related to seeing AIDS as a 'critical incidence'. AIDS, as 'the same' happened in all western countries and all prison systems at approximately the same time. This allows for comparisons to be made as to how different countries and jurisdictions reacted to the same issue. AIDS must be recognised as a special 'critical incident' because of its incurable and terminal nature. Yet the method of transfer is known, especially to those in control of prisons, and risk reduction, as compared with other epidemics, is simple and cheap. Condoms, needles and bleach are both cheap and simple to employ. Risk reduction is not simply a matter of economics and massive public expenditure. Therefore, it opens up the issue more clearly to an ethical debate.

Thus, my first point is that if AIDS is viewed as an extraordinary critical incident, it can be argued that the reactions chosen, with a corresponding extraordinary ethical clarity, can be said to mirror the ethical image of each society and of each prison system. By careful study of this special threat there emerges a fundamental evaluation of an ethical character - the general human decency of one or more of the systems.

This connects with my second point. How can prisons be more responsive to these ethical issues? There has been discussion whether the task of improving conditions for prisoners, including the issue of AIDS, is better based upon a judicial model rather than a medical model of problem perception, reasoning and conflict resolution. Norway provides evidence on this issue. This is because of the changes which occured in 1987 which made the medical profession more independent of prison authorities and because the AIDS issues are clearly and publicly understood. In addition, the Norwegian prison system is small and therefore easier to review. With the firm power base located outside the prison establishment there was considerable success for the health teams in forming and applying their prevention policies for HIV and AIDS. When the prison authorities showed reluctance to give priority to transportation of HIV prisoners to civilian medical facilities a complaints procedure was established involving the prison and Prison Board. This forced changes within the prison system. Likewise, the health authorities were able to stop the Ministry of Justice and the prison authorities from introducing a policy of double occupancy of cells on the grounds of hygiene and HIV prevention.

However, the history of the medical model dominating in total institutions is not an overwhelming success story in terms of human rights. Although the interests of the patient are, in theory, paramount, reality and various horror stories indicate otherwise. Opening the closed institution to more than one model of perception, discretionary judgment and conflict resolution, with a secure external powerbase is a good start. This move towards multiple models should also incorporate the reduction in authoritarian structures, increased prisoner contacts with the outside world and judgments of their conditions based not upon utilitarian concerns but according to civil standards of decency, fairness and human rights. Within this programme the struggle against HIV and AIDS has proved to be important.

# AIDS IN PRISONS IN GERMANY

JOHANNES FEEST AND HEINO STÖVER
*Department of Criminology,*
*University of Bremen*

In 1992 about 60,000 persons were held in German prisons. Of those, about 18,000 were held on remand. This reflects an overall imprisonment ratio of 72 per 100,000. The former West German rate was, and remains, about 75 per 100,000 while the former East German rate has dropped from almost 200 to around 20 per 100,000.

The German prison system is covered by the Prison Act 1977 which is federal legislation requiring state implementation. Until unification in October 1990 there were 11 state prison administrations which differed considerably. Now there are 16 state prison administrations. However, little is known, in terms of qualitative and quantitative data, concerning their operation although it would appear that there is, at the moment, only a limited problem with drugs and AIDS in former East German prisons. Because of limited information this chapter concentrates on the information known about the former German Federal Republic (West Germany).

The Prison Act 1977 prescribes an accommodation standard of one person per cell. However, because of exceptions to the norm for older institutions, provided by the legislation, only about two-thirds of German prisoners occupy single cells at night. Differences between states are marked. For example in Bremen there is 91 per cent single cell occupancy whilst in Saarland there is less than 50 per cent single cell occupancy.

Conjugal visits are not available in German prisons. But 'long term' visits by families of long-term prisoners are now being practised on an experimental basis in a few prisons. This recognises, at the unofficial level, the possibility of sexual relations between prisoners and their partners.

The average length of sentences is not documented in the official statistics. However, about half of the sentenced prisoners serve sentences between one and five years: more than another 15 per cent serve longer sentences, including more than 1,000 lifers.

Nine per cent of all convicted prisoners are sentenced for drug offences but it is not known how many other offences are drug related. According to official estimates 10 to 15 per cent of all prisoners are drug users.[1] Unofficial estimates are much higher. The authors' impression for Bremen is that about one-third of all male prisoners and almost half of all female prisoners are, in some manner, involved in drug usage.[2]

The quality of prison regimes differs greatly both between states and between individual prisons. While prisons in the southern states of Bayern, Baden Wurttemberg and Sachsen are, as a rule, tougher and more discipline-orientated, the city states of Berlin, Bremen and Hamburg are know for their relatively liberal regimes.

The most important feature of the German prison system is the development of what is known as 'Lockerunpen', (relaxations), which include home leave and work furloughs. Although this was virtually unknown 20 years ago, there are now, on average, more than seven home leaves per prisoner per year. In reality this means that more than a third of all prisoners go on home leave for the maximum of 21 days per year allowed by the law. The percentage is much higher in the states of Saarland, Berlin, Bremen and Nordrhein Westfalen and much lower in Bayern, Baden Wurttemberg and Niedersachsen. These relaxations affect nearly every aspect of the prison system, from sexual release to drug supply. It also affects the identified AIDS/HIV prisoners as they find it much harder, if not impossible, to obtain home leave. Similar restrictions pertain to known drug users.

High risk practices are more likely to occur among those prisoners who do not receive 'relaxations' because the possibilities of obtaining clean needles and practising safer sex are higher outside than inside the prison. The general public are urged to practice safer sex by regular TV commercials paid for by the Federal Ministry of Health, while condoms can be purchased in many shops as well as from vending machines in public toilets. Syringes and clean needles are available from pharmacies. In most cities clean needles and syringes are available, free of charge, on an exchange basis, from private organizations and/or automatic dispensers.

## DATA COLLECTION

There are an estimated 1,000 HIV positive inmates in German prisons. This estimate is based on large-scale testing in some of the states which shows a prisoner average of 1.2 to 3 per cent HIV positives. The HIV prevalence varies considerably from prison to prison. For example, it appears that state prisons in rural areas seem to have no HIV positive inmates whilst the rate in metropolitan areas is 8.8 per cent.[3] The

---

1 For details cf. H.Stöver, *HIV/AIDS-Prävention für Drogengebraucher Innen im Strafvollzug* (1993), 2 Kriminologisches Journal.

2 According to the director of Bremen prison, some 80 per cent of all inmates do have problems with their addiction. Half of them are taking hard drugs (Die Tageszeitung, 7 December 1992). Some figures indicate a growing number of drug users outside prison since the mid-eighties. This increase will eventually be reflected within the prison population.

3 K.H. Schäfer, *AIDS: Ansätze zu einer Problembewältigung auf der Ebene von Landesjustizverwaltung und Parlament* in M. Busch et. al. HIV/AIDS und straffälligkeit. Eine Herausforderung für Strafrechtspfledge und Straffälligenhilfe (1991), 181.

percentage is higher among female prisoners, being 4 per cent in Nürnberg. The vast majority of HIV positive prisoners are drug users: in the prisons of Berlin 95 per cent of the male and more than 99 per cent of the female HIV positives are drug users.[4]

Sexuality remains a major taboo subject in prisons. Consequently little is recorded about it. Typically the leading textbook on prisons refers to USA literature on 'wolves', 'fags', and 'punks' and adds that 'presumably these role models can be found in our prisons too, maybe in less clear forms'.[5] There are reports of male rapes as initiation ceremonies in juvenile prisons but this issue remains to be researched. Likewise, no research has been conducted on the effects of the safer sex AIDS prevention campaigns on prisoners. However, a survey conducted among HIV positive prisoners by the Deutsche AIDS-Hilfe,[6] which is the major support scheme, provides the following information: almost 25 per cent of the interviewees claim to have had sexual contacts during their time in prison; about the same number claim to have been infected by sexual contacts in prison or before prison.

During the 1970s and 1980s prison administrators denied that there was any use of illegal drugs within prisons. Therefore drugs were a non-issue. But drug deaths, drug traffic, and drug-related crime and growing brutalization forced a change in the official line. In most prisons it is now freely admitted that there is an active drug scene.

The survey by the Deutsche AIDS-Hilfe provides the following data from HIV positive prisoners. More than 90 per cent claim to have experience with drugs; more than 80 per cent say that there are illegal drugs available in their prison; more than 70 per cent claim to have been infected through syringe or needle-sharing. Empirical data shows that 40 to 50 per cent of those i.v. drug users with prison experience continue injecting drugs while in prison.[7] These findings also confirm the existence of an extensive drug market which enjoys easy access to common drugs.

According to a large-scale epidemiological study among drug users[8] about 19.9 per cent of the sample of 1,253 i.v. drug users are HIV infected. About 60 per cent of all i.v. drug users in this sample have served a prison sentence. Compared with only ten per cent HIV positives among the addicts who have never been to prison, 26 per cent of those with prison experience are HIV positive. Sixty-seven per cent indicated they continued to inject whilst in prison. These data are confirmed by another empirical study (n=660) on drug use.[9] It found that HIV prevalence among i.v. drug users with prison experience was nearly twice as high (23.7 per cent) as drug users

4 R. Rex, *Anforderungen an die medizinische Versorgung von HIV-Infizierten und AIDS-Kranken im Strafvollzug* in Busch et al., ibid., 190.

5 Günther Kaiser/Hans-Jürgen Kerner/Heinz Schöch, Strafvollzug (1992) 430.

6 Michael Gähner, *AIDS im Strafvollzug* Lichtblick (prisoners' journal) (March/April 1992), 6. The results are based on answers from 117 HIV positive prisoners (availability sample).

7 D. Kleiber, *Die HIV/AIDS-Problematik bei i.v. Drogenabhängigen in der Bundesrepublik Deutschland - Unter besonderer Berücksichtigung der Situation hafterfahrener Drogenabhängiger* i: Busch et al. (eds.) HIV/AIDS und Straffälligkeit (1991), 35. U. Koch, S. Ehrenberg, *Akzeptanz AIDS-präventiver Botschaften: Evaluation der Aufklarungs- und Beratungsarbeit bei i.v. Drogenabhängigen in der Bundesrepublik Deutschland* in Deutsche AIDS-Hilfe (ed.): AIDS und Drogen II. (1992) 53f.

8 D. Kleiber, see. fn. 7.

9 Koch/Ehrenberg (1992), 48.

without prison experience (12.5 per cent). The HIV prevalence of women with prison experience was three times as high as those women who had not been inside prison.

These figures indicate that many people become HIV positive whilst inside prison. This graphic description by a prisoner provides a plausible explanation:

'As far as drugs are concerned there are shortages, but there is always someone who has something. The problem is always with the pumps. In the remand prison there is hardly a chance to shoot together. So you ask someone, about whom you know that he shoots, to lend you his pump. Most of the time, these are rotten things with a blunt needle and used maybe fifty times over. But if you have got heroin, then you want to get your shot. You are not interested at that moment whether the needle is clean or not ... When I served time in 1984, we didn't yet know anything about AIDS. But the situation was such that for months we only had one syringe, and all the junkies in the house used it. That must have been the time when I got my HIV infection. Probably all the others too, about a dozen. Some of them have already died ... Last year, I was in the same (Berlin) prison again: nothing has changed; everybody is using one syringe, just as in 1984.'[10]

The suggestion that infection occurs in prison is confirmed by the study of the Deutsche AIDS-Hilfe. About 17 per cent of the HIV positives (in Berlin it exceeds 30 per cent) think that they became infected whilst in prison. The author of the study comments: 'Probably many justice ministries will say that this is a subjective opinion not supported by hard evidence. I ask myself, however, why these prisoners should give false testimony.'

Another indicator of the exposure to infection is the extremely high prevalence of the hepatitis B virus amongst i.v. drug users in several prisons. The hepatitis B virus is transmitted via needle-sharing and unsafe sex and can be seen as a marker for HIV infection risk.

ISSUES

Compulsory Testing and Voluntariness

Compulsory testing is legal only in the state of Bayern. But even there testing is carried out on a 'voluntary' basis with the explicit threat of forced testing as a possibility, at least, for high risk groups. Almost all prisoners are tested in Bayern; 92 per cent in Nürnberg and 97 per cent in München. The testing occurs on reception in prison at the medical examination. In Bayern it also occurs at the time of release from prison.[11] Even in the states where compulsory testing has not been introduced by law the percentages of prisoners tested are high. In Nordrhein-Westfalen the figure is 80 per cent and more than 90 per cent in Hessen. All prisoners are encouraged to take the test. But the principal reason for the high take-up is that those who refuse are treated as if they were HIV positive until tested. This is the explicit policy in the states of Hessen, Saarland, Baden-Würtemberg and Bayern.

---

10 T. Meyer, *Alles läuft so, als gäb's das Virus nicht* Die Tageszeitung 30 March 1989.

11 The test results are not published.

In some states such as Berlin the percentages are below 50 per cent. The extreme case is Bremen where testing is not only voluntary but anonymous as far as the prison administration is concerned. The governor of the local prison stated:

'This means that the prisoner can be sure that not even the prison doctor will be informed of the test result. The prisoner alone will get the result and he will have to decide whether to divulge the result or not. This works in the following way: the blood sample with a number is sent to the public health office; and the prisoner gets the result directly from them, not via censored mail or via the prison doctor.'[12]

This same prison governor told one of the authors, however, that he knows practically all the HIV positive prisoners, because they talk to him about the test results.

In most of the cases (90 per cent according to the DAH survey) it is the prison doctor who informs the prisoner of the positive test result. Usually, the doctor has neither the time nor the training for after-care, nor psycho-social support.[13] The problem is compounded because support strategies, developed in civil society over the last decade, cannot be applied within the prison environment.

## CONFIDENTIALITY OF PRISONERS' HEALTH STATUS

In Nürnberg the prison doctor informs the governor of positive test results. Health status is revealed by the governor to others only if there are reasons to believe that others may be endangered.[14]

In Nordrhein-Westfalen the doctor and governor are aware of the positive result. In addition those prison officers who are in direct contact with the prisoner are aware of the medical status. The prisoner's social worker and psychologist are also informed. 'Of course, everybody is advised that this has to be treated confidentially, but you know from your own experience that in the long run everybody is in the know.'[15]

In Hessen the prison doctor informs the governor who, in turn, decides who will be given the information. 'The circle of people in the know is kept very small. As

---

12 Ehrhard Hoffmann (Bremen) AIDS in Justizvollzugsanstalten (1989) 4 (Expert Hearing of the Enquete Commission of the German Bundestag).

13 AIDS-Enquete-Kommission des 11. Deutschen Bundestages: Endbericht. Deutscher Bundestag (ed.): AIDS: Fakten und Konsequenzen (1990), 284f.

14 Prisoners' mistrust of the medical system is high. There seems to be little basis for a trusting relationship between doctor and inmate although a good relationship is the basis of a successful coping strategy for a positive result. According to the survey of the Deutsche AIDS-Hilfe, most inmates consider the doctors and medical personnel to be insufficiently informed about HIV\AIDS and that the standard of prison medical care is lower than that in civil society (see, fn. 6).

15 Dipl. Psych. Romkopf (Gelsenkirchen), AIDS in Justizvollzugsanstalten (1989) 15 (Expert Hearing of the Enquete Commission of the German Bundestag).

a rule, the governor informs his deputy, the officer responsible for the particular wing, the guards in charge and the work supervisors.'[16]

If the test is conducted by the prison doctor the result is placed in the prisoner's medical file. This file is available only for medical purposes. In principle, the health status of the prisoner is confidential. It is known from court reports that some prisons have marked the general file of some prisoners with statements such as 'HIV Positive' or 'Avoid Blood Contact'. Even though some prisons have been ordered by the court to remove such labels the courts have also approved this practice in certain circumstances, for example, where it constitutes proof that the prisoner is HIV infected.[17]

It is clear that in practice confidentiality of health status is not honoured. Prison personnel are either informed officially and directly or acquire this information through the rumour network. The testing policy places a spotlight on those prisoners who are HIV positive. It suggests to the staff they need to know this information in order to undertake their daily routine work. This possibility of identification seems to provide a feeling of personal security and possible prevention. Thus, prison officers support a policy of extensive testing. In routine circumstances officers are not at risk, but the debate revolves around two issues: physically restraining a prisoner and/or giving first-aid to a prisoner. These possibilities influence the perception of degree of risk and underpin the support for identifying and controlling HIV positive inmates.

The policy of general testing and identification of HIV positive prisoners damages any possibility of 'normalization' towards HIV and AIDS. In turn, it increases existing anxiety among personnel and confirms the need to view particular prisoners as extraordinary.

## ISOLATION OR NORMAL PLACEMENT

Identified HIV positive prisoners experience a range of restrictions from state to state. Originally they were excluded from certain types of work such as the kitchen or barber shop. These restrictions have been lifted in some states. Normally, they are placed in single occupancy cells and may share a cell only if they inform the other occupant of their health status.[18] In Hessen prisoner's transport papers are marked 'Avoid Blood Contact'.[19] Prisoners find it more difficult to receive 'relaxations' such as home leave. The reason for this restriction is, presumably, the fear of adverse press coverage. However, on the other hand, seropositive prisoners may receive a special diet which includes milk products and fruit. Special medical attention is provided and in some states, including Bremen, they are given preferential access to the prisons' limited

---

16 Dr Sauer (Hessen), AIDS in Justizvollzugsanstalten (1989) 24 (Expert Hearing of the Enquete Commission of the German Bundestag). After this revealing definition of a 'small circle' laughter was recorded at the hearing.

17 OLG Koblenz, Zeitschrift fur Strafvollzug (1989), 121.

18 Dipl. Psych. Romkopf (Gelsenkirchen), AIDS in Justizvollsugsanstalten (1989) 15 (Expert Hearing of the Enquete Commission of the German Bundestag).

19 Dr Sauer (Hessen) Ibid., p. 23.

methadone programmes.[20] They may also be offered preferential access to the growing number of 'drug free areas'. These prisoners are visited by members of the local AIDS support scheme and they may receive condoms, usually on request from the prison doctor.

## EDUCATIONAL HIV/AIDS PREVENTATIVE MEASURES

Counselling of prisoners is handled mainly through written materials, which describe risk behaviour and HIV transmission routes. The propaganda's message encourages a complete change of behaviour. For example, a leaflet issued by the justice administration in Berlin states: 'Stop injecting, get off drugs! Stop tattooing and piercing your earlobe! Stop anal sexual intercourse!' But the demand for abstinence to prevent infection is unrealistic given the widespread drug use and homosexual activity in prison. The strategy of promoting abstinence is one-dimensional and reminiscent of the civil drug counselling system before the identification of HIV and AIDS in 1983.

Prevention, by personal communication, established as model projects in some prisons and researched in Bremen[21] is mainly confined to test-counselling and legal advice. These also fail to reflect the reality of everyday life of drug-using prisoners, which is the need to use drugs in a relatively safe manner and to avoid additional danger.

Some organizations such as the Deutsche AIDS-Hilfe demand a 'safer-use-training' for prisoners which should reduce the level of risk. The training involves how to use bleach or thermic disinfectants; how to inject hygienically; how to avoid overdoses after prison release; differential risks of different ways to consume drugs and the consequences of polytoxicomanic drug use.

The possibility of personal communication about HIV/AIDS prevention between a prisoner and the psycho-social prison service is limited, particularly if no practical preventative measures are made available. One without the other merely exaggerates the level of blame and shame rather than implementing the policies of 'safer sex' and 'safer use'.

Counselling prison officers remains even more of a problem. Some AIDS schemes are trying to develop continuing education programmes for officers because their knowledge of HIV transmission, infection, and the value of testing seems disappointingly limited.[22]

---

20 For details see, Horst Bossong and Heino Stöver, *Zur Praxis der Sustitutionsbehandlung in der Bundesrepublik Deutschland* in Bossong/Stöver (eds), Methadonbehandlung, Ein Leitfaden. (1992), 43-67.

21 Cf. Kaulitzki et. al., *Modellversuch AIDS im bremischen Justizvollzug*, Bremen (1991), (unpublished).

22 Cf. P. Lindlahr, *Fortbildungsveranstaltungen für Bedienstete im nordrhein-westfälischen Strafvollzug zum Bereich HIV-Infektion und AIDS*, Bonn (1991), (unpublished).

PREVENTATIVE MEASURES: CONDOMS, STERILE NEEDLES, BLEACH AND
METHADONE

Condoms are available in some prisons but clean needles and syringes are banned
throughout the German prison system. Nor do needle exchange schemes exist inside
prisons.[23] However, there is a growing body of opinion which favours the distribution
of clean needles as a way of controlling the spread of the HIV virus.[24] The movement
is assisted by the acceptance of needle exchange programmes outside prison as a
regular feature of HIV-AIDS prevention. The main legal argument against needle
distribution was that the distributors were liable as accomplices of the drug users.
However, this has been removed by section 29 of the Drug Law 1992
(Betäubungsmittelgesetz) which states that 'providing drug addicts with sterile one-way
syringes do not constitute the offence of furthering the use of illegal drugs'.[25]

Despite this change to the law and despite political demands to the contrary,
there remains strong resistance from prison administrations and state ministries against
the provision of sterile injection equipment to drug using prisoners. The main
arguments are that drug-free prisoners might be encouraged to start using drugs.
Providing sterile needles might be misunderstood as a signal to legalise drugs rather
than appreciated as a public health measure against HIV. Prison officers are concerned
that they are required to undertake contradictory tasks: on the one hand they must
search cells and confiscate drugs and equipment but, on the other, sterile needles
should be tolerated as a preventative health measure. Finally, there is the proposition
that syringes may be used as weapons.

Counter-arguments by supporters of needle provision are that these items are
already available in prisons and the shortage of such equipment does not deter
prisoners from using or starting to use drugs. Indeed, the reverse is true in that the
shortages lead to extensive needle sharing or the manufacture of even more dangerous
equipment such as sharpened ball point pens. Prison life is such as to bring people
inevitably into contact with drugs either through officially administered psychotropic
or sedative drugs or through the culture of prison life. The introduction of clean
needles would safeguard existing drug users from HIV and hepatitis B infection. To
date there is no evidence that needles have been used as weapons against staff.

Although prison staff are sceptical about these changes they are capable of
being convinced of the need for change, as is illustrated by their growing acceptance
of the dispensing of methadone. The message must be one of harm reduction not one
of supporting hedonistic drug use.

Nevertheless, currently there exists strong opposition to the provision of sterile
equipment. Consequently, certain experts and committees have offered a 'second best'

---

23 The legality of supplying sterile needles to prisoners is demonstrated by Wolfgang Lesting (Die
Abgabe von Einwegspritzen im Strafvollzug zur AIDS-Prävention- strafbar oder notwendig.
In:Strafverteidiger 1990, pp. 225-230.

24 For an overview see: Stöver, H., Schuller, K.: Vergabe von sterilem Spritzbesteck. Copenhagen,
WHO 1991. See also: Stöver. H, Schuller, K.: AIDS prevention with injecting drug users in the former
West Germany: A user-friendly approach on a municipal level. In: O'Hare et al. (eds.), The Reduction
of Drug-Related Harm. London, New.York, 1992, pp. 186-194.

25 Bundesgesetzblatt Teil I, 1992, p. 1593 f.

solution which is the distribution and training in the use of bleach as a disinfectant. This is not yet available in any German prison although the debate on its provision is a lively one. The major difficulty is that its use in prisons could be taken as tacit acceptance of drugs and equipment in prisons. In addition, bleach is not totally reliable[26] nor is it a substitute for albeit clean but blunt needles which can damage veins.

In the struggle to introduce an effective HIV/AIDS instrumental prevention strategy bleach may be seen as a step in the right direction. For five years this debate has raged and during this time i.v. drug users have been infected and have died. Another possibility is that of thermic disinfection which involves immersion heaters to sterilize needles. But such a development also needs instruction because users need to be told the time that equipment needs to be boiled.

Methadone has now become part of prison medical treatment by some doctors for i.v. drug users. In contrast to its use outside prison, the doctors see it as an alternative HIV/AIDS prevention strategy in that oral application and the blocking of the heroin craving is supposed to stop drug injecting and needle sharing. So, prison doctors who prescribe methadone explicitly argue against providing sterile 'works' for prisoners because it runs against the treatment programme. This is problematic as only a few prison doctors prescribe methadone for maintenance rather than for detoxification. Moreover, the cost of the programme means that it is still severely restricted in terms of availability, and even then some prisoners may 'top up' with other injectable drugs, and those not treated with methadone probably continue to practice high risk injections.

EARLY RELEASE

Normally, prisoners can be 'paroled' after having served two-thirds of their sentence and under exceptional circumstances after half of their sentence. There is a clause in the German Code of Criminal Procedure which allows for the instant release of a prisoner with a very grave illness, particularly if the prisoner's life is in danger.[27] This clause is rarely used because prison hospitals are employed in such eventualities. Even with terminally ill prisoners early release is not guaranteed especially if new offences cannot be excluded.

CONCLUSION

The AIDS issue was dramatised in the mid-1980s. This offered some hope for certain groups of prisoners including long-term drug addicts and terminally ill prisoners. The main change AIDS has brought about in Germany is the breakthrough for methadone programmes both inside and outside prisons and the development of low threshold services aimed at harm reduction. But the current dynamic for change appears

---

26 Lauf, R. (1992): Stellungnahme zur Desinfektion von Spritzen sichtiger Personen mit bleach. Universitäts-Krankenhaus Eppendorf, Hamburg 8.9.92 (manuskript).

27 Section 455, StPO.

exhausted. Increasingly the official response is that everything is under control and there is only limited need for further action.[28]

There remain major anomalies between the operation of strategies 'inside' and 'outside' prison. For example, outside prison the anonymous testing programme is voluntary except for 'problem groups' in Bayern. But prisoners are urged to take the test if only to avoid negative consequences, and for them employing the term 'voluntary' is questionable. Again, prison personnel perceive the test and subsequent identification as a form of damage limitation which contrasts with the perspective of 'normalisation' which can be observed in civil society.

A double standard is also noticeable in counselling, before and after the test, but essentially in the field of prevention. Outside prison comprehensive strategies for harm reduction for i.v. drug users are being developed but no similar programme is available within prison. Clean equipment for drug users is not provided, although this is done outside prison. Prisoners are subjected to moral appeals to stop practicing risky activities and are not offered practical support to reduce risk by using bleach or thermic disinfectants. Thus, HIV/AIDS prevention in prison remains unrealistic and unreliable.

There is a growing number of i.v. drug users in prison. They live with a risk constellation which is necessarily leading to a close correlation between imprisonment and HIV infection. But despite this relationship prison administrators and the responsible politicians do not publicly recognise that effective prevention of HIV is the only way to stop an increase in the number of HIV/AIDS prisoners.

---

28 In May 1992, a well structured conference, held in Hanover and organized by the Federation of German AIDS Foundations, made a forceful attempt to show the need for more action, for example on the question of sterile needles. Despite widespread invitations to justice ministries a disappointingly small number were represented and those few seemed disinclined to make extra efforts on that issue.

# AIDS IN PRISONS IN POLAND

MONIKA PLATEK
*Department of Criminology,*
*University of Warsaw*

Radical political changes which occurred in Poland in the autumn of 1989 are also reflected in changes within the prison administration. The administration has moved from being a servant of those in political power to being a servant of the law and legal process. One consequence is that the formerly secretive prison administration is becoming more open with its data, problems and procedures concerning prison administration. Many of those politicians who entered Parliament in 1989 had a personal and intimate knowledge of Polish prisons having themselves been, at one time, political prisoners! In addition, this new openness is a reflection of the democratisation of social life in Poland.

At the beginning of 1989 over 100,000 people were in prison. By the start of 1991 the number had dropped to around 40,000. In September 1992 the figure had risen to 61,340 of whom 15,493 were on remand. In June 1993 there were 60,679 licenced prison places and it seems likely that the new state will soon be facing the problem of prison overcrowding as the numbers committed to prison increase.[1] However, this increase has little to do with the actual level of criminality but rather it is the old ploy of filling the prisons as a form of visible security for the general population. The government is shown to be strong and active if the prisons are full! Such policies also damage control efforts concerning the spread of HIV and AIDS.

New Prison Rules were introduced in 1989. These rules create limited but nonetheless enforceable rights for prisoners. Access to court is created and the prison administration may be listed as a party. The Rules also recognised categories of vulnerable prisoners which include young offenders, drug addicts and women. Special attention is paid to the health care of prisoners.

---

[1] There has been a considerable growth in the number of foreigners held in Polish prisons over the past two years. In the 1980s the number was as low as six to nine a year. At the end of July 1992 the number had climbed to over 390 and at the beginning of August 1992 there were 427. 253 came from the former Soviet Union, 30 from East Germany and 17 from Romania. By the end of March 1993 the number had again increased to 670. More than 85 per cent are on temporary detention. J. Wilczynski, *Foreigners in Polish Prisons: Strangers Behind Bars*, Zycie Warszawy, 20 June 1993.

Currently there are 209 prisons and detention centres in Poland. Some of the centres are physically located within one or two detached units inside prisons. With more arrest cases some of the correction institutions have been changed into detention centres. The Prison Service in Poland is part of the Ministry of Justice and is administered by the Central Prison Service Office.

The Rules do not contemplate single occupancy of cells but impose a minimum space of 2.5 square metres per prisoner. However, at present this space requirement is not honoured. Prisons are of different standards and age. Some were built in the nineteenth and even eighteenth centuries. Most have adequate sanitary facilities. There are, however, some without toilets and running water. With the new problem of overcrowding there is a tendency to exceed the licenced capacity for cell occupation. Generally, very few prisoners enjoy a single cell. It is common for there to be two, three or four prisoners to a cell and in some prisons there are as many as eight to a cell.

Conjugal visits within the prison were not allowed but this has changed recently. There is also a developing home visit programme as well as facilities within prisons for conjugal visits.[2] The statistics show that before 1989 no more than 5,000 visits were granted per year to the 100,000 inmates. In September 1992 the number of home visits granted was 4,098 for up to five days to 4,053 prisoners; 10,483 inmates were given 16,386 visits for up to 24 hours. These figures are standard for the year although the visits increase during holiday periods such as Christmas. This liberalisation of home visits has, of course, implications for the spread and control of HIV.

The average period of imprisonment is changing. Before 1989 the average length was 22 months. It dropped after 1989 to one year and is now increasing. In October 1992 it had risen to 23 months. Although the number who are sent to prison is dropping their length of stay is increasing. The number of foreign prisoners before 1989 was less than 100 but by October 1992 the figure stood at 526 which albeit low by Western standards is a fivefold increase in Poland. Drug trafficking is the single largest crime for the foreign prisoner population.

Drug-related crime is a relatively new phenomenon and almost unknown prior to 1980, partly, perhaps because there was a ban on information concerning drugs. After that date information was available although it was irresponsibly produced. For example it stated how to make 'kompot' out of poppy seeds which were freely available in the country. However, as now, drugs and drug addicts are nowhere as significant as alcohol, alcoholics and alcohol-related crime. Nevertheless, the view of the courts has moved from relatively short sentences for drug related crime to much longer terms of imprisonment. This shift reflects Poland's new political position within Europe and responds to the routing of hard drugs from Russia, via Poland into Germany.

Drug-related prisoners are still most often those who are drug addicts. One cannot exclude the possibility that those who only deal but are not drug addicts might enter prison but this is rare for Polish prisoners. They continue to comprise a very small element of the prison population.

---

2 J. Wilczynski, *Visiting Rooms for Polish Prisoners: Windows to the Outside*, Zycie Warszawy, 21 February 1993.

In September 1992 there were 1,476 prisoners registered as requiring special medical attention. Within this group there were 142 drug addicts of whom 14 are women. The balance of this grouping was mainly comprised of alcoholics.

Because of the small numbers of addicts the rules of their special units are innovative and have been applied elsewhere. Thus, they serve both to maintain and improve general prison standards. For example, innovations such as own clothes, plants in cells, the right to make and receive phone calls, developing small flower and vegetable gardens have all come out of these units. The units employ specially trained and selected staff whose concern is more with the prisoners' psychological and social needs than with with security and prison discipline. In addition, educational programmes are encouraged and special activities are available.

## DATA COLLECTION

Prison life is tedious and revolves around the act and the relating of the acts of sex and crime. The idleness of the regime increases the need for drugs and alcohol. Official statistics say little about prison rape. The prison practice indicates that the more strict is the regime and the more crowded is the prison the greater is the likelihood of acts of rape and homosexuality.[3] As programmes such as home visits and a relatively relaxed prison atmosphere developed then the incidence of homosexuality declined. Nevertheless, because these stories were believed to affect both prisoner and staff morale official reports of such activities were not encouraged. Paradoxically, the official response was supported by prisoner self-reporting. They were reluctant to produce this type of evidence for fear of stigmatisation and the concern about peer group reaction.

After the political changes occuring post 1989 the penal system also experienced changes at all levels. Central administration was affected as new people entered from university positions with expectations of change and reform. Home leaves, work furloughs, homosexuality: these topics, and more, were on the public agenda and were freely recognised and discussed.

Currently, the prison statistics indicate a prison subculture but without detailed analysis. We can only assume that homosexual activities, that involve violence, are included in the figures of 181 cases between January and September 1992 as compared with 415 attempted suicides in that period. With the rising rate of incarceration one cannot be sure that the lenient and open line will continue. That this, in turn, might disguise homosexual activities and prison rapes as a 'drastic expression of prison subculture' is a matter of interpretation.

HIV and AIDS may yet affect the prison sub culture. The first prisoners identified as HIV positive were drug addicts and these continue to constitute the largest group. They are young, ill educated and working class. They are coming from

---

3 The problem is well known among practitioners and scientists yet little is written on the subject. See, however, P. Moczydlowski, *Hidden Life of Polish Prisons* (1992), Indiana U.P.; M. Platek *Prisoners' Subculture in Poland* (1990), International Journal of the Sociology of Law 4; J. Leszczynski, Z Problematyki Etiologii Przestepstw Seksualnych (Problems of Etiology of Sexual Crimes) Prawo i Zycie, (1973) 1.

the poor, eastern part of Poland. Their association with drugs arises from trading with Russian and other Warsaw Pact soldiers that were stationed in Poland.

The HIV and AIDS numbers remain small although rapid growth is anticipated. Very few were notified in 1989 and in 1991 the number rose to over 100 with an increase expected for 1992. The medical doctor responsible for health care in prison administration reports that the numbers of HIV prisoners doubles every three months.[4]

In 1988 AIDS in prisons was considered to be an issue of no significance. This was an attitude that prevailed throughout Polish society. WHO data was reassuring: 75 per cent of AIDS cases were reported in the USA and Africa while 12 per cent were located principally in Western Europe.[5] Thus, the virus was treated as an issue affecting foreigners.[6] Nevertheless, as early as 1986 AIDS was listed as a contagious disease in law with the resulting consequences of procedures concerning detection, notification, prevention and treatment.[7] The diagnosis of AIDS provides the grounds for compulsory outpatient treatment, unless the sanitary inspector orders compulsory hospitalisation for definite epidemiological or clinical reasons. The result is that there are no legal grounds for AIDS patients to be isolated either inside or outside prison.

In July 1989 the prison administration called a national conference on HIV and AIDS in prisons and houses of detention. It was known that some inmates were infected. The Central Prison Authority started receiving information concerning these prisoners in January 1990 and in June of that year the duty to notify of such prisoners was introduced. The data shows that the number of HIV carriers increased by several to over a dozen persons every month.

In 1990 some 105 HIV seropositive people were imprisoned of whom 46 were convicted and 59 were on remand. The steady state in terms of numbers in that year was between 60 and 70 people in the 30 prisons and houses of detention. Seventeen were subsequently released because of the onset of AIDS: a decision which had serious repercussions which are noted below. During the first three months of 1991 some 46 new prisoners who were infected with the virus were admitted. At the same time eight prisoners with AIDS were released. Today HIV and AIDS prisoners are found throughout the Polish prison system.

In mid 1989, about 250 HIV positive people were registered in Poland. In 1990 there were nearly 1,000 of whom 36 had developed AIDS. Most of them were drug addicts or homosexuals and the proportion of women was small. Drug addicts were the first people to be identified as HIV positive in prison. Originally there were no special units or rules for treatment or containment and there was no official

---

4 This information comes, on oral request, from the Central Prison Administration, Warsaw, but is not published in the Prison Statistical Information.

5 Sokolowska, M. (1990): Spoleczne i kulturowe aspekty regulacji prawnych w zakresie zapobiegania i zwalczania AIDS (Social and cultural aspects of legal regulations concerning protection and AIDS relief). In, Prawne Problemy AIDS (Legal Problems of AIDS) ed. A.J. Szwarc Wydawnictwo Prawnicze. Warszawa, 40.

6 Szawarski, Z. (1986). Epidemia Stachu (The outbreak of fear), Problemy No. 7.

7 D.Z.U. No. 40 poz. 197/1986 Nowela z 21 pazdziernika 1986 do Rozporzadzenia Rady Ministrow z 20 grudnia 1963 w sprawie ustakenia wykazow chorob zakaznych (Novelization of the act including AIDS into the list of contagious diseases).

expectation of the virus becoming a major prison problem. However, that was not the case and the system is now facing the issues of staffing, location of prisoners, treatment, confidentiality and costs.

The original response was to see HIV prisoners as a product of drug addicted prisoners and in a sense this was correct. However, in Poland, drug addicted prisoners have a profile of rarely being hostile to staff, not participating in the sub-culture of the prison and being generally responsive to authority. Thus, the small number of HIV prisoners were kept with the drug addicts and the issue of placement was solved. But as the number grew and the profile of the drug addicts changed post 1989 to become closer to the general prison population so the issues of HIV and AIDS re-emerged.

## SEGREGATION

A special ward for HIV inmates was established in July 1990 in Lodz house of detention. These prisoners were also introduced into the drug addicts special ward at Sluzewiec prison, Warsaw, where the addicts were willing to accept these prisoners.

The prisoners were allocated a complete floor of the prison with a separate walking area. Considerable freedom of choice was provided in terms of decoration of cells and the organisation of the ward. Normally the cells would house six prisoners but in that ward it was two or three to a cell. The spacious corridor was converted into an attractive and well equipped day room. New arrivals, often devastated by being told of their health status, found support from the staff which included doctors, nurses and psychologists. Cells which are kept open throughout the day were well maintained and kept clean. These wards benefit from a supportive attitude by staff.

These wards contrast with other experiences in Polish prisons where inmates have refused to share meals, toilet facilities or shake hands with HIV prisoners. Even medical doctors have refused assistance to these prisoners and encouraged general protest amongst prison staff against the policy of normal location of HIV prisoners. The impact of such actions was used to feed the prejudices outside prison where, for example, residents in a small town refused to have a hostel for children infected by the virus.[8]

These problems, based upon ignorance, continue to exist but appear to be ameliorating with the passage of time and growing experience. It is important, particularly for Western readers, to bear in mind that this account is related within a period of great political change. These changes have, in turn, affected the criminal and penal policies of Poland. For example, the creation of the HIV ward and the accompanying infrastructure was made possible not simply because of prisoners' requirements, as they as a group are relatively powerless, but because of the changes to penal policy. The system moved from being repressive and totalitarian and instead attempted to adopt the model of care and concern. The declining prison population and a prison staff given scope to try new ideas made such a significant change easier to implement.

---

8 Wilczak, J. (1992), Z HIVem w aktach. Oddzial specjalny. With HIV in files. Special Unit. *Polityka* No. 32 from 8 August 1992.

## TESTING

The issue of testing for HIV, both within and outside prison, is more a practical than a rights issue. By this I mean that if the reagents are unavailable in Poland, for reasons of cost, then the tests cannot occur. However, information about a person being infected can only be lodged in the medical record.[9] Prisoners on reception are commonly tested. Legal authority for such actions is found in Article 61 of the Code of Execution of Penalties (c.e.p.) which states there is a duty to undergo a medical examination. Whether this includes the obligation to give blood for a test is moot and has not been challenged in court as blood is routinely taken for tests for venereal diseases.

Confidentiality is provided not only for the benefit of the individual but also for the benefit of prison routine and good behaviour of the inmates. The attempt to maintain confidentiality is important because there is considerable bias, indeed hatred, towards HIV people. Discrimination is commonplace and is partly based on the belief that it is a problem of drug addicts, criminals, prostitutes and homosexuals. Given the strong Catholic influence within Poland it is seen by many as a specific punishment for a sinful life: 'An AIDS patient, it is said, is doubly dangerous: being a vessel of sin and impurity, he or she spreads physical and moral plague.'[10] The Polish Ombudsman has been strongly criticised by the representatives of the Polish clergy for advocating help for HIV and AIDS people and for embarking on a public health education programme. She has stated that the illness is neither God's punishment nor a sin and for this she received strong condemnation.[11]

Like all institutions, maintaining confidentiality is very difficult. For example, apart from those prisoners who disclose their health status the process of segregation is also a clear indicator.

Although most prisoners are already infected on arrival there are some who become so within prison. Most disturbing are those who knowingly infect themselves by injecting contaminated blood. Such blood has a value and is bought and sold within prison. The first press story was dismissed as fiction but later this practice was confirmed by staff at several prisons.[12]

This practice is explained, in part, by the fact that the first AIDS prisoners were released from prison and transferred to an open hospital. Perhaps prisoners sought to impress cell mates by their actions or sought early release to resolve personal matters. One prisoner said:

'It was only those with long sentences, rapists, robbers and murderers, who took HIV injections. I got some blood from infected addicts who told me that was the way to be released before time. Afterwards, I let some thirty others have some of my infected

---

9 Central Prison Administration letter from 1 July 1990 (inner order NE 1989/90, NL-1137/90).

10 Z. Szarawarski (1986) op. cit., p. 34.

11 S. Stechly (1992), Czy AIDS jest kara a grzechy? Is AIDS a punishment for sin? *Polityka* No. 32 (1840) from 8 August 1992, p. 7.

12 M. Mamczur (1990), AIDS - znaczy wolnosc (AIDS means freedom). *Sztandear Mlodych* No. 5, 26-28 October 1990. These facts were confirmed during the conference of prison administration staff in February 1991 in Lodz.

blood. Do I feel guilty about it? Hardly. Together with my blood, I always gave them pamphlets dealing with AIDS. Those who actually took the injection must have known what they were doing.[13]... Some addicts knocked on our cell wall, asking for cigarettes. They said they had HIV and I asked them whether this was the way to be released. Oh, yes, they said. Absolutely. Well then, I acquired a needle and a syringe and the addicts let me have an inch of their blood. I gave them cigarettes and tea for it. I couldn't find the vein and I feared I wouldn't get AIDS after all. So I asked the addicts for another inch.'[14]

The logic which prevails within civil society does not necessarily apply within prison. The injection of infected blood appears insane but actually raises a number of questions. For example, the issue of the effect of prison literature on informing of the dangers of AIDS comes to the surface. Although the literature is available the suspicion of prisoners of anything 'official' is so deep-seated as to negate the documentation. For some prisoners injecting HIV is merely another form of self-mutilation. Given that self-mutilation is commonplace in Polish prisons it raises the wider issue of the effects of isolation. If self-mutilation is normal within prisons, and thereby seen as an acceptable passport to freedom via HIV, this represents a defeat not only for the particular prison but also for the overall penal policy which lists resocialization as a principal goal.

## ISOLATION

It is not the intention of those prisoners who consciously infect themselves to keep others in ignorance of their predicament. Indeed, quite the contrary as they wish to benefit from the infection. Addicts are also supportive of HIV prisoners. However, for those other infected prisoners protecting their status it is difficult and many inmates are hostile to them. Prisoners are sometimes isolated for self-protection. There have also been occasions when HIV prisoners have been isolated as they have threatened cell mates by using their virus as a weapon of punishment.

## PRISONER PROFILES

AIDS prisoners are transferred to prison hospitals in Warsaw, Poznan and Gdansk. Simultaneously, steps are taken by the prison administration to move such prisoners to a general hospital. Prison hospital facilities are, like the prisons themselves, overcrowded and short of necessary medical facilities. Already it seems that only those prisoners who can afford the expensive medication will be provided with such. Given that prisoners are invariably poor or debt ridden that treatment will not occur. At a time of scare resources prisoners who infect themselves or are considered by the public to be a 'bad lot' will not be prioritized over other young people in civil society without criminal records.

HIV prisoners are usually under the age of 30. The staff are supportive and seldom wear protective clothing to deal with them. The attempt to treat them like other prisoners is illustrated by the fact that HIV prisoners have the same home leave

---

13 Ibid., p. 5.
14 Ibid.

provisions as other inmates. However, this has attracted the opposition of both some local authorities and also some doctors who are concerned about the possible deterioration of the prisoners' health.[15] Police share the same position on home leaves believing that such prisoners are particularly dangerous and should be subject to 24 hour observation or isolation.

The WHO recommendations that prisoners be placed on normal location are not viable in Poland. In practice, infected prisoners are kept in separate cells, use separate bathrooms and washing machines and have their dishes washed separately. They are not employed in the kitchens or laundry as this would likely cause protests from other inmates.

## PROTECTION

There is a ban on drugs, needles and syringes in prison. The staff attempt to support addicts and the prison sentence is often the longest period of abstinence. Nevertheless, as to be expected, drugs and needles are brought into the prison and are available to those who seek them. The policy is to try and keep them out as their presence runs contrary to the therapy that is offered.

Contraceptives are banned as are sexual relationships within prison. There is a move to change this rule as consensual homosexual sex is no longer illegal in Poland. But the sub-culture that shapes prison life mitigates against such a change. The macho-man image is not conducive to such sexual practices. Homosexuals are treated badly within prison by the inmates although it is acceptable to use them as passive partners. They are treated as 'objects' by prisoners. Therefore to accept the use of contraceptives recognises the rights of passive partners.

Although there are no drug-free units there are units with drug-anonymous and alcoholic-anonymous programmes. These commenced in 1990 as experiments but are now well established with qualified staff.

## CONCLUSION

The number of HIV and AIDS prisoners is growing but so is the level of awareness amongst staff and administrators. The daily contact with these prisoners has raised the level of staff tolerance particularly when compared with civil society. Like all prisons those in Poland struggle to achieve adequate facilities, resources, hygiene and health care.

However, should HIV be identified as a 'sin' then the solution might be perceived as punishment and prison. Thus, there is a close relationship between penal policy of a reformist nature and the conservative, church forces which operate in Poland. This relationship is not necessarily complementary.

Finally, there is a tendency for the prison population to expand slowly. It is possible to make substantive changes to the sentencing process to counteract the growth in prison numbers. For example, pre-trial detention could be dramatically reduced especially as cases are subject to delays of up to two years and sometimes even longer. The minimum space requirements for prisoners cannot be guaranteed in

---

15 Doctors in the Lodz debate held this view, supra. fn. 8.

all prisons because of growing space problems and, in turn, this raises the levels of tension and anxiety amongst inmates. Overcrowding leads to deterioration of hygiene, care and supervision. It also leads to the increased danger of spreading HIV and the resulting growth in the AIDS rate.

# AIDS IN PRISONS IN ENGLAND AND WALES

PHILIP A. THOMAS
*Cardiff Law School,*
*Wales*

'Prisons are an environment in which there is a great potential for transmission of the HIV virus'.[1]

England and Wales has amongst the highest proportion of the population in prison in Europe. There are 132 jails in England and Wales. In 1991 there were 45,900 prisoners and by the year 2000 the number is set to rise to 57,500 representing a 23 per cent increase in sentenced adult men and a 43 per cent increase in remand prisoners.[2] In 1991 the Home Office opened seven new prisons and proposals to shelve seven others were cancelled. The option to use prison ships, reminiscent of the Victorian 'hulks', and also army camps for emergencies has also been retained.[3] Despite the biggest prison building programme in British history, undertaken at a cost of £1 billion in the 1980s, projections indicate that the system will still be short of about 5,500 places by the turn of the century[4] and the Law Society warned the then Home Secretary, Kenneth Clarke, that police cells will still be employed to house prisoners in 1994.[5] In June 1992 there were 1,242 men and 18 women in police cells in England and Wales who should have been located in prison[6] and the cost to the Home Office in 1991-92 to the police for this 'lock up' service was £94.7 million. This means that the nightly cost of each prisoner at £250 is greater than the fashionable London hotels![7] On 13 August 1993 the total prison population for England and Wales stood at 45,426[8] although the figure is projected to rise to 50,000

---

1 Adam Sampson, Prison Reform Trust, *The Independent*, 6 June 1991.

2 Home Office, 28 May 1992. However, it should be noted that in 1988 the prison population had exceeded 50,000.

3 In July 1993 reports on the use of two ships from the Bibby Line for prison hulk purposes were debated in Parliament.

4 *The Guardian*, 29 May 1992.

5 LAG, June 1992, 28.

6 *Hansard*, 15 June 1992, vol. 209, col. 378.

7 *The Guardian*, 5 August 1992. However, between February and March 1993 police cells were used only once for overflow purposes. With the prison population beginning to rise again, particularly amongst juveniles, the pressure on cells is likely to increase. LAG April (1993) 5.

8 Figures provided by NACRO on 16 August 1993.

in 1994 as the courts are less willing to grant bail.[9] In addition, the current Home Secretary, Michael Howard, Q.C., has stated that 'prison works'. His get-tough policies will accelerate the growth of the prison population. Further, bail changes announced in November 1993 will inevitably increase the numbers held on remand in prison awaiting trial.

The prisons are predominately of Victorian design and construction and prisoners continue to live in overcrowded and degrading conditions. In the year ending March 1990 sixteen prisons were overcrowded by at least 50 per cent on average throughout the year and several were in excess of 100 per cent overcrowded at certain times.[10] Some prisoners are housed three to a cell which was designed for one inmate. The degrading system of 'slopping out' continues and although the Home Office has set December 1994 as the date by which this procedure will no longer be necessary it remains to be seen whether this target will be met. The prisons are powderkegs waiting to be ignited as indeed happened in April 1990 when Strangeways, Manchester, erupted in the most serious riot and longest siege in English penal history. Over 20 other prisons experienced disturbances at the same time and injury, damage and loss of accommodation was severe.[11] In addition, since 1980 it has become increasingly common for police cells to be used to hold remand prisoners. For example, in 1982 the average daily number of prisoners so accommodated was 47 and had risen to 1,557 in August 1991. These cells were not designed for such usage and the practice has been widely condemned.[12]

In December 1991 the Council of Europe published the Report of the first UK visit of inspection conducted by the European Committee for the Prevention of Torture and Inhuman or Degrading Treatment or Punishment.[13] The Report contained a scathing condemnation of prison conditions. For example, cells at Brixton and Leeds designed for one inmate frequently held three. Where this occurred the report stated 'prisoners were practically confined to their beds ... Additional cell furniture other than a small table and chair was out of the question. ... Ventilation was also inadequate.' Prisoners who might be locked in the cell for up to 23 hours were provided with a bucket to relieve themselves. On occasion, prisoners carrying their

9 *The Guardian*, 25 August 1993.

10 Prison Department, Occupation of Prisons, Remand Centres: Young Offender Institutions and Police Cells on 31 December 1991 (1992).

11 The Government ordered an Inquiry under Lord Justice Woolf (Prison Disturbances April 1990. Cm. 1456, 1991) and responded to the Report in, Home Office, Custody, Care and Justice: The Way Ahead for the Prison Service in England and Wales (Cm. 1647, 1991). Unfortunately, the rebuilt prison and its new regime seems not to have heeded the warning of Woolf and the inmates. Prisoners continue to spend up to 20 hours a day in their cells. Judge Tumin commented, after an unannounced inspection, that 'There was virtually no employment, no education centre and no space for full association. ... It is a matter of great public concern if decisions are now being made which could undermine a good regime in the full prison of the future'. *The Guardian*, 13 August 1992.

12 Her Majesty's Inspectorate of Constabulary Greater Manchester Police 1991 (1992). See also, Woolf Report, op. cit., chap.11., para. 152.

13 Council of Europe, Report to the United Kingdom Government on the Visit to the United Kingdom carried out by the European Committee for the Prevention of Torture and Inhuman or Degrading Treatment or Punishment from 29 July 1990 to 10 August 1990 (1991) Strasbourg.

buckets were forced to squeeze past others carrying their food on narrow walkways. 'This is both unhygenic and uncivilised.'[14] Overcrowding was a particular concern. 'It was a significant problem at Wandsworth, worse at Brixton and outrageous at Leeds.'[15] The situation in Brixton, Wandsworth and Leeds prisons was held to be 'inhuman and degrading' and by implication in breach of Article 3 of the European Convention for the Protection of Fundamental Rights and Freedoms. Frances Crook, director of the Howard League for Penal Reform, stated: 'The government has known for years that conditions are inhuman and degrading, and this must amount to deliberate maltreatment.'[16] The Home Office responded by rejecting the committee's allegations.

In June 1992, 'Helsinki Watch', the independent human rights monitoring organisation based in New York, issued a report on British prisons.[17] The Report stated that the prison riots in April 1990 'served as a desperate warning to the government and the public that the abhorrent living conditions in many prisons could no longer be tolerated.' Although the report recognises that reform has begun, it continued: 'Even though prison officials tried to convince us that massive improvements had been made, it was clear that, as one prison official stated during our visit "The British prison system is just coming out of the dark ages".' The prison authorities proved unhelpful in terms of access and the committee was denied entry into Wandsworth, Birmingham, Bedford and Maze prisons. In other prisons members were hurried along or obliged to tour with foreign students and they were unable to talk with prisoners who alleged physical violence by prison staff. The committee described the overcrowding, lack of sanitation and inadequate educational or work opportunities as mistreatment and some elements were in breach of United Nations minimum standards.

A description of an average dispersal prison comes from an official report.[18] Canterbury prison in south east England is Victorian in design and age. When inspected in March 1991 it was overcrowded by 50 per cent. Most prisoners were two to a cell without integral sanitation. Half of the prisoners were without employment and others were involved in sewing mailbags. Half of the prisoners were on remand and spent 20 hours a day in their cells. They had no work, no education and no access to books. Visitors were obliged to wait outside the prison in all weathers and when admitted used a cramped, collective visiting room, for up to half an hour, where there were no facilities for children, no carpets, curtains and no privacy.

In June 1992, Dartmoor prison, a 183-year-old Victorian establishment, was described by Judge Stephen Tumin, the Chief Inspector of Prisons, as a 'dustbin' which should be closed by the end of 1993 unless radical reforms occurred. The judge is reported to have been so appalled by the conditions he saw that he was close to

---

14 *Daily Telegraph*, 13 December 1991.

15 *The Independent*, 13 December 1991.

16 *Daily Telegraph*, 13 December 1991.

17 Prison Conditions in the UK (1992).

18 Her Majesty's Chief Inspector of Prisons, HM Prison Canterbury (1992). See generally, R. Morgan, *Following Woolf: The Prospects for Prison Policy* (1992) 19, Journal of Law and Society 231-50.

recommending its immediate closure.[19] He found prisoners scrubbing dishes with the same brushes they use to clean lavatories and food was left in open containers on the floor near waste and cockroaches.

Subsequently, in October 1992 the Chief Inspector of Prisons was obliged to issue a highly critical report indicating that prisoners are still suffering from overcrowding, disgraceful living conditions and inadequate medical provision. The report states 'Many points we have raised many times remain accepted but not remedied.'[20] It further warned of the problem of drugs which many inmates claim are easier to procure inside prison than outside.

The general concerns of Judge Stephen Tumin were again focused on a particular prison with his report on Wymott prison in Leyland. It appeared to inspectors that prisoners seemed to be in control of their wings at night. The report stated 'Prisoners appeared amazed that anyone should be trespassing on "their" territory and we strongly suspected that drugs were in open use. ... Drugs were acknowledged to be freely available. Inmates told us they were easier to obtain than outside ... Our tour of the six workshops was revealing. In the laundry we found some 10 inmates asleep, certainly not through overwork but possibly because of the influence of drugs and/or watching TV through the night. A similar scene was found in the light textile workshop ... It is hard to imagine a more corrupting environment in which to place an offender.'[21] The response of the then Home Secretary, Kenneth Clarke, was 'The prison's success in discovering drugs is testimony to the governor's pro-active policy in this area and the skill of his searching teams.'[22]

Within the newly established private prison sector there is evidence of dissatisfaction. For example, in the first private prison, Wolds, which was opened in April 1992, a report by the highly respected Prison Reform Trust, indicated unsatisfactory performances at a number of levels. The attempt to create a drug free unit for up to 50 prisoners had failed. The Trust has evidence that drugs are widely available inside Wolds and one drug expert commented that it was the only prison he had visited where heroin was widely available.[23]

One consequence of the dissatisfaction with prison conditions has been discussions within the Home Office, as voiced by the Home Secretary, Michael Howard, about establishing an even more austere prison regime.[24] Such a policy would run contrary to the recommendations within the Woolf Report and to the character of the reports issued by the Chief Inspector of Prisons.

---

19 *The Independent*, 2 June 1992. The Home Secretary, Kenneth Clarke, rejected the Report on the day of its publication.

20 *The Guardian*, 30 October 1992.

21 *The Guardian*, 17 November 1992.

22 The Prison Officers Association and the Wymott prison governor refuted that there were no-go areas in the prison and denied that drugs were easier to obtain inside than outside the prison. *The Guardian*, 18 November 1992.

23 *The Guardian*, 5 April 1993. On 15 August 1993 Virginia Bottomley, The Secretary for Health, indicated that the private sector will be allowed to build and operate between 60 and 65 secure units for juveniles.

24 *The Guardian*, 24 August 1993.

## PRISON POPULATION

The most obvious characteristic is the unenviable position that Britain has in the 'proportion of population in prison' table of Western European countries. This places intolerable pressures on space and prison living conditions. In addition, prisoners experience long periods of incarceration. About 35 per cent of prisoners discharged in any one year have served over 12 months. Half of all sentenced men released from prison, a third of women and 70 per cent of young offenders are reconvicted within two years. Like other prison populations described in this book the age structure is geared to the relatively young. Nearly 20 per cent are under the age of 21; a total of over 40 per cent are under 25 and nearly two thirds are under 30. Fifteen per cent of male prisoners and over 23 per cent of female prisoners describe themselves as black or Asian. In addition, 44 per cent of unconvicted prisoners were unemployed and over 40 per cent of prisoners have no formal educational qualifications. Fifty per cent of prisoners are married or living with a partner prior to imprisonment and 32 per cent of males had dependent children.[25] However, a NACRO survey of 10 per cent of the prison population found that nearly half were at risk of being homeless on release and 89 per cent were likely to be unemployed.[26]

The prison population is also far more likely to commit suicide. For example, between 1983 and 1993 the number of prisoners committing suicide has increased by more than 25 per cent and prisoners are seven times more likely to commit suicide than people living in the community. In 1990 there were 50 suicides. It is prisoners under the age of 25 who are most likely to take their own lives.[27] Frances Crook, director of the Howard League for Penal Reform, stated: 'The overuse of penal custody kills. The majority of people sent to prison are poor, vulnerable and young. They are not able to cope with the bleakness of prison life.'[28]

There is also a disproportionately high black prison population. Sixteen per cent of the total prison population in 1992 came from ethnic minorities, compared with their representation in the general population of under 5 per cent. In 1985 the proportion of black prisoners in the prison population was 12.6 per cent which rose to 14.6 per cent by 1988.[29]

Because of the shortage of secure units for juveniles there has been a growing trend to place young people in prisons. The 370 secure units within children's homes are due to be supplemented by a further 65 units which will be provided by the private sector through contracting out the building and operation of the extra units.[30] The new units may not be operational until 1996. In the meantime, the number of 15 and 16-year-old boys sent to prison to await trial stood at 1,162 in 1992 and this figure is set to rise for 1993. Since July 1990 some 20 teenagers have taken their own lives in prison establishments. However, section 60 of the Criminal Justice Act 1991 will

---

25 Prison Reform Trust, The Identikit Prisoner (1991).

26 NACRO, News Release, August 1993.

27 Howard League, Dying Inside: Suicides in Prison (1993).

28 *The Guardian*, 18 August 1993.

29 Race Policies into Action, NACRO (1992).

30 *The Guardian*, 16 August 1993.

make it illegal to remand this age group in prison to await trial. The earliest this section will come into force is 1995.

During 1990, some 3,176 women were received into prisons. In June 1990 remand prisoners constituted 22 per cent of the prison population which stood at 1,613 women. Nine per cent of women received as sentenced prisoners during 1990 had been convicted of drugs offences compared with four per cent of men. Twenty-five per cent of the women's sentenced population in June 1990 had been convicted of drugs offences, compared with eight per cent of the male prison population.

Prisoners are subject to being moved from prison to prison thereby producing the possibility of cross infection. Thus, the prison population is predominantly young, male, white, surprisingly 'mobile' and sexually active.

In addition to the large and rising numbers, British prisons house more people serving life sentences than are to be found in all of the other Western European prison systems. A survey established that the United Kingdom had 3,503 'lifers' compared with 2,688 in the rest of Western Europe.[31] One in every 13 sentenced prisoners is serving a life sentence. The number of life sentence prisoners increased four fold over 20 years. In 1970 the number was 730 which represented 2 per cent of the sentenced prison population. By 1990 the number had risen to 2,795 or 8 per cent of the sentenced prison population. A life sentence is indeterminate. The average period of detention after sentence for the 68 lifers released in 1989 was 12 years. Prisoners who have murdered police officers or prison officers, murdered during the course of terrorist acts, committed the sexual or sadistic murder of children or murdered by firearms during the course of robbery can normally expect to serve at least 20 years. In most long term prisons inmates are housed in single cells and some prisoners have their own cell key.

The issue of sentencing an offender who has been diagnosed as HIV positive was considered in R. v. Moore.[32] A man of 37 pleaded guilty to a number of burglaries. He had been diagnosed HIV positive in 1986 and there was a likelihood that he would develop AIDS within about two years. The court was informed treatment was available within prison but it would be easier if he were at liberty. The appeal court held that a sentence of five years was not too long given the nature of the medical evidence. It further stated that if the time were to come when for practical or reasons of humanity it was no longer possible to hold Moore because of his condition then the Home Office could deal with it under established procedures. Subsequently, in R v. Starke[33] the Court of Criminal Appeal stated that where a defendant suffering from AIDS had a life expectancy of between one and four years, it was not correct to reduce the sentence of four years imprisonment and this was a matter for the possible exercise of the royal prerogative of mercy.

---

31 Quaker Council for European Affairs, Life Imprisonment (1990). On 30 June 1991 there were nearly 2,900 persons serving a life sentence in England and Wales. This is an increase of 73 per cent on the figure on 30 June 1981. Prison Statistics England and Wales 1991 Cm. 2157 (1993).

32 *The Times*, 30 July 1990.

33 1992 Crim. L.R. 384 (CA).

DRUGS USE

As in other European and North American countries drug users constitute a significant proportion of prisoners. Figures for 30 June 1991 show that 2,850 prisoners were recorded centrally as being in prison sentenced for drug offences in England and Wales. This constituted nearly 10 per cent of the total sentenced male prison population for which an offence was recorded.[34] In 1984 there were 1,650 people in jail for drug offences. More recently, the Prison Service evidence to the Woolf Committee indicated that between 2,000 and 3,000 inmates have been reported by medical officers as having some degree of dependence upon drugs at the time of their reception into custody.[35] In 1990 some 2,739 prisoners were inside for drug related offences. The number of people with a drug problem entering prison has increased sharply since the mid-1980s: drug offenders increased by 20 per cent per year between 1986 and 1990. For women the figures are even more startling: 55 women in 1980 rising to 303 in 1990. Drug offenders account for a third of all convicted women prisoners.[36] In 1993 it is estimated that some 12,000 people who inject drugs will spend time in a British prison.[37]

The Prison Service has noted 'These figures are recognised as understating the scale of drug abuse in respect of people sent to prison.'[38] Evidence to the Woolf Committee from Professor Gunn, Department of Forensic Psychiatry at the Institute of Psychiatry, states survey work as finding, amongst the sentenced prison population, a level of drug use/dependency of 10.1 per cent for adult males, 6.2 per cent for male youths and 24.2 per cent for females. His criterion was the daily use of drugs of dependency during the six months period prior to the index offence. Thus, cannabis users were discounted.

Evidence indicates that there is serious official under-accounting of drug users in prison. It is not merely the difficult issue of quantifying criminal activity. In addition the formal recognition of the widespread existence of drug use within the prison could be perceived as an admission of failure by the prison authorities to control the behaviour of their charges.

The majority of prisoners do not identify themselves as drug users upon reception for fear of receiving different and unpleasant treatment. Some prisoners have been placed in isolation for the period of withdrawal yet had received no appropriate medication during this stressful time. Institutional procedures appear to pay insufficient attention to this problem even as a medical issue. Professor Gunn's report stated that 'prison doctors regarded drug and alcohol abuse as being outside their area of concern ... many prison medical officers lack interest or involvement in the care of substance abusers, whether their primary problem is drugs or alcohol.'[39] Dr Dolan, of the Centre for Research on Drug Behaviour, London, stated that studies on injecting drug users discharged from prison showed that up to 10 per cent carried the virus. She

---

34 *Hansard*, House of Commons, 26 January 1993, col. 686.

35 Woolf Report, op. cit., chap. 12 para. 339.

36 *The Guardian*, 4 July 1992.

37 *New Scientist*, 20 February 1993.

38 Ibid.

39 Ibid., chap. 12 para. 341.

calculated that about 60 drug abusers could be infected each year whilst in prison. Up to 900 jailed drug abusers could be at risk whilst in the custody of the prison.[40]

The Home Office, the responsible department for prisons, has claimed that there is a 'low incidence of intravenous misuse in prisons in England and Wales.'[41] It further claimed that 'Our evidence based on close surveillance suggests that such activity (needle sharing) is on a very small scale.'[42] Some prison governors rallied to this position of decrying the apparent widespread abuse of drugs. For example, the deputy governor of Stafford prison stated 'We think the possible use of IV drugs is very, very minimal.'[43] The governor of Saughton prison, Edinburgh, announced that 'I have no evidence that needles are shared.'[44] Not all senior managers are so cautious in their public statements over drugs awareness. In contrast, the deputy governor of Cardiff prison stated, when commenting on a death in prison as a result of a heroin overdose in April 1992, that: 'There exists a drug sub-culture which is almost impossible to stamp out.'[45] In England, the governor of Featherstone prison stated that 'he was at a loss about how to tackle the problem of drugs circulating among prisoners.'[46]

On the other hand, there exists a growing body of evidence indicating that the problem of drug abuse within the prison is both widespread and well known to all who live or work therein. For example, the National Association of Probation Officers stated that 617 needles or syringes had been found by prison staff between 1987 and 1989.[47] A survey by this organisation discovered a high incidence of drug abuse. The use of heroin by injection was reported in 25 of the 40 establishments surveyed. The multiple use of unsterilised needles is commonplace so that the equipment may become more important than the drugs. In two prisons the needles which were discovered were in a 'distressed state' and had been used by many people over a period of time.[48]

Prison users confirm the multiple use of drug injecting equipment. An ex-prisoner from Holloway, London, stated that she knew of five people with at least three sets of works and summed up the desperation of prisoners: 'When you need a fix you'll use any needle.'[49] Another ex-prisoner from Holloway, who had been convicted of armed robbery to feed her habit, said 'You always got something to sort you out. I had no qualms about sharing needles, much as I knew about AIDS.'[50] 'One

40 *The Guardian*, 21 July 1992.

41 Prison Medical Service: Third Report of the Social Services Committee, Session 1985-86 (1986) para. 8, HMSO.

42 Unpublished comments on recommendations of NAPO briefing paper, Prisons, Risks and HIV. See generally, P.A. Thomas, *HIV/AIDS in Prisons* (1990) 29, The Howard Journal of Criminal Law 1-13; A. Young and J.V. McHale, *The Dilemmas of the HIV Positive Prisoner* (1992) 32, The Howard Journal of Criminal Law 89-104.

43 Panorama, BBC 1, 1989.

44 Brass Tacks, BBC 2, 1989.

45 HTV news report, 31 July 1992.

46 *Birmingham Evening News*, 19 January 1993.

47 Woolf Report, op. cit., chap. 12 para. 347.

48 NAPO, Prisons, Risk and HIV (1989).

49 'The Killer Inside' Panorama, BBC 1, (1989).

50 *New Scientist*, op. cit.

ex-prisoner told a TV reporter 'I was lending my needle to 20 prisoners and I'm HIV. They knew I'm HIV.' [51] Yet another ex-prisoner stated 'I must have got it (HIV) in my last prison sentence as I was sharing needles in prison. There were two sets of works between 30 of us.'[52] Youths leaving custody in Merseyside have indicated that one syringe can be shared between 30 and 40 people within a single day in prison.[53] Dr G. Hart studied 50 men and women who spent an average of 20.6 months in prison since 1982. Forty-seven ex-prisoners had taken at least one illegal drug in prison and of these 33 had done so by injection. Twenty-six had shared injecting equipment. Four of them had anal sex whilst in custody and they had between four and 16 partners.[54] Another survey of 452 ex-prisoners showed that 40 per cent were aware that drug injecting took place on the wing or the landing where they had spent the bulk of their time in prison. Three quarters of those who practised drug injection said they had shared needles and syringes with others. One man said 'I shared in jail and cleaned the needle by flushing the toilet and holding it under the water.'[55] In May 1992 an inquest jury decided that a prisoner in Winchester prison died by misadventure as a result of a drug overdose.[56] During an amnesty on syringes at Oxford prison in 1988 both of the syringes that were handed in were found to be infected with the HIV virus.[57] In Wolds private prison one inmate stated 'Every so often you'll get a strip search but it's not very often. Drugs, you can put them down your pants, down your socks, in your pockets. I've seen people sneak in bottles of Bacardi. It's not as if they can put that down their socks or down their pants. It's just so easy.'[58]

The contrast between official and unofficial figures is well illustrated by the findings of a survey undertaken by the Prison Officers Association in 1984. Returns from members working in Liverpool prison showed that in 1982 there were 40 instances of drug discovery and in the next year the figure rose to 54. The official Report of the Director General's Office stated that those years showed only one discovery of drugs in that prison.[59] Nevertheless, the general proposition that the number of HIV prisoners correlates positively with the number of drug dependent prisoners would appear to apply in this prison system.

## SEX BETWEEN MEN

Homosexual sex continues to be a criminal offence in England and Wales although it was decriminalised under the Sexual Offences Act 1967 in that 'a homosexual act in private shall not be an offence provided that the parties consent thereto and have

51 Ibid.

52 Ibid.

53 R. Newcombe, *Prisoners and HIV Infection* (1987), Merseyside Drug Journal 10.

54 *The Independent*, 25 May 1990.

55 Centre for Research on Drugs and Health Behaviour Prisons, HIV and AIDS: Risks and Experiences in Custodial Care (1991).

56 LAG, June 1992, 28.

57 R.D.T. Farmer, Transmission of HIV within prisons and its likely effect on the growth of the epidemic in the general population (1989).

58 *The Guardian*, 5 April, 1993.

59 P.A. Thomas, op. cit., 9.

attained the age of 21.' The result is that gay men continue to be imprisoned. One hundred and seventy-eight men were taken into prison in 1989 for offences of buggery (anal intercourse) and indecency between men. In June 1989 the prison population for these offences stood at 375 men.[60] Official figures show that the number of males convicted of sexual offences has risen throughout the decade of the 1980s. For example, 25 men were convicted in 1980 under the Sexual Offences Act 1956, section 13, as amended by the Sexual Offences Act 1967, section 3 (2), which is concerned with men over 21 procuring or being party to an act of gross indecency with men under 21. In 1989 the figure had risen to 69 men. One hundred and eight men were convicted in 1980 of procuring or being party to an act of gross indecency with another man over the age 21. In 1989 the number of convictions for that offence had risen to 265 men.[61] In addition, assuming that homosexual men are imprisoned in similar proportions to heterosexual men but for offences other than those encompassed within the Sexual Offences legislation then approximately 10 per cent of the prison population at any one time is gay. Nevertheless, condoms are not available for prisoners for use within prisons[62] although this policy is under review.[63]

There is a body of evidence, particularly from the USA, which indicates that sexually active men may at times cross over the sexual boundary during their incarceration. Such a conclusion concerning the confinement of large numbers of young, sexually active males in a single sex institution is not surprising, particularly to those familiar with the British public school system! The prison regime continues to lock people up in multiple occupancy cells for extended periods of time. A survey of 4,000 prisoners produced returns indicating that 52 per cent had a cell to themselves. Sharing of cells was most common among remand prisoners, only 18 per cent of whom had a single cell. Twenty per cent said they had been locked in their cell for more than 20 hours on the previous day to the survey. The average lock up time was fourteen and a half hours. Thirty per cent of the prisoners felt that the most important improvement in prison life would be the introduction of conjugal visits which are not currently offered.[64]

Professor Gunn has suggested that overcrowded conditions increase the need for sexual contact.[65] A survey of 453 ex-prisoners showed that one in 10 admitted that sexual acts occurred in prison and of those who also admitted to participating in such acts they all described unprotected anal penetration.[66] Marcus Hellewell, who spent three years in prison, stated that during his imprisonment 58 men shared his cell at

60 *Hansard*, 11 June 1991, vol. 192, col. 509.

61 *Hansard*, 18 February, 1991, vol. 186, col. 17.

62 Peter Lloyd, Home Office Minister: 'Procedural guidelines issued to prison governors in November 1991 advised that the period leading up to release is an important time for educational measures and for individual counselling of HIV infected prisoners ... The guidelines also recommended that governors consider introducing schemes under which all prisoners released - and perhaps those going on home leave - have discreet access to a small supply of free condoms. Several establishments - including at least one for women - operate such schemes.' *Hansard*, 16 June 1992, vol. 209, col. 432-33.

63 Ibid.

64 The National Prison Survey 1991, Home Office, 1993.

65 *The Independent*, 20 January 1988.

66 Prisons, HIV and Aids op. cit.

different times. Seventeen had high risk sex with him and some of those were heterosexuals. He believed that up to 85 per cent of men have some kind of sexual experience in prison. He thought 'sex relieves the frustration and boredom of prison.'[67] T. Dan Smith, a former politician and ex-prisoner, talked of being 'confined in a cell with two homosexuals who proceeded to make passionate love for hours.'[68] The Advisory Council on the Misuse of Drugs has been given evidence which led it to state 'homosexual acts occur on a significant scale amongst male prisoners, including amongst those who are heterosexual when in the community.'[69] The Prison Reform Trust reported, on evidence from prisoners and prison staff, that between 20 and 30 per cent of prisoners in long term prisons may be involved in homosexual activity.[70] This figure is particularly important given the disproportionately high number of 'lifers' in British prisons. This claim was supported by the evidence of the survey conducted by the National Association of Probation Officers in 40 establishments where it was stated that sexual relationships were not unusual between prisoners. Bi-sexual activity was reported by 12 out of 40 probation officers.[71]

Again, the official position refutes the above claims of an active homosexual prison community. The Home Office is on record as saying that 'the number of cases of homosexual behaviour is thought to be low.'[72] The Home Office library has no classification explicitly covering homosexuality in prisons. Prison governors have made similar statements. J. May, governor of Dartmoor prison, said 'I don't think we have a problem and there is no great need for the free issue of condoms. In Dartmoor, obviously, we have some people who are homosexuals but it doesn't present us with any difficulties.'[73] Douglas Hogg, former Minister of State, Home Office, declared that 'We have no evidence of the extent of homosexuality in prisons.'[74] Subsequently, Angela Rumbold, Home Office Minister, stated that 'some prisoners were very likely to have sex in prison.'[75]

## TESTING

The number of prisoners who have died from AIDS is thought to be four between 1988 and 1990.[76] All deaths occurred in civil hospitals. The number of known HIV positive prisoners stands at any one time at around 70. Between 1985 and 1990 the number of prisoners reported as infected was 317[77] and the Home Office has

---

67 *The Independent*, 6 June 1991.

68 *The Guardian*, 20 February 1985.

69 AIDS and Drug Misuse, part 1 (1988).

70 U. Padel, HIV, AIDS and Prisons (1988).

71 NAPO, Prisons, Risk and HIV (1989).

72 Prison Medical Service: Third Report of the Social Services Committee, session 1985-86 (1986), House of Commons.

73 *Tavistock Times*, 19 February 1988.

74 Brass Tacks, BBC 2, 1989.

75 *The Guardian*, 11 February 1991.

76 Prison Reform Trust, HIV, AIDS and Prisons: Update (1991).

77 *The Independent*, 20 September 1990.

estimated that 0.1 per cent of the prison population is infected.[78] Such an official figure indicates an insignificant number of infected prisoners and certainly nothing to be overly concerned about. However, the former Director of Prison Medical Services has stated that these figures are incorrect and his estimate rose to between 350 and 500 prisoners.[79] Given that academics have been denied access to conduct research in prisons this figure remains a 'guesstimate'. However, Harry Fletcher, spokesman for the National Association of Probation Officers, has stated that 'the real figure for HIV in prisons is ten times the government's figure.'[80]

In addition, prisoners on reception are reluctant to announce that they are in categories which would result in isolation or treatment they perceive as detrimental. This attitude is no different from many gay men who avoid the test because, for example, they may be penalised thereafter for insurance or mortgage purposes even if the test proves negative. Currently, testing of prisoners is voluntary. Prisoners are subject to the mass and anonymous epidemiological surveys that are conducted but this is of value only for statistical purposes as particular inmates are not identifiable. In April 1992 it was announced that, in principle, approval from the Home Office had been received for voluntary anonymous testing to occur within prisons. This would be along the lines of those being conducted amongst pregnant women in antenatal clinics where unnamed samples are taken to establish the scale of infection rather than identify particular individuals at risk. Remand prisoners would be the first group to be offered this opportunity to test.[81]

On reception all prisoners are questioned to discover whether they are 'high risk' and blood tests are available to those who agree to the test. However, the meaning of 'voluntary' must be questioned. Some prisoners identified as 'high risk' have been isolated until such time as they volunteer for the test.[82] Wandsworth prison is such a place where those considered to be members of 'high risk' groups were isolated in the Viral Infection Restriction Unit (VIR) until tested and proved negative. Terry McLaren, Prison Officers Association secretary in that prison, stated: 'It is a one-off at Wandsworth and is a joint policy agreed by the government and the POA which has been in force since 1985. The Home Office has said it contradicts its policy but they are content to let it continue because I think they agree with us that there are benefits.'[83] The spokesman did not make clear who were the beneficiaries but it would appear reasonable to exclude the suspected prisoners. Those who were found to be seropositive were placed under a VIR order. Under this arrangement they are isolated from other prisoners and withdrawn from kitchen work or any other form of work where blood spillage was possible. Although the Home Office's policy, as stated by Douglas Hogg, is that HIV prisoners should 'participate as fully as possible in normal prison life.'[84] It was accepted by the Prison Medical Inspectorate that many prisons

---

78 NAPO, op. cit., p. 2.

79 Parliamentary All Party Penal Affairs Group, 29 November 1988. See also, Prison Service News, February 1989.

80 *The Independent*, 6 June 1991.

81 *The Guardian*, 3rd April 1992.

82 Padel, op. cit., *The Independent*, 25 May 1990.

83 *The Independent*, 25 May 1990.

84 *Hansard*, House of Commons, 16 March 1989, col. 295.

did not meet this requirement and less than half of all HIV positive prisoners were on normal location.

The Woolf report stated that a visit to the VIR unit in Wandsworth prison presented a number of inmates who either were HIV positive or were awaiting their results. They were housed in a small, dingy and airless basement. They had one hour of exercise, some classes and visits to the library. Otherwise they were confined to the basement. The Woolf report stated:

'It is hardly any wonder that, given the prospect of such conditions prisoners who may be concerned about the possibility of having the AIDS virus may be reluctant to express that concern to the prison authorities. We could not imagine conditions more likely to deter a prisoner from doing all in his power to avoid revealing that he was or might be HIV positive than those we saw at Wandsworth. The conditions were a travesty of justice.'[85]

The treatment of prisoners in VIR units illustrates why many were reluctant to embark voluntarily upon a process which guarantees experiences such as those which follow. One prisoner is reported as saying 'the test was forced upon me. Also counselling was not given or offered. I was held in isolation until the results were known.' What follows are a series of responses from different interviewees: 'If you get allocated to the blood test wing the only way the authorities will treat you as HIV negative is if you have the test. So they are twisting your arm.' One man indicated that 'Nobody would talk to us, nobody would even eat dinner with us.' Another said: 'I was not allowed to work in any area. I was banged up 23 hours a day. Not allowed to use the gym, the only exercise I had was short walks around a circular path.' Another said 'I had to eat off plastic disposable plates' and 'I had no exercise, only allowed to slop out once a day, no use of a bath at all, I had to use drinking water to wash.'[86] In 1991 it was reported that prisoners at Stafford jail infected with HIV were led on chains when they visited the local hospital. Handcuffs were attached to the escorting officer by a chain 'between six and eight feet in length'. The practice had been written into the jail's operational rules at the insistence of the local branch of the Prison Officers' Association because of 'residual fears' of the officers.[87] However, private correspondence with the Home Office indicates that local policy now conforms with Home Office guidelines. Such operational practices and institutional treatment negated the innovative procedures and counselling services which are being developed in prisons such as Bristol and constituted positive disincentives to prisoners who might consider taking the HIV test.

## CONFIDENTIALITY

The maintenance of confidentiality within prison presents particular problems. The closed society breeds internecine gossip. For example, the 'need to know' prison policy promoted by the Home Office which extends the doctor and patient relationship to include certain prison officers can result in this information being a source of both

---

85 Woolf, op. cit., chap. 12. para. 360.
86 Centre for Research on Drugs and Health Behaviour HIV prevalence and risk behaviour of 452 ex-prisoners in England (1991).
87 *The Guardian*, 27 September 1991.

power and punishment. Informing others of the health status of a prisoner could result in serious damage to that person's social standing and personal treatment within the institution. For example, as VIR is written on their files this identifies them to those with access to the file but who are not necessarily required to know under the rules governing restricted information. This presents the opportunity for gross misuse of power such as occurred in the women's prison, Holloway in London, where prison officers wrote 'HIV' in red letters on every prison noticeboard where a prisoner's name was listed.[88] Given the policy of isolation which affects most prisoners who are suspected of having or have the virus then the labelling process is automatic and self-evident. Such units have been called the 'AIDS wing'.[89] The Woolf report was critical of segregation and 'need to know' policies:

'We have no evidence either that disclosure - on a 'need to know' basis - to wing staff that a prisoner was HIV positive is necessary or desirable ... HIV prisoners must not and need not become the pariahs of the prison system. Prisoners must ... be helped not hounded.'[90]

However, it was announced in July 1993 that segregation of HIV prisoners would be formally abolished later in the year.[91]

HEALTH CARE

The Prison Medical Service has for many years been subject to intense criticism which included concern over poorly trained medical and nursing officers. In 1992 the prison health programme was radically restructured.[92] The name of the service was changed to the Prison Health Care Service for Prisoners. A formal recognition of the equivalence principle was made. This states that prisoners should receive health care at a level no lower than that available in civil society. This had been put into the AIDS context by Dr John Kilgour who stated 'What we must ensure in the prison system is that we reflect the attitudes, the ethics and the standards of care of the community at large in the face of the threat presented by the aids virus.'[93] It is hoped that these major changes will move the prison away from the punishment and towards a medical paradigm. However, the bottom line is clear. Ultimately, and essentially, the effective restructuring of prison health care necessitates adequate Treasury funding accompanied by a fundamental change in the attitudes and behaviour of those officers and managers who have traditionally applied the punishment rather than the medical paradigm to those in their 'care'.

---

88 *City Limits*, 6 April 1989.

89 Padel, op. cit.

90 Woolf, op. cit., chap. 12. para. 369.

91 *The Guardian*, 12 July 1993.

92 P.A. Thomas and R. Costigan, *Health Care or Punishment: Prisoners with HIV/AIDS* (1992) 33, Howard Journal of Criminal Law 321-36. This article provides a detailed account of the changes in the health care system for prisoners.

93 J. Kilgour, *AIDS and the Prison System* (1987), Prison Service Journal July, 17.

RESEARCH

The policy of the Home Office was to reject statements about the widespread use of drugs in prison and that homosexual acts occurred. This position was supported by the lack of hard, objective evidence to prove this proposal. However, the Home Office was also opposed to such work being undertaken in prisons thereby, by its very stance, making the testing of the proposal impossible.[94] This policy has been reviewed. In 1993 it was announced that prisoners in Brixton and Wandsworth prisons, London, are to take part in a survey of their knowledge, attitudes and risk behaviour. The research will cover sexual behaviour, drug injecting and tatooing. It is a pilot study for a larger Department of Health project. The Director of Health Care for the Prison Service, Dr Rosemary Wool, commented that the service needed to find out what influenced HIV risk behaviour 'in order to plan the next phase in our strategy to fight AIDS in prison. It is not clear whether prisons accelerate or decelerate the rate of HIV transmission. This survey will provide information on the nature, context and prevalence of HIV risk activities in prison.'[95]

Another study of the prevalence of the virus amongst inmates is being established in Wormwood Scrubs, Pentonville and Belmarsh prisons by the Home Office and the Department of Health. It will help in the provision of services for seropositive inmates and in prevention work although the prisoners with the virus will not be identified.[96] These developments suggest that progress is being made within the Prison Service to address, in a realistic manner, the issues that arise out of the need to control the spread of the virus. Bob Hawkins, coordinator of the Cleveland Street Needle Exchange, London, says 'there is a gaping hole in the strategy for preventing the spread of HIV. The strategy has been fairly effective outside but we are giving it away at the prison gate.'[97] Within the same article Graham Bird, an AIDS researcher at the University of Edinburgh, agreed by saying 'If we are serious about stopping infection outside, we must not ignore policies inside.' However, in response, Dr Wool, whilst acknowledging the gap, argues that it is closing, albeit 'painfully slowly'.

THE LAW

Paradoxically, it is the law itself which contributes to the problem of controlling the spread of the virus within prisons. The fact that the use of certain drugs and homosexual acts are illegal resulted in those responsible for prisons adopting a totally hostile attitude towards liberalising measures aimed to enhance the health and safety of inmates. Whether this hostility merely exploits the existence of the law or is based upon the particular principles it seeks to uphold is a moot point. Nevertheless, there is a conflict between what the criminal law demands and what public health requires. The Sexual Offences Act 1967 states '... a homosexual act in private shall not be an offence provided that the parties consent thereto and have attained the age of 21.' This

---

94 See, P.A. Thomas, *AIDS in Prison* op. cit.

95 *The Guardian*, 12 July 1993.

96 *The Guardian*, 21 April 1993.

97 *New Society*, op. cit.

decriminalising measure does not apply to prisons as the Home Office claims there is no 'private' space in these institutions. However, it is reported that the Home Office in 1993 dropped its assertion that homosexual acts in jails are always illegal.[98] Likewise the Misuse of Drugs Act 1971 prohibits the possession or supply of controlled drugs. In addition, the prison rules would see the above as breaches of internal discipline which would attract sanctions.

Home leave for prisoners is currently available for low or medium risk offenders irrespective of the nature of their offence after a third of their sentence has been completed. However, the system was reviewed in October 1992 after allegations that it is too lax and further calls to tighten the process have been made.[99] Government spokespeople have consistently refused to countenance the possibility of introducing condoms and needle exchange schemes into the prison system.[100] For example, Angela Rumbold, Home Office Minister, said that both were unacceptable and that 'the more responsible course is to bring home to prisoners the very high risk they take in sharing needles and syringes.'[101] The Home Office has stated that 'The Department is not contemplating anything in the nature of a needle exchange scheme for prisoners.'[102] This position reflects a more general condemnation of drugs as the enemy of society. For example, Tim Rathbone MP, at the Association of Chief Police Officers annual conference in 1992, stated 'Drugs misuse threatens the health and well being of individuals and families and communities everywhere. Even democratic practice is at risk in some countries.'[103]

In addition, the prison riot in September 1993 at Wymott, resulting in damage of buildings to the cost of £20 million, appears set to legitimate the introduction of an even stricter prison regime, longer sentences and a larger prison population. The concerns to reduce the prison population, which, for example, resulted in 2,000 prisoners being released in one single day in June 1983 were replaced by growth thereafter and will be exacerbated by renewed Conservative Party cries for more law and order. The latest prison disturbance provides justification for a prison policy which contradicts the recommendations of Mr. Justice Woolf and the import of the Criminal Justice Act 1991, both of which aimed to reduce the prison population.[104]

---

98 *Independent on Sunday*, 28 February 1993.

99 In 1992 about 35,000 home leaves were granted and 2,301 prisoners failed to return. It is thought that 17 serious offences were committed by absconders, including two murders, one rape and eight armed robberies. *The Guardian*, 14 August 1993.

100 However, home leave prisoners at Lancaster prison are offered condoms for their weekend absences from prison. Home leave is allowed for two short visits a year and one long home leave in the last four months of the sentence. Conjugal visits into British prisons are not allowed. *The Guardian*, 12 April 1991.

101 *Daily Telegraph*, 30 May 1991.

102 Home Office, Unpublished comments on recommendations of NAPO Briefing Paper, Prisons, Risk and HIV (1989).

103 *The Guardian*, 4 July 1992.

104 'The ethos has clearly changed. Ministers no longer discourage the use of imprisonment.' Vivien Stern, Director, National Association for the Resettlement of Prisoners, *The Guardian*, 8 September 1993.

More generally, the legal rules and associated moral codes make changes within the closed institution difficult. The status of prisoners is socially low, politically relatively unimportant whilst their legal capacity is limited. In addition, for officials to accept the reality of an existing or potential health explosion within prisons as a result of 'illegal conduct' opens them to charges of maladministration. The internal social codes which operate and sustain prison life sometimes clash with public perceptions of those structures and the substantive law of the land which is supposed to operate within the prison. Thus, the Official Secrets Act 1989, which includes prisons, works to keep enquirers out of prison investigations. In this sense, prison walls are as much to keep people out as to keep people in! Likewise, tautologous arguments about research can be employed effectively by stating that there is no research to prove the alleged seriousness of the claims, no research is possible because the researchers will be examining criminal activities amongst people of proven dishonesty, without such evidence there is no basis on which current policy can be changed.[105]

One approach to promote change is to recognise the closed prison as a 'bridgehead' for the virus into the wider community and therefore as an issue to be tackled for the sake of the public good. Pragmatically, this might be valid although this argument devalues and, I believe, denigrates the legitimate claim of prisoners to the freestanding right to health care and a clean and safe environment. Legal formalism and moral codes are at loggerheads with issues of public health and human rights. In this struggle the conclusion is obvious even though its achievement remains problematic.

---

105 Judge Stephen Tumin, Chief Inspector of Prisons, has called for immediate research into high risk behaviour. 'No government is going to introduce either condoms or a needle exchange service into the prison system without the clearest possible evidence that health care requires us to do so.' *The Guardian*, 27 September 1991.

# AIDS IN PRISONS IN THE NETHERLANDS

MARTIN MOERINGS
*Willem Pompe Institute,*
*University of Utrecht*

Why does AIDS in prison deserve special attention? Addicted drug users, acknowledged as belonging to one of the major high risk groups, are significantly represented in the populations of penal institutions. Prisons may be defined as total institutions wherein the residents are excluded from the outside world and compelled to share a common social environment. In total institutions, it is a well-established phenomenon that durable close association fosters sexual interaction between residents. Given the single sex characteristic of prisons, this homosexual contact includes those residents who choose heterosexuality in their 'normal life'.

A well-known and widely held opinion in professional circles maintains that the level of civilization in a given society can be estimated by the manner in which prisoners are treated. I include the imprisoned carriers of the AIDS virus in this estimation. To what extent has the threat of contamination led to draconian measures which signify a breach of human rights and a curtailment of those other rights which are ordinarily available in a prison environment?

The possibilities and patterns of interaction with persons who are HIV positive or suffering from developed AIDS within the penal system are restricted by the possibilities which are available in the outside community. If there is no provision of methadone for drug addicts in the general community, then there will certainly be no such provision by the prison service. Further, the actual prison system and its policies and possibilities for inmate-differentiation is of considerable significance. I begin with a brief sketch of drugs and AIDS in the Dutch penitentiary system.

## DRUGS AND AIDS IN DUTCH SOCIETY

The possession and/or sale of drugs is illegal, although possession for personal use is not subjected to prosecution.[1] The Ministry of the Interior pursues a policy whereby possession of a maximum of 30 grams of hemp products does not result in

---

1 J. Silvis, A. Hendriks and N. Gilmore, *Drug Use and Human Rights in Europe Report for the European Commission* (1992), 124-127.

prosecution even though it is formally illegal. There are approximately 1,500 coffee shops[2] or other places where soft drugs are sold or distributed, and, in most towns or cities, these places are tolerated as long as they do not sell their wares to under-age persons or engage in advertising. Under pressure from neighbouring countries, sale to foreigners is not tolerated.

The provision of methadone for drug addicts is legal. It is provided within the context of medical treatment authorized by a medical practitioner. As one aspect of the campaign against AIDS 60 local councils have needle exchange programmes.[3]

Even though the number of drug addicts in the prisons is high, especially in the category of first offenders who are detained because of drug-related crimes, the idea exists that they should remain outside the prisons so that they can undergo therapy. To this end, the Prosecuting Attorney often conditionally dismisses the case on the understanding that therapy in a residential or non-residential setting follows, or the judge imposes a conditional sentence which includes such a therapy. Thus, at least at first sight, treatment is exclusively voluntary. Nonetheless, the stick of prosecution and possible imprisonment backs up the prosecutor's or judge's carrot if the conditional therapy is terminated before completion. Moreover, voices are being heard from within political and criminal law circles which call for compulsory treatment for extremely problematic drug users.

In the period from the first diagnosis in 1982 until January 1993, some 2,478 cases of AIDS have been noted in a population of more than 14 million. These cases do not so much refer to intravenous drug users (8 per cent), but, in far greater numbers, to men with variable sexual contacts (78 per cent). Contamination via heterosexual contact accounts for 7 per cent of the cases.[4]

It is assumed that almost half of the registered AIDS patients have died from their illness. Half of the registered patients are residents of Amsterdam. It is estimated that 8,000-12,000 persons are HIV positive, although it is difficult to determine this number accurately because, among other reasons, no official register exists of persons who have become HIV positive.

Since the mid-1980's there have been a number of AIDS related publicity campaigns, some of which have been directed at the general population and others at specific target groups. Homosexual organizations have developed a broad range of preventative activities and information campaigns. In 1982 it was a diversity of groups from the Gay Movement which were the vanguard in the struggle against AIDS. These groups operated effectively precisely because the Gay Movement had developed into a relatively strong pressure group. The COC Dutch Association for the Integration of Homosexuality in Holland, for example, has for years been known as the world's biggest and best organized association of homosexuals.[5]

---

2 H. Kuipers, *An Inventory of the numbers and sorts of points-of-sale for cannabis in the operational territories of National and Local Police Forces (Inventarisatie aantal en soorten cannabisverkooppunten in werkgebieden van korpsen rijkspolitie en gemeentepolitie)*, (1982).

3 *AIDS-Policy in The Netherlands (Het Nederlandse aidsbeleid)*, (1992).

4 Based on data from the Chief Medical Inspector of Public Health.

5 *If you could only get it from working too hard! Ten years of AIDS and Gay Culture (Als je het nou van hard werken kreeg! Tien jaar aids en homocultuur)*, M. van Kerkhof, T. Sandfort, and R. Geensen, (1991), 138.

An essential aspect of the attention for HIV positive persons and AIDS patients is the informal care provided by Buddies. Buddies offer practical, emotional, and social support to AIDS patients, a third of whom make use of them.

## THE PRISON POPULATION AND AIDS

### The Population

There are 7,500 prisoners in The Netherlands. The prison population has doubled in the last ten years. This is due to tougher penalties being given for certain types of crimes, especially drug trafficking, and means that judges are not simply sending offenders to prison more frequently, but, rather, are imposing longer sentences. About 40 per cent of prisoners are on remand, mostly in local Remand Prisons, though some have to be held in police stations due to shortage of places elsewhere in the system. The average length of imprisonment is about two months, although sentences for drug trafficking and serious crimes of violence are longer, usually two years or more.

The prison rate is about 50 out of every 10,000 inhabitants. The Dutch prison population used to be one of the lowest in the world, but The Netherlands may lose this favourable position if the government continues to build new prisons to house the growing numbers of offenders sentenced to longer prison terms. The Netherlands' system can prevent overcrowding by the so-called 'walking sentence', whereby less serious offenders sentenced to imprisonment for, say, up to two months, wait at home until required to report to the prison. They may indeed have to wait for several months before they can serve their sentence.

Prisons are small, most providing space for 100-250 inmates. The vast majority of prisoners are male. There are only about 250 female prisoners (although this number has doubled in the last 15 years). Because of that small number there is a tendency to limit social research to male prisoners.

The population is heterogeneous as far as nationality and ethnicity are concerned, with approximately 50 nationalities found in the prisons. About half of all prisoners are foreign and/or members of another (non-Dutch) ethnic group.

## HIV POSITIVE PERSONS AND AIDS PATIENTS IN PRISON

How serious is the AIDS problem within this population? The extent of the problem, other than in the civil population where the issue is primarily one of males involved in variable homosexual contacts, is dependent upon the percentage of addicts employing intravenous methods in their drug-usage.[6] Approximately one-third of all prisoners are users of hard drugs at the time they enter the prison system, sentenced for trafficking or drug related crimes.[7] This data has been self-reported by the prisoners.

The percentage in some remand prisons is higher, especially in Amsterdam, Rotterdam and the Hague. It is estimated that the proportion of such users on remand

---

6 Ministerial Circular, 27 August, 1987, nr. 555/387.

7 V. van Alem, L. Erkelens, G. Schippers, M. Breteler & J. Becking, *The addiction problematic in penitentiary institutions (Verslavingsproblematiek in de penitentiaire inrichtingen in Justitiële Verkenningen, 2: themanummer: Differentie in detentie)*, (1989) 40.

in these cities is at least in the region of 60 per cent. Half of this group of users employ the intravenous method,[8] while approximately half of this group is estimated as being HIV positive. This approximation is based upon estimates of self-injecting users of hard drugs and is independent of the detention situation. On the basis of this approximation, we can calculate that roughly 500 prisoners, about 8 per cent of the total inmate population, are HIV positive. By virtue of the assumptions upon which this calculation is based, it is also appropriate to acknowledge my reservations concerning the numerical conclusion.

Civil servants recoil somewhat when confronted with these calculations and maintain that, given the figures from the 1991 Annual Report of the Ministry of Justice's Medical Inspectors[9] which reported that 172 detainees admitted being HIV positive when they entered prison, the actual numbers will be lower. Four hundred and five detainees requested HIV testing during their detention; 348 requests were supported by the prison doctor. Twenty-two of those tested proved HIV positive. On 35 occasions a doctor proposed that a detainee permit himself to be tested, and of these persons six proved to be HIV positive. In 1991, 24 (serving) prisoners were registered as suffering from AIDS: in 18 instances, the diagnosis was established outside of the prison, while the other six were diagnosed inside. In comparison with the preceding year, these figures show an increase across the entire range of categories.

When, in western countries, it became known that a possible AIDS epidemic could appear, homosexual men, most especially those who participated in anal sex, became the objects of significant interest and concern. There is, however, absolutely no reason to assume that this category of persons is of especial interest or concern with respect to estimates of the number of HIV positive persons in detention. Why should homosexuals constitute a relatively higher proportion of the penal system's inmate population than heterosexuals? It is a separate issue that anal homosexual contact can be relevant in terms of infection or contamination within penal institutions, and this is not logically correlated with exclusive homosexual preferences amongst prisoners. I shall return to this issue.

In other countries, too, the number of HIV positive persons is related to the number of intravenous hard drug users. This becomes even more apparent when research is directed at this category of people, not only with respect to compulsory testing but also with voluntary participation in screening. Drug injectors who share needles have good reason to assume that they belong to a high risk category. Paralysing uncertainty encourages the willingness to undergo testing, and, unfortunately, the data justify the fearful expectations. The media pounce on such data as something which assists in the construction of prejudicial images.

Selective testing thus encourages a strengthening of prejudice and an over-estimation of danger. I do not wish to trivialize the reality of the AIDS risk, but selective attention easily leads to the association of the problem with a specific category of persons and thereby to their stigmatization.

---

8 V. van Alem et al., op. cit., p. 49.

9 Medical Inspectorate of the Ministry of Justice, Annual Report, 1991 (1992).

## THE PRISON SYSTEM AND THE RISK OF CONTAMINATION

In what kind of penal environment must prisoners, who are HIV positive or suffering from developed AIDS, function? In addition, to what extent does the prison system include an enhanced risk of contamination?

A prison, as I have already stated, is a total institution wherein the residents are deprived of various freedoms and individual possibilities. There is no freedom of choice in terms of daily interaction with other people. Prisoners cannot always freely choose their friends, let alone their sexual partners. The prison residents are condemned to each others' company 24 hours a day. Cellular institutions offer, at the most, the possibility of retreat to the individual cell. In The Netherlands, however, we have the principle of communal regimes[10] so that prisoners work communally, engage in communally organized sporting activities, and sometimes share communal washing and toilet facilities. The nights are spent in individual cells, or, in those institutions with a more open character, in areas which are accessible to, and shared with, a number of other prisoners. Dormitories, too, in the less secure prisons, are an aspect of penal reality. But in remand prisons and in some high security prisons, they spend most of the daytime in their cells. Hitherto, each prisoner has had his or her own cell, but this is likely to change, at least for prisoners serving short sentences. This could have major consequences for the HIV/AIDS policy.

Prisons are divided into various categories. For example, there are those for short-term and long-term prisoners; for men and women; and for adults and juveniles. As far as security is concerned, they are divided into closed, semi-open and open institutions. Since 1990 prisoners considered liable to attempt to escape and to use violence during their escapes, are put in prisons with a so-called, special level of security. The inmates stay in small wings with a maximum of five other inmates. They do not meet inmates from other wings, they do not stay longer than six months in the same wing, and they can be transported to another institution without notice. The regime will be more strict if the Minister of Justice follows the recommendations of a Commission[11] which, among others, advised covering these prisoners' exercise space with a grid. This has been prompted by some sensational escapes with the aid of a helicopter.

The regime of the prison is directed at the resocialization of the prisoner. Previously, the authorities were optimistic about the possibilities to train and educate prisoners so that they could participate in society as ordinary, useful citizens after their release. However, in the 1980's, the Minister of Justice[12] had to accept that resocialization thus described appeared impossible, and, accordingly, he made a more pragmatic statement: imprisonment should limit and reduce the damage to the prisoner as far as possible, and must be carried out humanely. The aim of resocialization was not dropped, but reinterpreted as preparing prisoners for their release. This can also

---

10 The most important principles underpinning the prison system are contained in the Principles Act Beginselenwet Gevangeniswezen for the Prison System (1953).

11 *Commissie Hoekstra, Report of the Committee evaluating security policy in the Prison System (Rapport van de Evaluatiecommissie Beveiligingsbeleid gevangeniswezen)* (1992).

12 *Ministerial Memorandum, Function and Future of the Dutch Prison System (Nota Taak en Toekomst van het Nederlandse Gevangeniswezen)* (1982).

imply making them aware of the social problems they may face after release, such as unemployment, stigmatisation, complicated social relationships, etc.

Many outsiders appear amazed that drug use occurs within the confines of prisons. But it is precisely because prisoners naturally attempt to escape from the monotony and dependence of their confinement that the urge to use drugs is so great. Prisoners are extremely creative in constructing methods designed to smuggle drugs into the institution: visits are employed, the bribery of fellow inmates who receive a temporary leave-of-absence, and, occasionally, guards are corrupted. Drugs are easier to smuggle into the prison than the needles which are used to inject them. The fear of infection through use of contaminated needles is, therefore, not entirely ungrounded. Even though prison administrators in The Netherlands argue that, among the prison population, smoking and sniffing drugs is far more popular than injecting them, there is quite probably more use of shared needles within the penal system than outside it because intravenous use offers a more intense 'kick'.

Homosexual contact 'as a substitute for something better' can satisfy sexual needs - although I stress that my assumption remains the voluntary participation of both partners. In other countries, where prisoners sometimes remain for many years in the same institution, prison sub-cultures often exist wherein homosexual rape, sometimes durable relationships, voluntary or under threat, perform an important function.[13] The term 'rape' is frequently most appropriate in these circumstances, even though prisoners occasionally appear to participate voluntarily in return for protection or other favours. Homosexual contact is marginalized, being in the sphere of taboo behaviour even where it is not formally prohibited. Some governors are of the opinion that it is not a permissible behavioural option: that which may not occur, therefore does not occur - or it is denied!

Other governors are more tolerant; homosexuality is not a 'hot issue' for them. Prison personnel do not 'hunt and harass' prisoners as they once did. Surveillance of toilet areas is no longer (so rigorously) maintained, so there is more opportunity for 'a quickie'. But that is the limit because prisoners may not visit each other in the individual cells.

What is certain is that, in comparison with other countries, more possibilities are available in penal institutions in The Netherlands to maintain contact with the outside world, thereby the need for sexual release within the institution becomes less intense. In the prisons for long-termers, conjugal visits are possible: prisoners and their partners can spend two or three hours in a specially separated and private visiting room. In the open prisons, where residents can spend the last few months of their sentences, weekend leaves-of-absence are granted. Homosexuality from 'necessity' is less frequent in such prisons, but it will certainly remain a reality for those prisoners who have yet to be tried or still have long sentences to serve. Nonetheless, infection with the AIDS virus through homosexual activity is not the most significant concern within the penal system in The Netherlands. Drug addiction gives far more realistic cause for concern.

---

13 See, W. Wooden and J. Parker, *Men Behind Bars* (1982). American research in a medium-security prison shows that two thirds of all the prisoners have had at least some sexual contact during their imprisonment. Fourteen per cent of the total prison population experienced this sexual contact against their will. This research took place in an institution for less-violent offenders who had, by American standards, relatively short sentences. The prison has approximately 2,400 individual (one person) cells.

Having oneself tattooed is a popular activity in prisons; this is also not without risk. This activity is nowhere as intensively - or as primitively - pursued as it is in prison. If needles are circulated and communally used, then the danger is clear. Penal authorities in The Netherlands are under the impression that tattooing is less frequent than in past years. This impression is derived from the diminishing number of requests for cosmetic surgery designed to remove tattoos.

This sketch clarifies why prison authorities are apprehensive about the contamination possibilities of the AIDS virus. The factual data as presented in Section 2.2 are concerned with the number of incoming prisoners who are HIV positive. There are no data available relating to the transmission of the virus within the prisons.

## DRUG POLICY WITHIN THE PRISON SYSTEM

Drug policy is of significance within the prison system because drug users constitute the largest risk group among its population. Many detainees have drug problems when they enter a remand prison, and, in many of these institutions, methadone is provided for the first ten days of detention in order to combat the most serious symptoms of drug withdrawal. However, this provision is not made in all remand prisons. It is a medical decision which falls within the competence of the specific prison doctor. One of its consequences is that a prisoner can be transferred to another prison and thus from one day to the next lose his access to methadone. The Medical Inspectorate of the prison service does attempt to ensure uniformity of treatment, but, in the background, the influence of the local prison governor is of significance. Recently, for example, a governor authorized the appointment of a particular doctor because he knew that the person in question opposed the provision of methadone.

For HIV positive persons and AIDS patients there are clear arguments for providing - or continuing to provide - methadone: the person's physical condition is thereby optimized and such provision also reduces stress. More and more experts are becoming convinced that a good physical condition combats the development of the illness and delays the onset of symptoms. 'Cold turkey', on the other hand, increases stress. Personally, I would go a step further: while the official position regarding contact with prisoners is the assumption that every inmate could be HIV positive, it would be advantageous in terms of encouraging optimal physical condition and reducing stress if every drug-addicted prisoner was provided with methadone on request.

Even if the physical symptoms of withdrawal are over, in the prison environment the need/desire for drugs is great. They are used to combat boredom, for example, or to ease the uncertainty regarding the judicial process in which the prisoner is involved. The importing or possessing of drugs within a prison is a punishable offence and is sanctioned by solitary confinement. Cell inspections are held regularly, and, in some institutions, prisoners may be systematically subjected to clothing and body searches after receiving visitors. At the same time, in some prisons, smoking hashish is tacitly accepted; even the most inexperienced prison guard can smell the hash cloud in some recreation units.

Some prisons have developed so-called Drug Free Units drugsvrije afdelingen for (ex-) drug addicts who do not want to be tempted by the drugs on offer. Anyone wishing to be placed in such a unit must sign a contract permitting urine testing for drugs. The prisoners, in groups of 12-24 inmates, reside in units which have treatment facilities but which never provide methadone. Demonstrable involvement with drugs once placed in such a unit results in transfer back to a standard regime unit/prison.

It is also possible, under Section 47 of the Prison Regulations, for a prisoner be transferred to a drug withdrawal or treatment centre for the last six months of sentence. In this connection there are a number of so-called 'withdrawal-farms'. Further, voluntary placing and treatment in such an institution can be continued even when the period of detention is over.

## THE MEDICAL TREATMENT OF PRISONERS IN GENERAL AND HIV POSITIVE AND AIDS PATIENTS IN PARTICULAR

Medical care is of great importance for prisoners. As has already been said, a large number of them are frequent drug users who are sometimes in very bad physical condition because of a neglected bout of influenza or other minor illnesses or infections. Further, when 'cold turkey' is imposed rather than the provision of methadone, the subsequent withdrawal symptoms require medical supervision.

Prisoners are forced back upon their own resources, having considerable time with which to be preoccupied with themselves. Each physical complaint, regardless of how trivial it may be, can easily become an obsession, something which is emphasized for detained HIV positive persons and AIDS patients. And this takes no account of the physical and psychic complaints which arise as a consequence of detention itself.

On arrival, each prisoner is subjected to a simple medical investigation including a urine test as well as a Mantoux test for possible tuberculosis. The prisoner may refuse the latter test, but, in consequence, he would be isolated because of possible contamination risks until he has either undergone lung X-rays or accepted the test. With respect to drug users a degree of pressure is exerted on them to comply with a blood test in search of, among other things, the Hepatitis-B virus. Blood is not tested for HIV+, although a positive tuberculosis test, something which is increasingly being witnessed, can be a symptom of its presence.

Among prisoners it is becoming increasingly common knowledge that the number of T-4 cells, which are an indication of immuno-resistance to AIDS, can be investigated through a blood test. In the event that the number of cells is under a particular level, then this constitutes a reason for the provision of medication including an eventual (continuing) provision of methadone. Accordingly, more and more prisoners are demanding such an investigation of their blood.

The doctor associated with each prison is responsible for the medical health of the inmate population, although in daily practice prisoners have more contact with nurses. When the prisoner submits a request for medical contact the first response is usually a visit from a nurse who then deals with most complaints. Many prisoners are dissatisfied with the degree of attention given to their medical complaints, but the prison medical services respond to this with the argument that prisoners have the tendency to exaggerate their ills. Regarding a concrete complaint that the medical services refused to provide certain medication, their response was to argue that aggression against family doctors had substantially increased in society and fear of such aggression often appeared a reason for such a doctor to prescribe drugs - something not done in a remand prison.[14]

## MEDICAL CARE AND RIGHTS UNDER COMPLAINTS PROCEDURES

If prisoners do not agree with a decision made by the prison governor then they can avail themselves of their right to lodge a complaint with the Complaints Commission of the Supervisory Committee (Commissie van Toezicht). This Commission tests the governor's decision against the applicable Regulations, which may be the Prison Regulations specific to the relevant institution, national law, or even international laws/treaties such as the European Declaration on Human Rights. Thus, for example, the Commission could overturn the governor's decision to relocate a prisoner exhibiting aggression towards prison personnel - possibly as a consequence of AIDS - in an isolation unit/cell. Both the prisoner and the governor can appeal to the Central Committee for the Application of Penal Sanctions Centrale (Raad voor Strafrechtstoepassing), located in The Hague, against a decision from the Complaints Commission. In this way there is some control exerted over the decisions taken by local governors or by their subordinate personnel.

However, decisions taken by the medical services do not fall under the complaints procedures; such decisions are not taken by the governor or in his name. The medical services are autonomous in their medical decisions. A prisoner cannot lodge a complaint with the Complaints Commission against failing to provide methadone; the most that can be done is a complaint to the Medical Disciplinary Council which is charged with assessing the medical activities of the relevant doctor. Should such a doctor be adjudged to have behaved in a less than responsible manner, then a judgement resulting in reprimand or suspension can follow. Even leaving aside the long period between medical complaint and its adjudication, the prisoner making such a complaint has little satisfaction from such a professional outcome.

Because, in their opinion, the Complaints Commission often colludes with the prison governor, prisoners do not have complete confidence in their right to complain. Nonetheless, these rights can offer them certain guarantees, such as an alternative if the prison doctor refuses a request for an AIDS test, which are not usually available in medical decisions.

On the one hand, the prison doctor is autonomous in decision making, but on the other hand is also a servant of the institution and carries out functions which are in the interests of good order and discipline within it. For example, the doctor advises the governor in regard to certain decisions such as re-location in isolation. The doctor has the duty of informing the governor to what extent continuing detention in isolation might be regarded as medically irresponsible. Also, a medical judgement is required before the governor awards a temporary pension because of loss of pay due to illness. Thus, the practice of a prison doctor involves a combination of irreconcilable interests: the medical welfare of the individual prisoner against the institution's interests in order, discipline, and security. If these conflicting interests were separated, then the

---

14 E. van Rijssen, *Work-trainee's Report from the Remand Prison in Utrecht (Stageverslag Huis van Bewaring in Utrecht)* (1992) 19-20. See also, M. Zijl, *Medical care in the prison (Gezondheidszorg in de bajes)* (1993).

medical care of prisoners, including HIV positive persons and AIDS patients, would be better guaranteed. Doctors, for example, when they are exclusively responsible for medical activities, would be more likely to judge such things as the provision of methadone on exclusively medical grounds. This argues against doctors being in the service of the Ministry of Justice and in favour of their offering their services alongside their regular practices as general practitioners. Such a move could possibly advance the debate concerning needle exchange.

## OFFICIAL PENITENTIARY POLICY RELATING TO HIV POSITIVE PERSONS AND AIDS PATIENTS

A number of years ago an anxiety psychosis developed amongst prison personnel: even touching an AIDS patient or an HIV positive person, for example during a body-search, was feared as potentially contaminating. The provision of information made the problem open to discussion, especially as this occurred at the same time as the identification of the first AIDS patient within the prison system. That first AIDS patient, incidentally, was a member of the prison staff. Some of the prison governors were of the opinion that it took too long for the Minister of Justice to establish guidelines for the prison service. The ministerial Circular of August 1987[15] is at this moment the authoritative document for policy in the closed institutions.[16] Compulsory testing for HIV is positively discouraged; preventive measures are preferred. According to the Circular: 'Given the manner in which contamination can occur, attention should be focused on aggressive behaviour whereby wounds can occur as a consequence of biting or scratching, or through so-called penetrative accidents as a consequence of pricking or cutting during body searches or cell inspections. However, the chance that HIV contamination could occur in these latter examples should not be overestimated'.

The specific policy in penal institutions is directed at a number of concrete areas: hygiene, the provision of information, regime, and psycho-social care. With respect to hygiene, for example, the management is expected to ensure that sufficient quantities of work, surgical, and kitchen gloves are kept in stock, that they be made freely available, and that their use should be actively encouraged. The prison personnel are advised to wear work gloves when dealing with sharp objects such as glass splinters, razor blades, or cutlery. To prevent unpleasant shocks such as contact with injecting kits or sharpened knives during cell inspections, the same advice is offered concerning the use of work gloves. During cleaning work, body searches and the provision of first aid, it is recommended that kitchen or surgical gloves be worn.

With respect to the provision of information, the prison doctor must inform incoming prisoners about the dangers of specific activities and the transmission vectors through which HIV contamination is realistically possible. Folders and brochures, in different languages, should be extensively and uncomplicatedly available. For the benefit of prison personnel and inmates, regular information meetings should be organized. The labelling, isolation, and/or concentration of prisoners known to be HIV positive is considered to be totally unacceptable. Prisoners known to be HIV

---

15 Ministerial Circular, 27 August, 1987, nr. 555/387.

16 Idem.

positive are not subjected to a special regime, and, in principle, this is also the case for AIDS patients unless their medical requirements necessitates it.

Within the prisons, condoms should be made available, at regular shop prices, to any prisoner who wishes to obtain them. Regardless as to whether or not the individual involved is actually HIV positive, if threats of contamination with allegedly infected blood are made, then, according to the Circular, such activity should be considered as constituting a threat to inflict grievous bodily harm and the appropriate interventionary and disciplinary steps should be undertaken.

A rough synopsis of the opinion held by governors within the prison system is: 'AIDS is not a significant topic at the moment, although there is certainly a latent anxiety amongst both personnel and inmates'.[17] However, as soon as a putative case of HIV positive or AIDS becomes known, or some sort of incident occurs, then those latent anxieties among personnel and inmates are made manifest. 'AIDS is a controllable problem', is how one governor expressed it.

POLICY IN PRACTICE
NO PROVISION OF CLEAN NEEDLES OR INJECTION KITS

The Circular recognized that the extent of the problem is inextricably related to the percentage of users of intravenously taken hard drugs. But that recognition remained at the level of a simple acknowledgement, and there is absolutely no question that a programme designed to address the issue of this HIV+ transmission vector has been or will be based upon the knowledge which we already possess. The possibility of providing clean needles or injection kits was not even mentioned. 'The Ministry of Justice behaves as if this aspect of the AIDS problem is not relevant; it is swept under the carpet. There must be a fundamental discussion concerning this issue', says Lemmers, a former member of the management team in a penal institution. He continues: 'When the issue of providing clean needles has been mentioned, then, until now, the only response from the Ministry of Justice has been to reiterate that drug use within the prison system is prohibited. And they are fearful of appearing to condone such behaviour. Within the Public Health system, this is a response which was long ago recognized as unacceptable; these institutions and their personnel deal with the practical issue of exchanging new needles for old ones'.

It is difficult for judicial agencies, which are pre-eminently responsible for ensuring that the law is respected and maintained, to participate in an experiment involving the exchange of needles and/or injection kits. Nonetheless, denial is no solution to the problem. One of the arguments which is often used against such an exchange is that needles are occasionally employed as weapons, but this ignores that used needles can have the same function - not to mention the additional risk of contamination. The defensive arguments are rationalizations, comparable to those used against the free provision of condoms.

---

17 J. Willems, G. Schippers and M. Breteler, *AIDS and Detention (Aids en Detentie Vakgroep Klinische Psychologie en Persoonlijkheidsleer)*, (1992) 10.

THE PROVISION OF INFORMATION

Every institution has access to information films. The intention is that the personnel share and communicate their insights with the prisoners, although it is debatable if this actually occurs. Is it not more realistic that the personnel remain primarily obsessed with the question: 'How do I ensure that I am not exposed to too much risk?'

In addition to the film, information is occasionally provided to prisoners by outside experts: doctors, and also, for example, staff workers from the Schorer Foundation which supports the interests of homosexuals.

In some institutions more systematic information meetings, aimed at all prisoners, are held by the Consultation Bureaux for Alcohol and Drugs (CAD). Their approach aims at behavioural change, dealing with such subjects as safe sex and the safe use of drugs. What nonetheless remains as a substantial hindrance is that safe sex, as it is propagated, is incredibly difficult to achieve in practice largely due to the continuing taboo relating to homosexuality. Even when condoms are available they are not likely to be quickly requested. It is an even greater problem with respect to the safe use of drugs as long as they are illegal and as long as needle exchange is not open to discussion. Published information in a number of different languages is supposed to be available, and sometimes is. This latter information is of a general nature and not directly related to the specific situation of detention.

I have serious doubts concerning the efficacy of this informative material. Within the prison system, roughly half the resident population consists of foreigners or possesses a different cultural background to that presumed by the information content. Many prisoners cannot effectively read or write, even in their own native language, while the information which is provided is primarily written. The information is not directly related to the detention situation, and, of equal importance, it bears little relation to the wide diversity of cultural backgrounds found in the prison system. With respect to drug use and homosexuality, other techniques are occasionally employed. Homosexual contacts are not always part of a common cultural heritage; sometimes they have a position in a culture which is substantially different to that found in Dutch society. For example, providing there is no emotional involvement with the partner, and one adopts only the 'masculine, active role', anal sexual contact with a person of the same gender is a relatively accepted cultural phenomenon in certain countries bordering the Mediterranean.

The experiment in one of Amsterdam's remand prisons where information was provided by welfare groups outside the prison to groups of Turkish and Moroccan prisoners, in their own language and in a situation where prison personnel were not present, was a positive development. There was a high attendance at the meeting, and participants dared to openly discuss the issues and to pose questions. After an intermission there was a written quiz, prepared in Dutch, which could be filled in with an 'AIDS-pen' upon which the telephone numbers of information lines were available. There was a reasonable response to the quiz, although many people have doubts concerning the effectiveness of condoms in providing protection against HIV transmission. AIDS is still often perceived as a homo-sickness, and many misunderstandings relating to HIV tests remain. Every prisoner is tested for tuberculosis upon arrival, and many think that an HIV test is also involved: if they hear nothing concerning the result of the test, then they think that they are healthy.[18]

The prizes for the quiz were T-shirts with the slogan 'Safe-sex, Stop AIDS' printed on them. In the future, such prizes will be somewhat less sensational because few prisoners dared to walk around wearing one.

Providing information to drug-using prisoners is made more important by the fact that they belong to a high risk group which is difficult to contact outside the confines of detention.

## THE USE OF GLOVES

Prison policy states that every prisoner is potentially HIV positive. If prisoners fight with each other or with members of the prison personnel, then frequently blood is spilt. Care of wounds and application of dressings occur with the use of gloves, as does the cleaning up of blood. Gloves are also worn during large-scale searches for drugs or other contraband. In comparison with a number of years ago, the atmosphere appears less stressed and there are better estimates made concerning the realism of the risks. This implies that the provisions of the Circular are not always strictly enforced: such a development is comparable to the relative relaxation which is noted by other professionals.

## AVAILABILITY AND PROVISION OF CONDOMS

Prisoners must be able to obtain condoms at shop prices. Although the Circular is clear on this point, the practice is different. Not all of the governors are equally pleased with this guideline. As long as homosexuality remains in the sphere of taboos, the provision of condoms will meet with resistance. A number of prisoners also showed anger at the possible provision of condoms. Their 'masculinity' was threatened: 'What is my wife/girlfriend going to think? That I'm a homo?'

'Of course, everyone knows that sexual contact in a penal institution is not permissible and that it is also almost impossible', says a highly-placed civil servant.[19] A member of the governor's staff argues: 'Sexual contact is forbidden here, so how can I provide a condom-dispenser?' Because of the permanent surveillance in many penal institutions there is hardly any chance of the privacy which is necessary for sexual contact, and this pragmatic restriction implies a prohibition.[20] This connects with the taboo surrounding homosexual contact which still flourishes in the macho culture supported by so many officers and prisoners. There is no identifiable written regulation which prohibits homosexual contact, yet some governors continue to condemn and forbid it: sexual relations cause unrest in the prison; they are detrimental to good order and discipline. This latter argument is sufficient reason for some

---

18 E. Cinibulak, *The provision of information to non-indigenous prisoners (Voorlichting aan allochtone gedetineerden, Studiedag Aids & Detentie)*, 28 January 1993.

19 E. Besier, *The AIDS Circular (De Aids-circulaire)*, in, *Balans* (1987), 11, p. 24.

20 C. Kelk, *The AIDS virus within penitentiary walls (Het AIDS virus binnen de penitentiaire muren in, Penitentiaire Informatie)* 1 (1988), 1.

governors to impose disciplinary reports on prisoners who engage in sexual contacts, and, on the basis of those reports, to subject them to disciplinary measures.

Prisoners themselves often maintain that condoms should not be available: 'They aren't necessary; there's no sex here.' Another inmate argues: 'If condoms are available, then sex will appear to be approved. That doesn't strike me as a good thing because then rapes will take place.' Nonetheless, four of the 25 inmates interviewed in a remand prison maintained that sexual contacts between prisoners occur; they had heard this from other people or had witnessed it themselves. Eleven respondents considered it possible or stated that they did not know, while 10 other inmates said that such contact does not occur.[21]

In some prisons, the medical services provide condoms. There is little use made of this provision. This does not surprise me: it does appear to be a high barrier which has to be surmounted! Some members of the medical services are not prepared to cooperate with the provision of condoms in this manner. They argue that this medicalizes their use. In the Bijlmer prison, condoms are available in the shop in which prisoners do their weekly shopping. To date, not one prisoner has made use of this provision.

In several prisons, condom dispensers have been installed. Some of these were in place prior to the Circular which acknowledged the AIDS era, installed as a consequence of the provision of conjugal visits early in the 1980's. Condom dispensers are not encouraged by the Ministry of Justice; they focus too much attention on sex. And this could suggest that anal sex with condoms is safe. On the one hand it would give warnings about potentially lethal anal sex, and on the other hand stimulate anal sex by the provision of condoms. In the meantime, special condoms for anal sex are being produced, but they are not available in the penal institutions.[22]

Precisely what level of security is achieved if no condoms are made available? A refusal to undertake suitable measures can reflect denial of a problem; this is also Thomas' argument concerning the policy in English prisons.[23] Denial is more likely to result in an increase than a decrease in high risk sexual activity. The same argument applies to drug use.

## DISCIPLINARY MEASURES AND PUNISHMENT

If a prisoner threatens a fellow prisoner or a member of the prison staff with a needle or with blood, regardless as to whether or not they are infected, then that prisoner can be subjected to a disciplinary response. For example, solitary confinement lasting several days or weeks can be imposed. The isolation is imposed as punishment and not because the prisoner is a carrier of the AIDS virus. In some countries there is a special regime for HIV positive persons and it is also possible that prisoners can be subjected

---

21 E. van Rijssen, *Work-trainee's Report from the Remand Prison in Utrecht (Stageverslag Huis van Bewaring in Utrecht)* (1992) 19-20.

22 J. van Woerkom, *HIV and AIDS-prevention and care in prison: theory and practice (HIV en AIDS preventie en zorg in de bajes: theorie en praktijk, Studiedag AIDS en Detentie)*, 28 January 1993.

23 P.A. Thomas during his reading of an unpublished paper, at a staff conference, Aberystwyth, Wales, 25 June 1989.

to compulsory testing. Quite frequently, special regimes and compulsory testing go together.

In The Netherlands, one prisoner has been subjected to a compulsory AIDS test: he had bitten a member of the prison staff 'to give him AIDS'. The governor considered that this action had created a situation where the circumstances were out of control, and, to provide clarification for the bitten staff member who was confronted with the question 'Am I going to get AIDS?', the prisoner was compelled to undergo an AIDS test. The test result was negative. 'Unfortunately', said the governor, 'the prisoner didn't make a complaint to the prison's Supervisory Committee. Had he done so, we would have established whether or not our response could function as a legitimate model for similar situations.'

I pose the question, incidentally, as to whether or not biting is dangerous: contact with blood does not necessarily have to occur, although, in this specific case the prisoner did have bleeding gums. But, within the prison system, even apart from the question of AIDS, biting is in itself a sensitive issue. After being bitten, one routinely undergoes medical treatment which includes a tetanus injection. A governor or management team could reason that even if there is no danger of blood transmission, it is possible that a test should follow in order that the bitten staff member, or the partner of that person, be relieved from the anxiety and stress of doubt.

## THE RIGHTS OF IMPRISONED HIV POSITIVE PERSONS

Many social scientists and politicians assert, at least in their public pronouncements, that the essential characteristic of imprisonment consists of the loss of liberty. The fact that prisoners are deprived of their freedom, one of the most substantial 'goods', gives expression to the reality of their punishment. Apart from this deprivation, prisoners should have as many as possible of the other rights which are available to free citizens. The legislature attempted to establish this position in the Constitution: a prisoner can be restricted in the exercise of constitutional rights only to the extent that such exercise conflicts with the maintenance and execution of imprisonment itself (Article 15, sub 4, Constitution of The Netherlands). The question arises as to whether, with such a vague yet far-reaching formulation, the legislature has actually managed to achieve restraint in secondary prohibitions and restrictions.

## NO COMPULSORY TESTING

An AIDS test taken against the will of a prisoner is in contradiction with the constitutional guarantee of privacy (Art. 10, Constitution) and the right to physical integrity (Art. 11, Constitution). However, exceptions to these rights are also possible. According to the Supreme Court, Hoge Raad, a prison governor, on the basis of his managerial function, may impose restrictions on a prisoner's right to privacy, although such an imposition is itself restricted to the protection of public order. The European Court of Human Rights has established that such a restrictive imposition is applicable to certain groups, among them prisoners. Another condition for exception to the right of privacy is that a substantial social urgency exists, with the restrictive condition that proportionality exists between method and goal. Weighing the interests of those involved against each other, there is as yet no justification for such impositions with respect to compulsory AIDS tests.[24]

The restriction of constitutional rights is a subject which cannot be dealt with in a couple of paragraphs, especially as certain specific constitutional rights can be in apparent contradiction with others. For example, the right to the physical integrity of one's person, which would provide a prohibition against compulsory testing, might be balanced with the government's constitutional duty to implement measures designed to protect and foster public health (Article 22, Constitution). In this instance, the individual prisoner's rights to privacy and the physical integrity of his person appear to conflict radically with the duty of the government to ensure that the AIDS virus does not contaminate other people. In other countries, it is on this governmental duty to public health, that advocates of compulsory testing base their arguments - and not always without success.

Fortunately, in The Netherlands, partly because the current government simply and unconcernedly dismissed the idea, we have not (yet) arrived at a discussion of compulsory screening. Also, the prison system in The Netherlands, with only one prisoner per cell, does not necessitate such a screening programme. However, should the discussion concerning 'two prisoners in one cell' once again emerge, something which, given the shortage of cells even after the current substantial prison building programme is completed, remains a realistic prospect, then it is probable that new voices arguing for compulsory testing will be heard. Contemporary extensive budgetary cuts with respect to the penal system will have a substantial negative impact on the prevention and/or treatment of AIDS within that system: such an impact will be at the expense of the legal and social rights of prisoners. Other countries already offer us a negative example.

TESTING ON REQUEST

There must be no compulsory testing, but does a prisoner have the right to be tested on request? Prisoners will regularly make such a request but the response is not always directly acceded to by the relevant authority. The prisoner is well advised of the psychological consequences attendant to the knowledge that one is HIV positive, especially for someone who, confined in a cell for many hours each day, is forced back upon personal resources. For this reason, a certain policy of discouragement exists.

In the opinion of some prisoners, they may not be tested, but official organizations add a nuance to such a view, i.e. testing if prisoners still wish it following pre-counselling. Informed consent is required. The result of the test is given to the prisoner by the medical service with the utmost discretion; personnel are not informed without the express consent of the prisoner. Nonetheless, according to Jeannine van Woerkom of ACT UP!, an organization of AIDS activists in Amsterdam, a prisoner's HIV status is sometimes made public without consent or involvement.

---

24 C. Kelk, *A number of juridical aspects of the AIDS-problematic in the detention situation (Een aantal juridische aspecten van de aids-problematiek in de detentiesituatie), Studiedag Aids en Detentie* (1993).

In general, HIV positive persons are more negatively responded to by fellow prisoners than by personnel. On one occasion, a prisoner was admitted with the announcement 'Man has AIDS' on his transport papers, and, via personnel, other prisoners from the wing upon which he was to be placed became aware of this information. Some of these other prisoners refused to go into the cells as long as the HIV positive person remained on the wing. Interaction with HIV positive persons by other prisoners is generally characterized by anxiety and a certain aloofness, sometimes even by aggression. Accordingly, medical services advise inmates to keep their HIV status secret.[25]

CONCLUSION

The government does not only have, as far as that is feasible, the duty to respect the constitutional rights of prisoners and to refrain, also as far as that is feasible, from breaching those rights, but, also, it has the more positive duty to substantiate the acknowledgement that the execution of imprisonment should be as humane as possible and that the unavoidable damage which imprisonment brings should be restricted to an irreducible minimum.[26] In addition, there is a legally established governmental responsibility to ensure that prisoners are prepared for their return to civil society (Article 26, Principles Act for the Prison System). In my opinion, the provision of condoms is appropriate in terms of Article 26, and the provision of information appears to me to be equally relevant in these terms. Contrary to what many free citizens appear to think, imprisonment does not inevitably include the loss of various rights which those citizens consider to be self-evidently available to themselves. Or, in perhaps more appropriate language: in a democratic and constitutional State, a prisoner retains all rights other than those expressly removed by law by virtue of being in prison. Precisely because of the necessary restriction of a limited number of the constitutional rights of prisoners, the government should ensure that the circumstances of detention be carefully regulated in order that imprisonment does not constitute an inhumane experience.

In the context of AIDS, the government of The Netherlands cannot be accused of using its concern to suppress the danger in order to undermine the existing legal protections available to prisoners. Given the more positive task of preparing prisoners for their return to civil society, which the government has specified for itself, there remain a number of concrete areas in which the response has been inadequate. Specific matters and areas which call for attention and improvement include the provision of group-specific information: educational information for foreigners and members of ethnic minorities. The existing material should not simply be translated; it should be made relevant. Account should be taken of the different cultural backgrounds and the

---

25 J. Willems, G. Schippers and M. Breteler, *AIDS and Detention: an exploration of the AIDS-related problematic among senior personnel, prison officers, and prisoners in a number of penitentiary institutions in The Netherlands (AIDS en detentie, een exploratie van aids gerelateerde problematiek bij hoger personeel, penitentiarire inrichtingswerkers en geditineerden in enkele penitentiaire inrichtingen in Nedlerland Nijmegen)* 1992, pp. 17-18.

26 Nota Taak en Toekomst van het Nederlandse gevangeniswezen (1982), 22.

differential linguistic competence, also in terms of the individual's native language, which prisoners possess. Information in picture books or comics could be useful.

The provision of person-specific information. This should be concerned with addressing individual uncertainties, anxieties, and difficulties related to safe sex practices. HIV positive persons have a right to personal counselling.

The resolution of the dilemma that homosexuality is prohibited while condoms are nonetheless available by acknowledging and accepting that homosexual contact does exist, at least to a certain extent, and that it will continue to do so.

The acknowledgement that intravenous drug use does exist as a practice within the penal system, thereby enabling the emergence of an open discussion concerning the (possible) provision of sterile needles.

# AIDS IN PRISONS IN BELGIUM

JOHN DE WIT
*Journalist,*
*GAZET VAN ANTWERPEN,*
*Antwerp*

General penal reform in Belgium is much needed and long overdue. Consequently, it is unsurprising that the treatment of prisoners with AIDS and HIV is unsatisfactory.

In 1992 the Belgian government earmarked 28,360,000,000 belgian francs for the Department of Justice. This sum represents 6.6 per cent more than in 1988 when Melchior Wathelet, Minister of Justice, came to office. This figure is 1.7 per cent of the national budget although in 1966 it was 1.85 per cent and in 1976 had stood at 2.31 per cent. Currently, almost six billion francs are provided for Belgian prisons.

The majority of Belgian prisons were built in the style developed by the nineteenth century philanthropist, Edouard Ducpétiaux, as represented by Tongres prison in 1844 and Audenaerde in 1919. They are cellular jails of the Pennsylvania type which involve total isolation and discipline for the individual prisoner. Despite rebuilding, especially after the introduction of communal regimes, the core of the penal system is unaltered. There are four open prisons but 82 per cent of prisoners are kept in closed prisons. Cells measure 4 by 2.5 metres often with only one, small window as is found in Saint-Gilles prison which was almost completely destroyed in the riot of 1987. Some five years later Senator Willy Kuijpers stated,[1] after visiting the prison, that matters had not improved. The Board of Public Works had rebuilt 18 cells but then moved onto another prison, Vorst, and did not return to complete the work at Saint-Gilles. The result is that the prison hospital, to which prisoners are brought from other institutions for treatment, remains inadequate. Paint and plaster are flaking from the walls from the central control tower. Temporary wire netting is used as a 'safety net' to protect those who pass underneath. Birds foul central areas and when a prefabricated building was put up, involving opening the sewage system, the result was a serious rat infestation. Cells are dark and dirty. Only 30 out of 500 cells have sanitation. In most cells there is a chemical toilet which is cleaned once a week, on Saturday. An unbearable stench pervades the entire building and the prisoners call it 'Chanel Pénitentiaire'.[2]

The prison population on 30 June 1993 comprised 7,742 prisoners kept in 5,811 cells in 31 prisons and detention centres. Overcrowding is a serious problem

---

1 'Senator Willy Kuijpers bezoekt gevangenis van Sint-Gillis. Minister Wathelet schafte uniek onderzoekscentrum af als lopende zaak' in: *Gazet van Antwerpen*, 24 March 1992.

2 It is called after the Parisian mannequin, Coco Channel, who gave her name to the perfume.

particularly in the large city detention centres. Paradoxically there remain empty cells because of the shortage of prison staff to supervise all cells. In the new prison at Bruges there are as many as 300 unoccupied places. Yet in Antwerp all recreation rooms have been utilised to house detainees. It is not unusual for single occupancy cells to be used for two, three or even four prisoners in an area of two by four metres.[3] After a number of spectacular incidents, including the escape of three criminals from the Saint-Gilles prison in May 1993 and also the suicide of Patrick Haemers, Minister Wathelet announced in June 1993 an ambitious plan to renovate prisons. From 1994 until 1997 he wishes to spend 925 million francs on renovation. In addition, he wishes to see a new prison built in Andenne at a cost of 1.3 billion francs.

The reasons for overcrowding are numerous. There has been a significant increase in the number of illegal immigrants. Overstayers are imprisoned for a maximum of one month before deportation. On 30 June 1993 there were 340 illegal immigrants detained in 31 prisons. In 1991 the figure stood at 242. This issue was addressed by Inspector General Harry Van Oers who wrote to the Minister of Justice suggesting alternative means of dealing with illegal immigrants.[4] The term of imprisonment was raised to two months. It was also decided to establish specialised detention centres for illegal immigrants. These prisoners are unpopular with prison staff, who see them as a welfare not criminal problem, as they cause extra paper work and do not speak the language. They produce irrational operational behaviour in that, for example, in Saint-Gilles 20 illegal immigrants were sent out of prison in order to make room for 16 new illegal immigrants coming into the prison the same day.

The growing remand population also causes overcrowding despite legislative reform in December 1990.[5] During December 1989 there were 677 warrants of arrest; in December 1990 this had dropped to 398 as a result of the reform. But in February 1992 the number rose to 696. Another problem is the spectacular rise in long sentences in Belgian prisons. In 1985 there were 739 people convicted to five years or more. In 1991 the figure had risen to 1,185. This represents one sixth of the total daily prison population.

There is also an increasing number of drug addicts in prison. One in four inmates are imprisoned for acts which are directly linked to drugs, such as drug dealing or use of drugs. In 1970 this percentage was 1.21 but by 1982 it had risen to 6.5. However, by adding together offences which are drug related, such as theft to sustain a drug addiction, it is estimated that as much as half of the prison population is included. An unpublished pilot study in the open prison of Hoogstraten, near the Dutch border, produced surprising results. Hoogstraten holds only first-time offenders

---

3 'Veertien maal meer tuberculose in Strafinrichtingen dan erbuiten' *Gazet van Antwerpen*, 11 March 1993.

4 'Overbevolking in Belgische gevangenissen nijpend' *Gazet van Antwerpen*, 13 April 1992.

5 In 1990 Parliament passed a law to restrain remand prisoners. Alternatives were established and remand prisoners whose likely punishment would not exceed one year in prison could not be remanded. Before 1990 this term was three months. The new law also created an extra control on remands that lasted for more than six months. Thereafter, an extension is to be discussed in a public forum. Nevertheless, critics considered these reforms to be inadequate. Boutmans, E. e.a. *Het ontwerp-Wathelet tot herziening van de wet op de voorlopige hechtenis verandert niets aan het misbruik van het voorarrest, Panopticon*, 1990, 3, 243-57.

who have no drug history. In fact, the survey found that 34 per cent of the inmates said they had proof that needles were used for drugs in the prison and this was confirmed by 25 per cent of the prison officers. Thirty-eight per cent of the prisoners indicated that they had used drugs prior to prison entry and half of them admitted to using drugs in Hoogstraten. One out of four took heroin, one in two used cocaine, and the same figure used amphetamines. Four out of five smoked marijuana. The prison administration decided, in its wisdom, not to publish the results of the survey.[6]

Drug trafficking and drug use have been forbidden since 1921. Unlike the adjacent country, The Netherlands, where soft drug use is tolerated by the authorities, in Belgium many users of such drugs are imprisoned. Eight thousand two hundred and seventy-seven people were arrested in 1990 for drug offences of whom 5,945 were dealers. The policy continues to be repressive although in 1993 the Home Office spent 56 million francs on prevention on the programme entitled 'contracts of security' which is a joint venture with local municipalities aimed to reduce feelings of insecurity.

Experimental use of methadone is allowed but remains unregulated. However, doctors who prescribe it are liable to be punished. Dr Baudour of Brussels was sentenced in 1985 to 18 months imprisonment for such an action. Prosecution policy varies from province to province. In Flemish Brabant and Limburg the provision of methadone is illegal; in the province of Antwerp it is allowed according to well defined conditions; in the province of Liege doctors are free to prescribe it. In Flanders methadone experiments are conducted in two institutions in Antwerp, both in substitution programmes where the dose of methadone is gradually reduced until the addict is free of drugs and methadone and also in maintenance programmes for three groups of persons: pregnant heroin addicts, HIV carriers and long term addicts.[7] Yet in all of Belgium it is only the city of Charleroi which has signed the 'Resolution of Frankfurt' which seeks more lenient drug policies.[8] It is possible that a common prosecution policy will emerge after the decision of the Council of State Conseil d'etat on 11 February 1993 that the Order of Doctors cannot forbid distribution of methadone by doctors as this would breach their freedom to provide therapy.

Since 1989 Antwerp's drug addicts can obtain clean needles in the 'Free Clinic', an organization that helps people with problems on an alternative base. In this experiment, which has the approval of the local public prosecutor, addicts are taught to clean their needles and information on further help is provided. In Brussels the organization 'Doctors Without Frontiers' Medecins sans Frontieres and the French

---

6 J. Orenbuch, *Dossier: drogues et prisons* in Stigma, November 1990, Brussels: S. Todts, *HIV en tuberculosescreening in de Antwerpse gevangensis* in VRGT-Nieuwsbrief, Vlaamse Vereniging voor Respiratoire Gezondheidszorg en Tuberculosebestrijding, February 1993, 2-5: *Gevangeniswezen bezorgd over aids en tbc*, Gazet van Antwerpen, 11 March 1993.

7 *Criminoloog Tom Decorte wil een landelijk instituut voor drugproblemem*, Gazet van Antwerpen, 30 September 1992.

8 The European signatories are Frankfurt, Amsterdam, Hamburg, Zurich, Arnhem, Kallithea, Rotterdam, Teramo and Charleroi, 22 November 1990. *Frankfurtse resolutie wil liberaal drugbeleid* Gazet van Antwerpen, 26 November 1991. Regarding Charleroi, see, Van Cauwenbergh, Plan d'action contre la drogue et pour l'aide aux drogues, 27 November 1992, Charleroi 15p. See also *Voor Tobback staat Charleroi model in aanpak drugs*, Gazet van Antwerpen, 18 November 1992.

speaking community wanted to run a bus for a needle exchange programme. It was due to start on 1 April 1993 but was stopped by the mayor of Koekelberg. Such a service already exists in the Wallone city of Charleroi. Nevertheless, only 7.7 per cent of HIV infected males and 5.5 per cent of infected females on 31 December 1992 were infected through the use of needles. In Belgium there is not (yet) an epidemic of AIDS amongst drug users as is found in some other countries.

Within prison there are no drug therapy programmes and addicts have no treatment. However, in Dendermonde and Verviers, both of which house recidivists, there are experimental drug-free wards for a few inmates. The unit opened in Dendermonde in April 1991 and 26 prisoners have attended three times a week for urine tests. Those who test positive are excluded from the ward. A special regime operates in these units and work is guaranteed (Gestandaardiseerde Instellingsstructuur: GIS). Governor Mentens of Dendermonde stated that the ward is effectively drug free.[9] The more recent unit at Verviers has yet to publish data.

Since September 1992 all inmates of those two prisons are tested for drugs before taking leave and on their return.[10] Failure to pass the test or refusal to take it means loss of future home leave. In the experimental period of three months only four people in Dendermonde were tested positive in the drug tests. The general administration advised the Minister not to apply it generally as this would result in an extra cost of 30 million francs. The Minister of Justice wants to segregate drug addicts by locating them in two prisons at Wortel and Saint-Hubert.

## HIV AND AIDS PRISONERS

The conditions experienced by these prisoners must be placed in the context of all prisoners in Belgium. For example, a law on the legal status of prisoners, such as has existed in the Netherlands since 1953, is unknown in Belgium. The General Rules of Penal Institutions contain 'rights' only to religious and moral support and to private correspondence with certain authorities.[11] The General Rules are essentially a set of discretions exercised by governors. Furthermore, each prison, since May 1983, is required to make only one copy available to prisoners. So, for example, in Merksplas there has to be only one copy although the population rises to around 1,000 prisoners. Before 1983 even the one copy was unavailable to prisoners. However, given that 17.3 per cent of inmates neither speak nor read French or Dutch a significant number of prisoners are effectively excluded from appreciating what the Rules offer.

The prisoner complaint process is ineffective. Complaints may be lodged with one of the two Inspector Generals of the penal system or the King may be petitioned as well as the Presidents of the Parliamentary Chamber and Senate and the Minister of

---

9 R. Mentens *Een drugvrije afdeling in de gevangenis van Dendermonde: een pilootproject*, Panopticon, 1992, 244-53.

10 Prison leave for three days was introduced in 1976. When the leave process is not abused, and only 0.05 per cent of leaves are considered as failures, then a prisoner is allowed to leave prison every three months for three days. In 1991 there were 6,796 leaves for 1,873 prisoners.

11 Algemeen Reglement van de Strafinrichtingen, Koninklijk Besluit from 21 May 1965 (Belgisch Staatsblad 10 August 1971). See also, P. Claes, Rechten van de gedetineerde, 1989, Liga voor Mensenrechten, Gent, p. 58.

Justice. However, such actions rarely achieve the desired result. In addition, in each prison there is an advisory committee whose task is to control the board of the prison. The committees are comprised of leading local residents whose average age is 67.5 years. Comparable committees in The Netherlands consider complaints concerning disciplinary measures, violations of privacy of letters, breaches of the right to receive visitors and 'other rights which may be obtained by practice'. In Belgium these committees are ineffective. Some consider as little as three cases a year. They contrast sharply with their counterparts in The Netherlands.

The inability to apply effectively the prison rules is, in part, a consequence of understaffing and lack of equipment. This is well illustrated by the issues of prison visiting, educational and medical care. In March 1987, Willy Kuijpers, member of the European Parliament, visited the Vorst prison in Brussels.[12] It had 634 inmates housed in a prison licenced for 402 men. Between 200 and 350 visitors were expected on the particular day of his visit and there were 20 small visiting cubicles. Visitors started queuing outside the prison at 6 am. Kuijpers reported talking with a 72-year-old grandmother who had left her house at 4 am to visit her grandson. He saw two women carrying babies queuing outside the gates and met a woman who had travelled from Spain in order to have 20 minutes of visiting time. In 1993 the situation covering visits changed in Vorst.

Nevertheless, remand prisoners are separated from visitors by thick, sheet glass but if an open visit is allowed, for example in the canteen, most of the prisoners are strip searched before returning to the cells. Visiting rules vary from prison to prison so, for example, in some prisons books from visitors are banned. Three in ten prisoners receive no visitors.

Education and recreation for inmates is poorly organised. In 1984 this budget was transferred from the Ministry of Justice to the communities. The French speaking community offered educational courses because 12 per cent of prisoners are illiterate and a further 15 per cent have serious reading problems. Courses, offered by the organisation Adeppi, were followed by 228 prisoners in 1987. In Flanders the educational budget hovered around zero and the federal Minister of Justice was obliged to intervene. One in four of the Flemish prisons continue as educational wastelands and only half of these prisons organise literacy courses.

Finally, medical care remains inadequate predominately because of the shortage of qualifed personnel which, in turn, impacts upon the provision of care for AIDS prisoners. Inmates who are seriously ill, from whatever cause, are transferred to the Medical and Surgical Centre at Saint-Gilles. There was a surgical ward of 22 beds and a ward for internal diseases of 15 beds. Both were destroyed in the riots of 1987.[13] Planning developments programmed two renovated operating theatres for December 1990 but the work did not commence until April 1992. According to the head surgeon, sterility could not be guaranteed until recently and the sterilizing unit was already beyond its guarantee period before it became operational. The invasion of

---

12 *Gevangenis van Vorst*, Fatik 25-26, August 1987, 2-5.

13 The former Minister of Justice, Jean Gol, placed British football fans in new cells after the Heysel disaster in 1985. These modern, comfortable cells were shown on television which resulted in riots in other Belgium prisons.

rats and birds has resulted in half the patients being treated elsewhere with only minor operations occurring in the Centre.

The consequences of poor health care are predictable and a number of deaths have occurred. Suny Okon died in 1984 after a tooth extraction. In 1986 a drug addict and minor drug dealer, Geert Wijffels, died in Bruges prison. He was refused access to a doctor 15 times. Two weeks before his death a counsellor noted his very low blood pressure. He was held in an unheated cell whilst the outside temperature stood at -25c. When in 1987 the director general of the Belgium prison system, Julien De Ridder, was confronted with this case in the European Parliament he commented 'prison is the most radical form of prohibition for drug addicts.'[14]

## AIDS

Melchior Wathelet, Minister of Justice, stated that 60 prisoners are HIV positive which constitutes about 1 per cent of the daily population. These prisoners are on normal location. There is no compulsory testing for new arrivals but a voluntary test is available.

The recent history of AIDS control is that in the middle of 1985 the conservative Minister of Justice, Jean Gol, commissioned a survey of AIDS-related issues in Belgian prisons. He announced that seropositive prisoners should be neither isolated nor discriminated.[15] This decision was reaffirmed within the Council of Europe.

Circular letters of 5 July 1985 and 6 September 1985, which still apply, state that prisoners who are likely to be involved in high risk activity should be offered a test.[16] The prisoner has the right of refusal. The letters also give instructions on conduct when a seropositive prisoner bleeds. The medical officer must be informed; contaminated areas and objects must be disinfected and relevant personnel must wash with disinfectant. Toilet articles must be destroyed when the prisoner is placed elsewhere or released from prison. The prison staff are also reminded about the confidential nature of the prisoners' health status.

The Order of Doctors of Medicine states that seropositivity is covered by the professional obligation of confidentiality: only doctors may receive information on the HIV status of prisoners.[17] A Royal Decree of 1 March 1971, concerning prophylaxis of contaminating diseases[18] states the competent authorities have to be informed of certain diseases in order to prevent them from spreading. Furthermore, according to

---

14 J. De Wit and L. Van Outrive, *Gevangeniswezen en abolitionisme 2*, Liga voor Mensenrechten, Gent, 1989, p. 78.

15 At a national conference on AIDS in prisons, 28 August 1985.

16 The complete text of these circulars to prison governors and associated commentary is found in F. Pieters, *Het jaar van het virus: AIDS-virusdragers in de Belgische gevangenissen*, Panopticon, 1986, 558-69.

17 H. Nys, *Recht en aids: besmetting, opsporing en preventie strafrechtelijk en gezondheidsrechtelijk beschouwd*, (1988) Panopticon, 8-23. V. Janssen, K. Lalieux and P. Mary, *La situation des détenus séropositifs our sidéens* in M. Vincineau, Le Sida: Un défi Aux Droits (1991), 129-76.

18 *Koninklijk Besluit betreffende de profylaxe tegen overdraagbare ziekten*, 1 March 1971 (Belgisch Statsblad, 23 April 1971).

the circular letters, HIV carriers have to be locked up in individual cells. This means that their health status is widely known beyond medical circles. According to some governors it is impossible to keep seropositivity confidential within a prison system given its power structure. Thus, in reality, confidentiality does not exist.

In another circular letter of 16 October 1985, Minister Gol gave the prisoners a right to choose their own doctor.[19] Previously, this was a right only for remand prisoners. Prisoners are personally liable for the doctor's fees and the prison medical officer has the right to assist during the consultation. Thus, the right is impaired and difficult to exercise. In many prisons it is simply impossible to choose one's own doctor.

## HOMOSEXUALITY

On 27 December 1989 the incoming Christian Democrat Minister of Justice, Melchior Wathelet, dispatched a circular letter to prison governors which provides for prisoners buying condoms in the canteen.[20] The intention was to produce a policy in accord with that of the Council of Europe.[21] The letter implies acceptance of the practice of homosexuality in prisons. But acceptance is not universally supported as is illustrated by the prisoners at Lantin who protested about being labelled as gays. They stated that the numbers of homosexuals did not differ from those outside the prison and the real problem was that of dirty needles. 'If the Minister of Justice wants to prevent AIDS from spreading in prison he should be concerned about dirty needles. Drug addicts in Lantin are often obliged to use dirty needles or make others with a ball point pen.'

Although homosexuality is legal in Belgium such a bold acceptance from a Christian Democrat Minister was unexpected. Until a change in the law in 1985 it was illegal for men to have intercourse with men if under the age of 18. For heterosexual sex the age is set at 16 years. In 1982 a bill was introduced in Parliament to penalise all discrimination on sexual or relational preferences. In 1993 a Bill was introduced to create a partnership-regulation for gays. As of now, none of these Bills has passed into law. Until the early 1980s homosexuals were also discriminated against in prison in that they were not admitted to open prisons. It was left to Minister Jean Gol to abolish this discrimination.

## SIDATORIUM

Until recently Belgian prisons had a 'sidatorium'[22] or AIDS ward. This was located in Lantin as a result of prison officers threatening to strike in December 1985. The prison medical officer advised that cells in the psychiatric ward be dedicated to housing five seropositive prisoners. The public became aware of this quarantine ward in 1989 when some of those prisoners sought a court hearing on the ward

---

19 Fatik, 18 December 1985, 12-13.

20 Circular letter, 1548/XII, 27 December 1989.

21 Recommendation 1080 (1988) on a co-ordinated European health policy to prevent the spread of AIDS in prisons, adopted in the assembly on 30 June 1988.

22 This term was coined by the French, extremist politician, Jean-Marie Le Pen.

conditions.[23] For example, they were denied the facilities of a hairdresser or dentist. They were not allowed to go to church mass and there was no confidentiality concerning their identities. Judge Robert Bourseau did not consider that the AIDS ward was a breach of their rights and, indeed, stated that they were better provided for in that ward. They were given a TV set and had cooking facilities along with an extra 500 Belgian francs for canteen expenses. The judge felt that positive discrimination had been exercised in their favour. Their denial of the opportunity to work did not constitute discrimination as 60 per cent of prisoners are not offered work. The Liege court held that HIV prisoners constituted an 'undeniable danger' and that it was logical and just to treat them in this fashion as it was in the public interest. However, on 22 March 1990 the special unit was closed following the intervention of the socialist member of the Committee of Justice of the House, Laurette Onckelinx, who protested against discriminatory practices. Three prisoners were given conditional freedom and two were sent to another prison and one was sent to the medical centre of the prison at Saint-Gilles in Brussels.

Early or temporary release from prison, granted by the Minister of Justice, has been possible since 27 February 1951 for reasons of terminal or serious illness.[24] The government has declared that prisoners with AIDS should be transferred to special hospitals and those terminally ill should be released.[25] This decision reflects the advice of the Council of Europe.[26] In practice, this temporary release for serious illness is rarely applied. In 1992 only 13 persons were released for these reasons. If one releases a person the day before his death, the state is exempt from responsibility for the funeral expenses. The personal history of Christian B. suggest what this means. He was remanded in custody in Vorst. For two days in September 1985 he was kept without food or water in an unheated cell where windows were broken. It was some weeks before he saw a doctor of his choice and soon after he died.

The treatment of HIV positive prisoners is illustrated by the case history of Jean-Luc S. He was sentenced on 6 June 1990 by the court at Dendermonde to three years and three months in prison for drug dealing. He appealed and his sentence was raised to 12 years. A blood test indicated a positive status but the prison doctor did not undertake a physical examination. In August 1991 a second opinion from a civil doctor was obtained. S. was diagnosed as having ARC, hepatitis B and C, herpes and chlamydia. Nevertheless after this diagnosis his position within prison remained unchanged. On 30 September 1991 he requested early release on grounds of serious illness but by 23 October there had been no decision. On 8 November S. brought a court action against the state. On 23 January 1992 Judge Pilate held that early release of S. would be premature. The prison doctor had found only slight anaemia while the applicant was suggesting ARC. The judge was not willing to compare the contrasting medical findings as they were 'irrelevant'. According to the judge, there were

---

23 Devrieze v. the Belgian State, Kort geding, 31.674/89, Rechtbank van eerste aanleg, President Robert Bourseau, Liege, 1 February 1990. J. De Wit, *Sidatorium van Lantin niet in strijd met de mensenrechten, Uitkomst,* March 1990, 17-19.

24 Bulletin Bestuur Strafinrichteningen, 1951, p. 195.

25 Circular letter, 27 December 1989.

26 No. R 1080 of 30 June 1988.

adequate medical facilities in prison. They could be enhanced by bringing in civilian doctors. As a result, there was no reason for early release on medical grounds.

After the judgment, S. appealed for release. He was placed under observation for three months in an Antwerp hospital. This cost the state more than one million francs. The Court of Appeal held that there was no case to release S. on medical grounds. Nevertheless, the Minister of Justice signed, on 9 June 1993, a Royal Decree, in which he gave S. an act of grace which reduced the sentence by six years. His release date is now February 1997 although parole eligibility commences in March 1994.

## CONCLUSION

In Belgium one per cent of the prison population is known to carry the HIV virus which represents almost 60 people. They are treated as regular prisoners although single cell accommodation is used, if available. The treatment of HIV prisoners must be understood to be located within the generally dismal treatment of all prisoners in Belgium. It is an issue which has been neglected for many years and the liberal reform of which, like other European countries, attracts no votes.

The prisons are old and have no modern sanitary facilities. There is limited availability of skilled personnel. Most prison officers commence work without training. There are only 45 social workers available to work with the 20,000 people who pass through the 31 prisons on an annual basis. Medical services are inadequate.

The prison population is growing and has outstripped prison facilities. The increased numbers are accounted for by more illegal immigrants, remand prisoners and those receiving sentences in excess of five years. One result is cell overcrowding with two or three people located in a single cell. Furthermore, problems are created by the substantial growth in numbers of prisoners who enter as drug addicts. The HIV prisoners are relatively helpless and the complaint procedures are extremely limited and limiting.

Minister Melchior Wathelet, who is not only the head of the Justice Department, but is also Minister of Economic Affairs and Vice Prime Minister, has plans to renovate all the old buildings. Wathelet also wishes to double the number of trained prison social workers and improve the training of prison officers. He plans two special closed institutions for illegal immigrants and has the intention of having drug addicts treated outside prisons. However, on this point matters remain unsettled. Wathelet's circular letter stating that an 'adequate answer' will be provided for everyone found with drugs will inevitably put even greater pressure on the prisons. The minister wishes to prosecute all who are found with drugs, users and dealers, excepting first-time users or if it is a habit without prejudice for society. All illegal drugs will be treated in a similar manner. The prosecution will demand that all dealers be remanded in custody. The prison population is set, once again, to rise as a result of illegal drugs in society.

Prisoners' rights and the complaints procedure remain woefully inadequate. A group of university professors are making a study which is due to be finished by 1996. Even then, there is no guarantee that the recommendations will be implemented.

More generally, the issue of prison conditions and reform is not on the political agenda. Belgium still has no reliable statistics on criminal trends which means that policy changes are often a result of panic decisions arising out of spectacular or shocking incidents. The influence of criminologists and rational policy formers is limited. It is within this framework that HIV positive prisoners are located. The healthy prisoner is located in a depressing institution ignored by politicians and society alike. But the AIDS and HIV prisoners are treated even worse.

# AIDS IN PRISONS IN ITALY

ADOLF CERETTI AND ISABELLA MERZAGORA
*Department of Criminology,*
*University of Milan*

The grim situation of AIDS in Italian prisons can best be understood by simply studying the relevant figures. Official statistics of the Ministry of Public Health, updated to September 1991, place the number of seropositive persons in Italy at 10,584, which places Italy second only to France within Europe. Sixty-seven per cent of these persons acquired the condition through IV drug dependency and 15.8 per cent as a result of homosexual activity. At the same time, from 1 January to 25 September 1991, 29 per cent of those entering jail were drug addicts. On 30 June 1992, this percentage had risen to 31.67.

It should be noted that, for at least 14 years Italy has experienced a steady growth in the proportion of drug addicts to the general prison population: in 1979 this percentage was nine, by 1986 it had already reached 19.43 per cent and has continued to increase as shown in the following Table.

TABLE 1

| Year | per cent IV drug users among inmates |
|------|--------------------------------------|
| 1986 | 19.43 |
| 1987 | 17.09 |
| 1988 | 24.13 |
| 1989 | 25.21 |
| 1990 | 28.80 |
| 1991 | 29.00 |
| 1992 (first six months) | 31.67 |

Another turning point was the passage of a new law on 26 June 1990, known as Law n.162. It radically reversed the official attitude towards drug addiction, making it an offence to be found in possession of an illicit substance, even in small quantities and intended for personal use, i.e., not for sale to others. Such possession had since 1975 not been punishable by law.

Not surprisingly, this new law has resulted in many more drug dependent individuals going to jail. This is exacerbated by the tendency for growth in the number of drug users within the general population. This is due mainly to 'indirect' crime resulting from the 'compulsive model' that especially heroin carries with it. Such an increase has, in fact, already been authoritively reported by the President of the Brescia *Tribunale di Sorveglianza*, who stated: 'The drastic decision of our lawmaker's to impose Law 162/90, in compliance with the international agreement reached at the December 1988 New York convention, is causing, as might easily have been anticipated, a considerable increase in the number of drug addicts, either awaiting trial or convicted that are held in our penal or correctional facilities or under house arrest.'[1]

As to homosexual activity in prison, even though no reliable data is available and one suspects that there is undue alarm it is unanimously held to be widespread. This is an obvious corollary of heterosexual contacts.

Thus, both major risk factors for AIDS infection flourish within the prison walls, with drug addiction clearly taking first place. In the case of female prisoners a survey made in a Roman prison revealed that drug addiction accounts for 90 per cent of the seropositive inmates.[2]

There were 3,497 asymptomatic seropositive persons incarcerated during the first five months of 1991, which is equal to 13.35 per cent of those jailed during this same period. As of 30 June 1992, the seropositive detainees has grown to 3,844, i.e., 13.63 per cent of those admitted. It is interesting to note that women make up 10.5 per cent of these cases. Closer examination shows that in 1991 of this group of IV drug users, 405 had ARC and 81 overt AIDS. More data shows an increase in the percentage of seropositive persons among inmates, as well as in the number of those in a more advanced stage of the disease. In 1989, 125 inmates of the Italian penal institutions presented with overt AIDS, whereas in 1990 the combined total of inmates presenting with ARC and AIDS numbered 437.

Moreover, statistics concerning seropositivity are probably underestimated, since up to the present time - and we will revert to this later - testing for HIV is voluntary according to Italian law, and only 43.35 per cent of those incarcerated during the first nine months of 1991 agreed to screening. Furthermore, the percentage shown is an average over widely differing geographic situations in the country, so that the incidence ranges from 15 per cent voluntarily screened inmates in the Lazio region to 59.2 per cent in Lombardy and 89.7 per cent in Liguria, to name only a sampling of three of the 20 regions into which Italy is divided.

---

1 G. Zappa, A. Nastasio, *AIDS, carcere e misure alternative, in corso di pubblicazione in Marginalità e Società* (1992).

2 F. Bevere, *Il problema AIDS nell'istituto femminile di Roma-Rebibbia* in F. Ferracut (a cura di), Trattato di Criminologia, Medicina Criminologica e Psichiatria Forense, vol. 12: *L'intervento medico e psicologico sul testimone, sull'imputato e sul condannato* (1990).

Finally a few general remarks are necessary concerning Italian penal institutions. The overall picture is appalling. Our prison population is growing at a steep rate. It rose by 35 per cent during the year from December 1990 to December 1991. Under ideal conditions, our penal institutions are designed to house no more than 28-29,000, whereas at the end of April 1992 the total population numbered 41,600. This obviously reduces the average available space per inmate down to a bare 3 square metres. The situation had become worse by 30 June 1992, when the prison population reached 44,108.

As to the legal status of this population, in 1991 more than half (56.7 per cent) were in jail awaiting trial, compared to the 39.8 per cent already convicted and the 3.5 per cent under special surveillance. Regretfully, these percentages are far from indicative of a smooth, humane, penal system nor an adherence to the fundamental principle of personal guarantees on which the system was formally based.

## RISK FACTORS

In order to evaluate correctly the heightened risk of HIV infection incurred by prisoners, one must also remember that the laws do not allow any controlled intake of illegal substances, although they foresee controlled distribution of methadone. Neither do they foresee the distribution of sterile needles, or condoms, on the grounds that not only drug consumption, but also sexual activity is prohibited on prison premises. Even single cells are, in fact, considered 'public space' both because cells are at all times open to inspection by guards and because, being the property of a public administrative body, they constitute 'public territory'. Sexual intercourse, therefore, is punishable by Penal Code provisions which prohibit 'obscene acts' (those which offend prevailing concepts of morality and modesty) in public or on premises open to the public.[3] Aside from the obvious hypocrisy of this ruling, all homosexual activity in prison is definitely outlawed (even though Italy has no laws prohibiting homosexual practices per se), whereas heterosexual contacts are virtually impossible due to the total separation of men from women in prisons and the absence of 'conjugal visits'.

Aside from problems due to drug dependency and homosexuality, detention obviously entails a greater degree of promiscuity than life on the outside. In Italy there is no obligation to keep a prisoner in a single cell 'except in special cases for the purpose of insuring proper order and security, or for the prisoner's own safety'.[4] The result is almost always extreme overcrowding. The risk of infection is further enhanced by a code of conduct typical of prison subculture - as we know from our long experience working in prisons as criminologists - which prescribes sharing personal articles with cellmates: in the case of razors or toothbrushes, this can lead to infection.

Furthermore, prison security imposes certain regulations that are at odds with the most elementary precautions guarding against the spread of infection. For example, experts in infectious diseases advise the use of chlorine bleach as a

---

3 Art. 527, Penal Code: Obscene Acts 'Whosoever commits obscene acts in public or in premises open to the public is liable to a prison sentence of. ...'

4 This merely states that 'the number of those detained or incarcerated in penal institutions and in prison facilities must be limited and in all cases allow for the best possible care of the individual.'

disinfectant, but this is not supplied in prison on the grounds that it may be used to harm oneself or others.

Another typical prison subculture ritual is tattooing, normally done in anything but sterile conditions. This custom, however, fortunately seems to be on the decline.

Finally, it is well known that prison life often includes episodes of physical violence, both among inmates and between them and the prison officers involving the shedding of blood. In addition, in prisons (although this differs from prison to prison) illegal drug traffic is rife and there is therefore widespread, shared use of syringes.

All the above are probably not peculiar to Italian prison life but it is definitely aggravated by severe overcrowding. It is important, however, to avoid exaggerating risk situations, thereby disregarding considerations of solidarity: An inmate's position, in fact, makes him particularly vulnerable to uncontrolled fears. Prisoners can be more eloquent on this matter than any number of panel discussions: 'Ever since I learnt I was seronegative I started worrying about getting infected. I had never given it a thought before, but now, if anyone uses my fork or my towel, it makes me very nervous (there are four of us in a cell, and we're all drug addicts). I know it's not really that important, and that things are exactly as they used to be before I became aware of them, but I can't help noticing and worrying, now that I know.'[5]

## RULES AND REGULATIONS

An approach to addressing the problems within prison involves a number of basic premises, namely: (a) health care is a fundamental right both for the individual and the community and, as stated in the constitution (Art. 32), must be safeguarded and fostered by all-round interventions, not merely medicalized; (b) this safeguarding should be ensured through adequate prevention and sanitary education campaigns that should reach all aspects of both individual and social life. This applies even more emphatically to AIDS which has been defined as a behaviour-dependent disease.

Faced with the quantitative situation described above the Italian legislature has mainly abided by the general precept that the important thing is to get as many people as possible out of prison, whenever appropriate and feasible. This has been, and is still done, using laws designed to release from detention those suffering from particularly serious illnesses. Further laws specifically targetted at persons with AIDS are being promulgated.

As a result, inmates may now have the following options depending on whether they are awaiting trial or have been convicted:

If they are still awaiting trial, and their condition is not too serious they may
(a) either be admitted to the clinical facilities available within the prison itself;
(b) sent for diagnosis and treatment to a public hospital, in the custody of prison guards, or
(c) confined to home under house arrest.

---

5 From a statement of prisoner C., in San Vittore prison, in L. Frigerio, *Nella stessa barca. Cosa succede a Milano.*

The choice of a solution hinges on the need to mediate between the demands of proper justice and those of proper care for the individual. Art. 274 of the Procedural Penal Code states that the accused may be subject to home confinement provided there are no essential reasons connected with the inquiry which mitigate against this action nor any likelihood of his tampering with evidence that make this inadvisable, nor any danger of the prisoner escaping, committing further serious offences involving a weapon, or belonging to an organised crime ring such as the Mafia. Furthermore, article 275 states that 'custody in jail cannot be inflicted if the accused is in a particularly severe state of health'. Recently, new rules have been laid down stating more precise criteria according to which no prison custody can be continued for anyone with overt AIDS.[6] This condition is to be certified by the finding of a number of T/CD4+ lymphocyte equal to or lower than 100/mmc. This result is to be obtained in two consecutive tests, to be carried out at an interval of 15 days, one from the other.

If the prisoners have already been convicted and their health is sufficiently poor to make it incompatible with prison life, the 'Tribunale di Sorveglianza'[7] may approve:

(a) assignment to house arrest, which involves house confinement and allows leave therefrom only for therapeutic requirements. This applies only in the case of a prisoner sentenced to a term of two years or less;

(b) remitting the serving of a prison term until such a time as the prisoner recovers and, in certain cases, indefinite remission. This is almost always automatically applied in cases of overt AIDS, and in some Italian courts, notably in Florence, also in the case of people suffering from ARC. Postponement of the prison sentence applies to a convicted person suffering from an 'incurable' or 'life-threatening' disease (and HIV disease obviously qualifies as such, whatever phase it is in), on the grounds that anyone whose health is so severely impaired will be in no condition to do further harm, and can be released from custody without danger to the community. In especially serious cases (a number of T/CD4+ Iynphocite equal to or lower than 100/mmc), The Ministry of Justice, in two circulars dated 13 April and 2 May 1992, states that the convicted person is to be admitted to a public health institution.

(c) in the case of drug addicts wishing to undergo rehabilitation, the court may allow them to serve out their sentence, if this does not amount to more than three years, confined to a live-in therapeutic facility or regularly attending a statutory local rehabilitation day centre.

Further to existing norms designed to deal with cases of severe pathologies, to be considered case by case, prisoners with AIDS or AIDS-related diseases are also the recipients of a number of measures aimed at achieving the lowest possible level of incarceration. This is due also to the fact that health care as provided within the prison facilities - originally planned for a prison population not comprising such a large proportion of seriously or chronically ill individuals - has been found grossly

---

6 D.L.11 Settembre 1992 N.374 e D. 27 Settembre 1992.

7 This is a board made up of two judges and two experts in criminology, psychology or psychiatry, having jurisdiction over the manner in which a sentence is to be carried out, and competent to pronounce alternatives to a term in prison.

inadequate and unable to cope with a groundswell of epidemiological pressure whose effects are even more devastating in the prison environment. The main shortcomings are a lack of sufficient clinical facilities of this kind and their logistic inadequacies. These centres are known as Centres for Clinical Diagnosis and Care (Centri Diagnostici Terapeutici - CDT). Unfortunately, for a prison population expected to reach 48,000 (official estimate) or 50,000 (unofficial data) during 1992, only 13 are presently operating, most of them providing second-rate services at best. To mention only a few examples: the CDT in Genoa anticipates 100 beds, but is only partly functioning, chiefly due to lack of nursing staff which is one of the chief drawbacks of health care in penal institutions. In the San Vittore penitentiary in Milan, the real operational availability of its 86 beds is about 50 per cent at any given time. Milan's prison at Opera has a CDT of a new and particularly progressive design and is considered the show-case of the Italian prison system. It has yet to start functioning, although the jail itself has been in operation for over five years.[8]

Special institutions, operating a policy of 'mitigated rigour', have been planned to house drug addicts, since they are such a large part of the prison population and their crimes are not usually of a serious nature. However, since persons suffering from AIDS or related pathologies should be cared for outside any sort of detention facility, the idea is that even these special institutions would be inappropriate for such cases - apart from the fact that these 'mitigated rigour' structures, which the Ministry of Justice plans to set up in 31 penitentiary sites, have not started functioning, due to lack of personnel.

In view of the erratic and patchy quality of the health care centres within penal institutions, the Ministry of Justice has also moved to implement new rules for prison routine. For instance, a careful completion of the inmate's clinical case file is required, and detailed clinical criteria for admission to hospital has been circulated. Moreover, the prison administration views with favour the setting up of multi-professional teams in which a variety of specialists cooperate.[9] Cooperation with physicians from outside the prison system such as specialists in infectious diseases and immunology, is also anticipated. Such teams should also include psychologists and educators. Educators, by working in close contact with the inmates, would also have a first-hand knowledge of the relational dynamics of prison life.

The role of the psychologist and that of the educator takes on special significance due to the special emotional stress experienced by a person with AIDS within a closed institution.

As Agnoletto - President of 'The Italian League for AIDS Fight'[10] pointed out,[11] awareness of seropositivity brings on important changes in a person's psyche, even in the perception of time. Becoming aware of only a limited span of time (in the words of one sufferer) 'does not even know what the expiry date is' deprives the person with AIDS of any extended life expectation and affords only a day-to-day existence into which to fit all personal aims and aspirations. If this existence

---

8 F. Buzzi, *Tavole della legge*, Viaggio attraverso le circolari che regolano las salute dei detinuti, Day After (1991), 22.

9 Circular n. 3194/5644, 16 February 1987.

10 *Lega Italiana Lotta all'* AIDS - LILA.

11 V. Agnoletto, *Intervento al convegno per gli Operatori Penitenziari*, Milan, 16 May 1992.

constitutes life in prison, not even this meagre leeway is allowed the sufferer and incarceration risks make his plight absolutely unbearable.

However, the Prison Authority was not primarily obeying considerations of this sort but rather those of a more generically humanitarian type and the wish to keep proper discipline within the penal institutions when it acknowledged the shortcomings of prison health care. It was mainly these aspects that inspired some of the more important provisions for the treatment outside the prison of AIDS-related conditions.

In a number of Circulars proscribing a compulsive, non-differentiating policy of segregation, the Prison Administration recommends admitting prisoners with overt AIDS (CDC class IV: B, C1, D and E) to statutory hospital care.[12] For prisoners with ARC (CDC class IV: A or C2) and LAS (CDC III), admission to hospital, in the opinion of the National Committee on AIDS, is not considered obligatory.

Partly overruling a tendency to segregate and produce extreme hardship, a Circular was issued extending the need for treatment outside prison to HIV positive inmates who are in a 'clinically acute state, requiring the same essential care as those with overt AIDS'.[13] Hospitalization is also deemed necessary when any AIDS-related pathology is present or when there are complications that cannot be dealt with in the prison health centres.

With explicit reference to the special risk situation prevailing in penal institutions, the Circular also states: 'Since there is a high risk of opportunistic or other infections, and seeing that the prison environment, on account of the unavoidable promiscuity, offers multiple occasions for contact with the pathogenetic agents responsible for such infections, a person with AIDS must regularly and frequently be tested for them'.[14]

In short, the Administration is well aware of the need to provide these inmates-patients with proper treatment and isolation, but admits that these two fundamental requirements are virtually impossible to achieve in prison, which are neither designed, managed nor supervised in a way to achieve these goals. Furthermore, once again, humanitarian concerns prevail and this can only be welcomed - with the recognition that keeping an inmate in such adverse conditions 'hastens the death of a prisoner suffering from AIDS'.[15]

It should be pointed out, however, that the public hospitals, themselves in a state of chronic overcrowding, view with the utmost disfavour these admissions forced upon them by the Prison Authority. Such persons are seen as disruptive of hospital routine because of their double identity as severely, indeed, incurably ill patients and prisoners. A special cause for complaint is the fact that they are under 24 hour police surveillance, so that there is a constant violation of the privacy of other patients on the ward, as they are often examined by the medical staff under the watchful gaze of prison officers.

Thus, there is an all too often mortifying shunting back and forth of the AIDS-afflicted prisoner between jail and hospital. It results in a 'passing the buck' exercise,

---

12 n. 3127/5577, 27 June 1985; 272/5722, 12 October 1989.

13 3320/9770, 25 July 1991.

14 Circular 3297/5747, 13 December 1990.

15 G. Zappa, op. cit., fn.1.

officially motivated by humanitarian and health care concerns, but in fact based on the need to maintain smooth functioning and discipline within both institutions.

Here again, we should stop to listen to what such inmates themselves have to say about prison and hospital medical care: 'For four whole days I got about by hanging on to my bed and propping myself up against the wall of my cell, because I wasn't able to stand upright. Then I was sent to the prison medical centre and from there to hospital, under constant surveillance. I had just barely managed to get used to prison life while I was still all right, but the moment I realized I couldn't walk by myself any longer, it was terrible.'[16] And again: 'Paradoxically, the jail considers the HIV positive prisoner a patient and in the best of cases shunts him off to hospital. The hospital, in turn, considers him a prisoner, someone who should properly be in jail. So, there is a double identity issue here, with neither identity giving adequate consideration to the seropositive person's needs.'[17]

This state of affairs engendered a bizarre idea within officialdom. Given the lack of beds in public hospitals, it was suggested that the proper place for people with advanced AIDS, whether prisoners or not, was the military hospitals. This was proposed by the then Minister of Health in November 1991 and met with vigorous opposition, mainly on the grounds that a military hospital is simply a prison in another guise and amounts to a solution based on segregation rather then on any concern for proper health care.

A more rational idea appears to be at the root of the general rules which apply to drug-addicted prisoners. These are based on the premise that a prisoner's condition as a patient should take priority over the condition as a prisoner. A prisoner is to be considered as any other citizen, having a right to avail himself or herself of all the possibilities available to a free person. This requires cooperation, not a conflict of competence, between those in charge of running the prisons and those staffing the statutory health services. With this in mind, an attempt has been made to establish what has been called a 'therapeutic link' between the prison authorities and the public health service. This is the idea behind Article 96,[18] which states: 'The Local Health Units[19] in concert with the penal institutions and in collaboration with the health facilities operating within the latter will provide for the treatment and rehabilitation of drug-addicted and alcoholic inmates'. This would appear to shift the problem into its proper perspective, as far as priorities and special competence are concerned: The prison will not be left alone to face the problem and, in fact, will be seen as a 'container', whereas 'providing' will be the task of the community on the outside.

## TESTING FOR SEROPOSITIVITY IN PENAL INSTITUTIONS

If the problem of tracing AIDS persons in prison has been the cause of considerable debate, by far the most controversial issue is whether or not testing inmates for HIV should be made compulsory.

---

16 From a statement from prisoner B, suffering from AIDS-related neuropathy, San Vittore prison, Milan. L. Frigorio, op. cit., fn. 5.

17 From a statement from prisoner C. Ibid.

18 Comma III T.U. 9 October 1990 n. 39.

19 Local Statutory Health Care Units: Unità Sanitarie Locali - USL.

First, we indicate that our Constitution specifically refers to health care in Art. 32, establishing the right to health as a fundamental human right both for the individual and the community as a whole.[20] This not only means adopting measures considered apppropriate for safeguarding society, but, in some cases, albeit with extreme caution, curtailing individual liberty with a view to ensuring the health both of the individual concerned and of the community at large.

An example of measures designed to safeguard society is the Compulsory Sanitary Intervention[21] which is resorted to without the person's consent, on the grounds that the person is manifestly a source of danger to himself or to others. However, the Constitution also rules that 'the law may not in any case encroach on what is considered proper respect for the individual'.

Aside from the need to reconcile these two fundamental requirements - safeguarding, that is, the community and guaranteeing proper respect for individual rights - there is also the problem of bridging the possible conflict between the inviolability of personal liberty (as prescribed in Article 13 of the Constitution, interpreted in this case as the right to control one's own body) and the right to enforce sanitary intervention, even those that entail physical constraint of an individual.[22]

As to the specific question of whether HIV testing should or should not be made compulsory, this poses no special problem when a medical intervention is routinely performed on all members of a specific category of citizens, as is the case with the mandatory vaccination of pre-school children. It is far more debatable whether or not such a mandatory procedure should be imposed only on certain predetermined classes of individuals, on the assumption that they might be a source of danger to the community. The issue also calls into question the fundamental 'principle of equality' whereby a difference in treatment may only be adopted for specifically justifiable reasons.[23] It has therefore been argued that submitting only the prison population to mandatory testing, or worse, only those who are known drug addicts or homosexuals, would be discriminatory and in breach of this principle, all the more so in view of the 'moral' onus that in any case accrues to these categories of citizens.

Actually, 'the real problem is not that treatment be made mandatory, but rather under what conditions treatment will be provided and what consequences it will have for the individuals concerned. There is, in fact, a considerable risk of setting off a chain reaction by singling out, labelling and excluding, judicially and in everyday life,

---

20 Article 32 of the Italian Constitution, comma 1: 'The Republic considers the right to health to be a fundamental human right of the individual and it acts in the interests of the community by also assuring free medical care for the indigent'.

21 Trattamenti Sanitari Obbligatori T.S.O. Private citizens may be subject to Mandatory Sanitary Treatment (Trattamenti Sanitari Obbligatori T.S.O.) according to article 32, comma 11 of the Constitution, which states: 'No one may be compelled to submit to any kind of medical intervention, except for reasons of a legal nature. The law can in no case go beyond the limits of proper respect for the person.'

22 Article 13 of the Constitution, commas 1 and 11, states: 'Personal liberty is inviolable. No form of detention, inspection or searching of the person or any curtailing of personal liberty is allowed, except by virtue of a properly justified judicial act, and then only in the special instances and manner forseen by law.'

23 Article 3 of the Constitution.

such a large group of citizens, with easily foreseen repercussions'. This holds true if such sample-taking were a decision left to the discretion of a single Prison Authority and not a general law applying to all those incarcerated.[24]

Furthermore, forceful arguments against such discriminating and ghettoing have been voiced by international and European health authorities, as well as by the WHO. It cannot be claimed that screening would be done in order to safeguard the community from a particularly dangerous health hazard, since infection does not come about simply as a result of seropositive and seronegative people living in the same community. Thus, one cannot place only prison inmates in a risk category while disregarding other situations on an equal level of 'danger', such as barracks, hospitals or schools, and ignoring individuals at large, who are equally in a position to spread the disease.

It has also been remarked that compulsory screening might paradoxically hinder a gradual and salutary shift in the direction of self-responsible behaviour on the part of citizens as a whole (drug addicts, for one, are known to be especially rash about taking risks) whereas it might even prompt individuals whose behaviour is risky of going underground in order to avoid being recorded. Inappropriate behaviour of this kind could also be the result of compulsory screening of health care providers, since there are known to be cases of 'false negatives' and that some improper standards of health care are prompted by anxiety about 'false positives'.[25]

Another objection to curtailing individual liberty by making HIV testing mandatory has been raised by the National Health Board [26] on the ground that such an encroachment is not justified by therapeutic considerations for the benefit of the individual, since there is at present no generally accepted therapy for AIDS.

For these weighty reasons, the legislature has allowed only voluntary testing in prison as applies throughout civil society. The law that sets out a 'Programme of Urgent Measures to be Taken for the Prevention (Prophylactics) and Fight against AIDS'[27] in comma III of Art. 5 states that 'no one can be obliged without his consent to undergo any medical analyses for ascertaining the presence of HIV infection except for strictly clinical purposes and in his own best interest'.

This same article leaves a loophole for screening without the subject's consent 'for strictly clinical purposes and in his own best interest', and goes on to say: 'Such analyses as are necessary for evaluating the incidence of HIV infection within the framework of an epidemiological survey are permitted only if samples taken are rendered anonymous with no possible way of tracing the identity of the person tested'.

It must also be said that not all authorities oppose compulsory testing in prison for the HIV antibodies. The Prison Authority, for one, has called consistently for compulsory screening of all inmates and has argued its case as follows: it would make reliable epidemiological survey of the prison population possible since, as we stated earlier, at present only 43.3 per cent of this population voluntarily submit to the test

---

24 G. Zappa, 'Prevenzione dell' AIDS e misure coercitive della libertà personale - Problemi giuridici' in AIDS: La Sindrome da Immunodeficienza Acquisita: Conoscerla per Prevenirla (1991), 311.

25 P. Cattorini, *Proposte di screening per l'infezione da HIV. Riflessioni etiche preliminari ed analisi della situazione carceraria* in AIDS e Situazione Carceraria ed. P. Cattorini, (1990), 59.

26 Consiglio Superiore di Sanita.

27 n. 135, 5 June 1990.

and non-official data has it that this proportion is even smaller, about 30 per cent so that the real prevalence of seropositive persons in our prisons is widely underestimated. Making the test obligatory, these sources hold, would also provide more reliable evidence of the danger of infection while in jail. Furthermore, in the view of the Prison Authority, effective prophylactics could only be ensured, also for the prison staff, by such mass screening. Making the test compulsory for all those entering prison would, according to the Prison Authority, eliminate rather than foster discrimination, to the extent that not only drug addicts and homosexuals would be 'advised' to take the test, but it would be given automatically to everyone.

The Association of Prison Doctors[28] voices similar concern and notes that all those who enter prison are obliged by law to take the Wasserman reaction for syphilis, which has not been considered a violation of individual rights or discriminatory. Also, as these doctors remark, AIDS has been added to the list of widespread contagious diseases that physicians are obliged to report to the health authorities, albeit subject to professional confidentiality.[29] As to the objection that the test is useless, there being no known cure for the disease, the AMAPI considers this a lame excuse. We find it interesting to state the conclusions this group of doctors reached during their 1991 convention, not only because these practitioners have such an important role but also on account of how their conclusions were worded: 'This obstinate refusal to recognize the need of making testing mandatory in prison, a milieu so fraught with risk, is tantamount to appointing the prison doctor to be the unwitting yet instrumental executioner of death sentences.'

Something of a compromise - and one that must be viewed with considerable perplexity, let alone alarm - has been proposed by the Ministry of Health's 'National Committee on Fighting AIDS'. This authoritative body suggests that should it not be possible to obtain 'informed consent' from a majority of the prison population, despite the assurance of anonymity, it might be possible to use blood samples collected for other reasons (for instance, vaccination against hepatitis B) and use them for HIV screening.

Aside from the fact that such a stratagem would go against the guidelines established by the EC, which state that no medical intervention may be adopted for a purpose other than that declared when requesting consent (and 'informed consent', after all, means just that) we consider that it is appropriate to speak of violence and the violation of basic human rights in connection with such a deceitful procedure.

## INFORMING AND PREVENTING

Over and above the problem of what strategies are correct for caring for the seropositive inmate, and of whether or not testing in prison should be made mandatory, international experts and those in Italy agree that correct and widely available information about AIDS is one of the most effective means of prevention.

Correct information implies not only making available knowledge of how to avoid risk behaviour but also publicizing information that can help prevent mass

---

28 Associazione dei Medici Penitenziari - AMAPI. See AMAPI, *Test obbligatorio per l'HIV in carcere*, in Medicina Penitenziari (December 1991), 10-11.

29 Circular n. 5, 13 February 1987.

hysteria, which is all the more likely to run rampant since the disease calls up deep-seated, ominous archetypes from our collective subconscious such as guilt, contagion, blood and sexuality.

In this connection, it is interesting to verify the abysmal ignorance on the subject shown by the results of a survey made by a prison doctor who questioned inmates and officers in the prison of Noto, Sicily.[30] He asked them what they knew about how the disease is transmitted. Answering a questionnaire that foresaw several possible answers to each question, only 13.3 per cent of the prison officers said they would greet a close friend they had not seen for some time and knew to be seropositive with a hug; 60 per cent would only shake hands and 26.7 per cent would only voice a greeting. Of the inmates, 20 per cent would simply say 'hello' without any physical contact; 45 per cent would go so far as to shake hands, and 20 per cent give their friends a hug. However, 5 per cent would pretend they had not seen him. Asked whether they would work alongside an HIV positive person 34 per cent of the inmates said no, and 46 per cent of the prison officers also said they would refuse. This can easily be understood if one considers that 16 per cent of the inmates, when asked who could become infected with the virus cited 'alcoholic', and only 29.4 per cent answered 'anyone'. Asked how AIDS is transmitted, 84 per cent of the inmates answered 'by the use of articles such as razors, nail scissors, and toothbrushes', 8 per cent named social contact, 21.3 per cent perspiration, 9.4 per cent named food and 50 per cent mosquito bites. Of the officers, 53 per cent said they would not allow their children to use a public swimming pool.

However, as we had anticipated, information is also a means of calling attention to risk behaviour, and we would add that 26.4 per cent of these inmates, (so wary of mosquito bites) said they had sexual intercourse with prostitutes when on licence; 48 per cent would have sex with a perfect stranger, and of these 8.4 per cent said they would not use any protection.

Along these same lines, a study carried out on 544 drug addicts, 43 per cent of whom had been incarcerated at least once, 10 per cent (some of them seropositive) reported they had shared razors and toothbrushes with their cellmates. Exchanging used needles was admitted by 9 per cent, homosexual acts by only 2 per cent.

One is forcefully reminded of the authoritative statement issued by the WHO which points out that the Prison Authority is responsible for providing correct information to the inmates.[31]

There is considerable evidence that prison can often be the place where a person first becomes aware of his seropositive condition. This is especially true in the case of those - mainly drug addicts - normally not very cautious or concerned about their physical well-being. Such awareness comes as a result of being given the opportunity in prison to undergo the test for HIV antibodies. Once seropositive individuals have served their term, however, they should be taken in charge by the civil statutory health facilities in order to ensure continuity of therapy. This was attempted, for example, in an experimental programme at the Rebibbia Women's Prison in Rome where in the period from November 1985 to March 1988, 652 inmates

---

30 C. Corrado, *Indagine conoscitiva sulle informazioni in tema di AIDS su detenuti e agenti di custodia*, Atti Conferenza Nazionale: AIDS e Carcere Rimini, 6-8 May, 1988.

31 WHO, Special Program on AIDS, Geneva, 16-18 November 1987.

aged 18 to 44 were tested for HIV antibodies.[32] Two hundred and twenty-three of them were found seropositive (34.25 per cent). Ninety per cent of these were drug addicts. They naturally received all the health care available within the prison walls, but - and this is relevant to our discussion - once they had served their sentence, a therapeutic programme was drawn up to keep them under further proper sanitary control. Through an agreement with the Clinic for Infectious Diseases of Rome University they were given a document containing useful clinical information concerning their condition. Such patients could then be regularly examined at the university outpatient clinic, free of charge and without any cumbersome registration procedure or long waits for appointments, and with their clinical history available in full detail. A link was thus established between the prison and the statutory health services.

CONCLUSION

The outlook for AIDS in prison is depressing especially since the scenario within which two such dramatic predicaments (incarceration and AIDS-related disease) interrelate is constructed of different and conflicting issues. On the one hand we have AIDS, which by all definitions is not merely a medical condition to be dealt with using 'technical' instruments. On the other, as we have said, AIDS fills our imagination with powerful connotations of deeply rooted fears (contagion, blood, sexuality, guilt, death). It is difficult to reduce such notions to rational terms.

Prison, for its part, is tied in with equally strong anxieties and irrationalities of its own and has an overtone of punishment, vengeance, exclusion. One of the most lively and heated debates developed during the recent decades around the concept of prison. This involved much discussion around prison abolition, which is not necessarily synonymous with doing away with punishment, of creating alternative measures to incarceration (i.e. diversion) or, vice versa, of revitalising new forms of retributive justice. The discussion rose to high levels of intellectual, political, civil and emotional tension and peaked during the early eighties, at which time the movement known as 'freedom from the need to imprison' got under way, the name of which explicitly frames its objective.

However, what happened in the wake of those years of high civil tension is also well known. In Italy, its effects were first exacerbated by a series of massacres in which the State itself was widely reputed to have had a hand, then by terrorism, and gradually by the increasingly defiant arrogance with which organized crime, especially the Mafia, worked hand in glove with official centres of power. Judge Falcone was such a victim. He was a judge always in the front line in the war against the Mafia, who had successfully unravelled many of its plots.

All this has dashed many hopes, and at least temporarily, visions of a society in which such distressing events could be less pervasive. Even so, the AIDS emergency will not allow us to dismiss the debatable notion of 'reasons for imprisonment' and obliges us to concentrate on the issue of allaying fears and guilt feelings, both of which are poor counsellors when it comes to drawing up prison policy.

---

32 F. Ceraudo, *Principi fondamentali di Medicina Penitenziaria*, Centro Studi della Presidenza Nazionale AMAPI, 1988.

Unfortunately, we feel that we are speaking only for ourselves, since similar considerations do not appear to be reflected in official thinking on the matter. In the best of cases, this has apparently been based on humanitarian sentiments and on the need to keep proper discipline in prisons or, at worst adroitly side-stepping the whole problem by physically removing the sufferers to some other place. This last rationale accounts for the shameful shunting back and forth that goes on between the prison and the hospital of people no one wants to take charge of, with no consideration whatsoever for the real needs of either the individual or the community - needs that are admittedly difficult to harmonize.

Still, simply negating the issue or sweeping it under the carpet are not adequate strategies for the individual, much less for the community, and we can only hope things will not get to the point where, paradoxically, better solutions for the problem of seropositive and AIDS-afflicted persons in prison will actually be sought and found only once the situation of proper prison management gets completely out of hand.

If we confine our discussion to what we have outlined here, the main issue, obviously, is still that of rendering HIV tests compulsory for prisoners. Compulsory testing would immediately usher in a widespread difference of treatment for inmates and their confinement in special sections of prison or other correctional institutions. It would also mean implementing a wide range of alternatives to prison confinement. All this, however, follows the paradigm of the 'technocratic' solution which likes to think of itself as 'virtuous'[33] but avoids tackling the far greater problem of laying open to thorough discussion the State's need to punish and to safeguard the community. On the other hand, such an attitude on the part of officialdom really would protect seronegative prisoners from the far from hypothetical risk of infection while in jail. It would empty our penal institutions of the embarrassing and worrisome presence of people who are dying.

The fact is, however, that this is true of any severely ill person, and everyone's conscience is soothed, rather hypocritically, by renouncing the State's prerogative to inflict punishment only when it is obvious that a definite sentence, one that cannot be appealled, will be forthcoming.

Furthermore, for AIDS as for any other severe illness, such 'false consciousness' means ignoring, or not wanting to become aware of, how much the hardship, stress and distress of prison life combine to aggravate the sick prisoner's condition. It is established that stress enhances depression of the immune system, thereby hastening the progress of the disease. In this sense, and resorting once again to an apparent paradox, he who has an overt AIDS condition, or is in the terminal phase of the disease, would benefit from physical, environmental and medical attention (and these are not even very costly), whereas the plight of the seropositive prisoner would steadily worsen during detention. HIV infection cannot be defined as a specific disease but it can become one and prison confinement can be a contributing factor. Incarceration speeds the progress of the disease from the infectious stage into the full-blown malady. It contributes to the disease itself and hence is instrumental in leading to the sufferer's death. Carefully considered, the contradiction between the right to life

---

33 M. Pavarini, *L'umana convenienza. AIDS e carcere: Quale soluzione?* in La Grande Promessa (1991), 28.

and the right to punish is a far more crucial issue where seropositive inmates are concerned than in the case of those who have ARC or overt AIDS.[34]

Thus, apart from there being a strong presence of hypocrisy, the proposed solution leaves the problem of social defence untouched. One of the present authors was professionally involved in the following case: an inmate presenting with overt AIDS was allowed, as per existing norms to serve the remainder of his term outside prison, in order to have access to proper medical care. He was a drug addict, and upon his release, attempting to get the money for his drugs, he held up his victim by 'pricking' him with a needle infected with his blood.

This act of AIDS terror is something that can happen again. We do not wish to sound cynical but we also feel that sentimentality is out of place, and we ask ourselves the nagging question: how is one to strike a proper balance between safeguarding the health of the individual and that of the community?

After so much criticism, do we have anything positive and constructive to suggest? We feel it is not our task to provide 'technical' solutions. As scholars we think it is our duty to insist on exhaustive discussion of the global problem rather than devising minor and random tactics that ignore or by-pass the truly crucial issues underlying decisions and actions. One of these crucial questions, we repeat, is the knotty one of balancing an individual's health requirements against those of the community. This may even turn out to be a problem to which there is no overall solution: an irreconcilable antinomy. Still, we feel it is less misleading to acknowledge such extreme incompatibility than to pretend the question does not exist.

---

34 Ibid.

# AIDS IN PRISONS IN SPAIN

JUAN TERRADILLOS BASOCO
*Department of Criminal Law,*
*University of Cadiz*

The Spanish prison population in January 1992 stood at 38,300.[1] Like other European countries this reflects a steady growth in the number of prisoners. In 1985 the figure was 22,500 indicating an increase of 70 per cent. The current rate of imprisonment is around 82 per 100,000 which places Spain in the middle of the EC incarceration rate.

The percentage of female prisoners has grown from around eight in 1990 to 12 per cent in 1991[2] which is on the high side when compared with the rest of Europe.[3] Whilst the incarceration rate is increasing at a rate of 10 per cent a year the rate is faster for female offenders. For example, in Cataluña, between 1987 and 1992, the number of female prisoners has doubled.[4] However, the number of youth offenders in custody, during the same period, has decreased by more than 20 per cent.[5] The percentage of remand prisoners has also decreased in the recent past by 37 per cent throughout Spain.

The educational attainment is low: 9.4 per cent are total illiterates, 46.9 per cent have failed to finish primary education, 29.9 per cent have finished it. The rest have achieved superior levels.[6] Thus, the typical Spanish prisoner is a young male, the average age on entering prison has increased from 27.7 in 1989 to 30.4 in 1991. In 1989 many have had employment althought 44 per cent were unemployed on entering prison. This percentage has decreased to 32 per cent in 1991.[7] Twenty-nine per cent lived with a partner or wife and 47 with other relatives.[8]

---

1 Defensor del Pueblo, Informe anual 1991 y debates en las Cortes Generales. I. (1992), 202.

2 Report Situación socio-sanitaria de la población interna en centros penitenciarios 1991, (1991) 16 Refat 3.

3 E. Giménez Salinas, *Droga/Sida: nuevo objetivo en el punto de mira penitenciario* (1991), 5 Eguzkilore 122.

4 The Generalitat (Government of Cataluña) is responsible for prisons in its province. This explains why data specific to Cataluña is provided in this chapter.

5 Centre d'estudis jurídics i Formació especialitzada, Evolució de la població penitenciària. Catalunya 1985-1991 (1992), 1.

6 Report cit., 2.

7 Ibid., 3.

8 M. Martín Sanchez, *Programa de prevención y control de enfermedades transmisibles en Instituciones Penitenciarias* (1990) extra 1, Revista de Estudios Penitenciarios 57.

## PRISONS

Spanish prisons are old and inadequate. In 1988 the 'Defender of the People' (Spanish Ombudsman) categorized 37 prisons as old, 16 as normal, and 26 as totally modern later than 1979.[9] In 1991 the situation has not changed.[10] In response, the office of Public Administration (Dirección General de Instituciones Penitenciarias) published a plan in 1988 to modernize Spanish prisons. The objective is to bring all prisons up to the minimum standard, required by law, by 1994.

Another major issue is that of overcrowding. The commitment of the criminal justice system to imprisonment as a principal form of punishment has been noted by the 'Defender of the People' which in turn exacerbates the issue of prison overcrowding.[11]

The report of the Prosecutor to Prisons Supervision (Fiscal General de Vigilancia Penitenciaria) in 1991 noted that four, five or even six prisoners are housed in less than 8 square metres of cell space in the first, third, fourth and sixth galleries in the 'Cárcel Modelo' prison in Barcelona. These galleries housed 1,600 inmates.[12] The Ley General Penitenciaria (Prisons Act), Art. 12.2 establishes that the prisons should house less than 350 inmates each.

In 1991 there still remained large collective cells in Algeciras, Palma de Mallorca and Vigo prisons and in the women's sections of Santander, Oviedo, Cáceres I and León prisons.[13]

Each prison is obliged to have at least one medical doctor who has psychiatric skills as well as a dedicated room for psychiatric observation. This is of especial importance for drug addicts and those inmates suffering from infectious diseases.[14] However, again, the situation is unsatisfactory. Even official publications have recognised the shortfall. The Public Prosecutor has noted that prison medical units fall short of legal requirements in terms of equipment necessary for dealing with HIV prisoners and the introduction of civilian doctors from public hospitals does not make up the shortfall.[15]

Another unsatisfactory feature of Spanish prisons is that there is no strict separation of remand and convicted prisoners. The reality of prison overcrowding and the frequent moving of inmates from prison to prison makes this impossible.[16] One result of this mixing of prisoners is that medical treatment is even more difficult to

---

9 Defensor del Pueblo, Informes, estudios y documentos. Situación penitenciaria en España (1988), 157.

10 Defensor del Pueblo, Informe anual 1991 y debates en las Cortes Generales. I. (1992), 201.

11 Ibid., 202.

12 C. Jiménez Villarejo, *Aproximación al problema del SIDA en las prisiones*, in Ministerio Fiscal y sistema penitenciario, ed. Centro de Estudios Judiciales (1992), 146.

13 Defensor del Pueblo, Informe anual 1991 y debates en las Cortes Generales. I. (1992), 202.

14 Ley General Penitenciaria, Art. 36.1 and 37. Reglamento Penitenciario (Prisons Rules), Art. 139.

15 Fiscalía General del Estado, consultation n° 4/1990, Nov. 5.

16 J. Alarcón Bravo, *El tratamiento penitenciario en el primer decenio de la L.O.G.P.* (1989) extra 1, Revista de Estudios Penitenciarios 17.

deliver and the incidence of contagious diseases is both more frequent and extremely difficult to control.

DATA COLLECTION

At the end of the 1980s there were about 5,000 reported cases of AIDS in Spain. In September 1990 this number had risen to 6,210 according to the figures of the Ministry of Health. Other researchers increase this figure to 7,047.[17] This means over 150 cases per million people. The death rate is 35.7 per cent.[18] Between 1990 and 1992 the rate of new cases of AIDS in Spain is four times the median rate of Europe.

In 1991 the rate of cases per million people in the self-governing communities was: Galicia, 106; Asturias, 114; Castilla-León, 58; Madrid, 284; Extremadura, 83; Andalucía, 121; Cantabria, 154; La Rioja, 164; Aragón, 104; Castilla-La Mancha, 65; Valencia, 114; Murcia, 85; Baleares, 234; Cataluña, 326; Navarra, 150; País Vasco, 306 and Canarias, 87.[19]

Eighty-three per cent of these cases are males. No women were reported as having AIDS before 1984. Thereafter there are two distinct phases. The first, 1984-1985, showed women as less than 10 per cent of the total but between 1986-1990 this rose to between 17 and 18 per cent. AIDS is found predominately amongst young people with 35 per cent of the cases presenting in the 25 to 29 age group and 82 per cent in the 20 to 39 age group. Paediatric cases of AIDS represent 3 per cent. Of these, 60 per cent of the children were infected by the mother. Fifty-five per cent of these women are intravenous drug addicts and 9 per cent were infected by sexual contacts.[20]

In Spain the issue of HIV infection is closely associated with the misuse of drugs rather than homosexual activities. Seventeen per cent of AIDS patients are intravenous drug users. Three per cent are both drug users and homosexuals.

AIDS AND THE LAW

The 'Ley General Penitenciaria' (Prison Act), of 1980 explicitly states in Article 3.2.4 that the prison administration must look after the life, the well-being and the health of prisoners. The Spanish constitution, in Articles 2 and 43.1, states that the Office of Public Administration has the responsibility to ensure that public health is guaranteed by such preventive methods and services as are necessary.[21]

Moreover, the Ley General de Sanidad (Health Act) of April 25 1986 guarantees the right to medical assistance in equal conditions for the whole population. Discriminatory behaviour by public servants is a crime according to Penal Code, Art. 181 bis.

---

17 Nájera-de Andrés, Juventud y SIDA en España (1990) passim.

18 J.M. de Miguel, *El problema social del SIDA en España*, (1991) 53, Revista Española de Investigaciones Sociológicas, at p. 75-76 and 87.

19 Política Científica (1991), 27.

20 De Miguel, op. cit., 76-95.

21 H. Hormazábal, *SIDA y Derecho Penal* (1992) 1 Cuadernos Jurídicos 10.

Equivalence of health care is laid out in Article 8 (c) of the 'Reglamento Penitenciario' (Prison Rules) which states: 'The medical attendance for prisoners will be organized on the same conditions as offered to civilians'. In addition, based on the WHO recommendations, HIV positive prisoners must be kept on normal location and not segregated.[22]

Drugs are banned within prison under Article 109 of the 'Reglamento Penitenciario'. It is categorized as a serious offence 'to introduce, take out or possess in the prison, objects that are forbidden by the prison rules, the use of toxic drugs, psychotropic substances or narcotics, except by medical prescription'.

Articles 94 to 98 recognise the possibility of conjugal visits, that will take place in designated rooms, with a visiting time of more than one hour and less than three.[23] The partners of the inmates are not allowed to bring bags into the prison and they have to undertake a personal search. In spite of these controls, the conjugal visits are still used, on occasions, to bring drugs into the prison. [24]

Article 60 allows the release, on licence, those prisoners who are 'seriously sick and have no possibility of cure'. Prisoners with AIDS have been released early on humanitarian grounds. However, the release process is lengthy thereby decreasing its effectiveness. Indeed, it has been suggested that the discretion is operated more on the basis of reducing prison death statistics than on humanitarian grounds.[25] As a consequence of that Article 4,000 prisoners were released in 1991.[26]

## TESTING

The quality of health care in prisons is inadequate and the need has been undervalued.[27] For example, medical staff receive particularly low salaries which often have resulted in the medical staff taking second jobs on a 'moonlighting' basis. Since 1989 the position has improved.[28] The number of posts for doctors has increased from 150 to 375. Equally important is the increase in full-time jobs, meaning 37.5 hours a week, as opposed to the previous commitment of three hours a day.[29]

The position of HIV testing is based on the interpretation of the Constitution, Arts. 9 and 10[30] that systematic and indiscriminate testing, whether in or out of prison, is unconstitutional. This is accepted by the Health Ministry. This constitutional

---

22 Jiménez Villarejo, op. cit., 148.

23 Terradillos-Mapelli, *Las consecuencia jurídicas del delito* (1990) 169.

24 Moreno-Porta-Rovira *El proceso de drogodependencia en el medio penitenciario: un modelo alternativo* (1991), 245 Revista de Estudios Penitenciarios 59.

25 C.M. Romeo Casabona *El SIDA en las prisiones. Transmisión del SIDA entre reclusos* (1991), 7 Jornadas penitenciarias andaluzas 60.

26 El País, 9 April 1992.

27 Defensor del Pueblo, Informe anual 1991 y debates en las Cortes Generales. I. (1992), 204.

28 R. de la Torre Martínez, *Reforma de la asistencia sanitaria en los centros penitenciarios* (1990) extra 1 Revista de Estudios Penitenciarios 15, 20.

29 M.J. Dolz Lago, *La cárcel, factor patógeno? (Límites de la asistencia sanitaria penitenciaria)*, in Ministerio Fiscal y sistema penitenciario, ed. Centro de Estudios Judiciales, 1992, 84.

30 Tribunal Constitucional case 37/89 February 15.

provision also denies the possibility of general health screening. The office of Public Administration has attempted to introduce the WHO recommendations relating to AIDS but their implementation has been fraught with difficulties because of the lack of human and material resources.[31]

In 1988 a 'Programme for preventing and controlling infectious diseases' was established by the Penitentiary Administration. Its first phase is dedicated to prevention and control of syphilis, hepatitis B and HIV. If AIDS is diagnosed, treatment including AZT, is available. This may be administered in conjunction with civilian hospital involvement. This programme commenced in March 1989. Of a prison population of 27,023, some 25,202 inmates were offered the test and 19,946 took it. This meant that 80 per cent of prisoners were tested.[32] The results of the programme showed that 28 per cent of those tested were HIV positive.[33]

Other statistics, from respected institutions such as the Carlos III Health Institute, Madrid, indicates that prisoner HIV positive percentage is 30. Other studies, conducted in different prisons, show a range of infection of between 29 to 57 per cent.[34] The most complete research[35] shows a range on entering prison of 28.4 per cent in 1989, 24.2 per cent in 1990 and 20.6 in 1991 which reflects a remarkable decline. The Public Administration estimates that in 1992 the number is around 7,800 infected inmates.[36]

In 1989, the National AIDS Case Agency for Penitentiary Administration indicated that of those infected 93 per cent were male and 7 per cent were female. Distribution by age was as follows: under 20 years, 1.4 per cent; from 20 to 24 years, 15.4 per cent; from 25 to 29 years, 46.2 per cent; from 30 to 39 years, 22.2 per cent; over 40 years, 2.7 per cent. This data which relates to the prison population mirrors the figures which apply in the general population.[37]

The number of deaths in prisons from AIDS now represents half the total number of deaths. In some provinces the percentage is higher and in Cataluña it is 56 per cent.[38] The principal risk factor in prisons is the intravenous use of drugs. Figures suggest that drug abuse accounts for 93 per cent of the infection rate; sexual relationships responsible for 12.7 per cent; blood transfusions for 6.9 per cent and tattooing for 6 per cent.[39]

Thirty-eight per cent of occasional heroin users in prison are infected with HIV and this rises to 61 per cent amongst the regular users. If more than 2 grammes are consumed daily this percentage increases to 67. Of all infected inmates 68 per cent carry tattoos.[40]

---

31 Jiménez Villarejo, op. cit., 141, 145.
32 Martín Sánchez, op. cit., 51 and 56.
33 Ibid., 57.
34 Giménez Salinas, op. cit., 123; Romeo Casabona, op. cit., 50; De Miguel, op. cit., 77.
35 Report cit., 2.
36 *El País*, 9 April 1992.
37 Martín Sánchez, *Sistemas de información sanitaria en Instituciones Penitenciarias* (1990) extra 1, Revista de Estudios Penitenciarios 77.
38 De Miguel, op. cit., 81.
39 Martín Sánchez, op. cit., 78.
40 Ibid., 58.

It is commonly accepted that drugs constitute the biggest single risk of infection in Spanish prisons. The report of the Defender of the People in 1988 stated: 'The rates of narcotics usage in Spanish prisons is in direct relation to the rate of drugs traffic in the area where the prison is located.'[41] According to data obtained in 1988 by the 'Programme' 44 per cent of prisoners questioned[42] stated that they had used intravenous drugs at least once.

In Cataluña, during 1989, the prison medical service made 10,535 addiction tests on reception of new prisoners. The results were that 81 per cent were addicted to tobacco; 44 per cent to heroin; 32 per cent to alcohol; 24.5 per cent psychopharmaceutical drugs; and 22 per cent to cocaine.[43]

Foreigners comprise a significant proportion of the Spanish prison population: 4,500 being 15.4 per cent of the total.[44] This percentage increases every year. Foreigners are most likely to end up in Spanish prisons as a result of drug trafficking offences as the figure of 46.5 per cent indicates. There are even cases of North-African immigrants who commit misdemeanours so they can enter prison to organise inside drug traffic where the profit is five times higher than outside.[45] However, the level of HIV infection is 5 per cent.[46]

CONCLUSION

Given the dangers regarding health and, in particular, AIDS which are inherent within the Spanish prison system it is necessary to address the deep seated causes. A system is required which addresses the issues of realistic punishment and alternatives to prison rather than simply incarcerating those who offend.[47] Such a new programme would entail employing extra-prison treatment of offenders and to seek to change the nature and level of risk practices of prisoners. For them, the danger to their health is increased by the very institution to which the state has committed them.

As stated, Article 60 of the Reglamento Penitenciario, which is also included in the Project of the Penal Code, allows those prisoners who are seriously or terminally ill to be given early release. The authorities should interpret this article in a humane manner so that prisoners may be allowed to seek better treatment in civilian hospitals and look for a better quality of life in civil society. In addition, the powers laid down in Article 57.1 concerning extra-prison treatment need to be employed more vigorously.[48]

Such developments are not matters of discretion but of obligation. Human dignity and social reintegration, as laid down in Articles 10 and 25 of the constitution

---

41 Defensor Del Pueblo, op. cit., 55.

42 Martín Sánchez, op. cit., 56.

43 Giménez Salinas, op. cit., 122; V. Martin et al., *Seroepidemiologia de la infección por VIH-1 en un penal catalá'* (1990) 4 AIDS 1023-1026.

44 I. Sánchez Yllera, *Extranjeros en prisión: doble condena*, (1990) 10 Jueces para la Democracia, 65.

45 Moreno-Porta-Rovira, op. cit., 59.

46 Martín Sánchez, op. cit., 57. P.A. Thomas, *The Dealer* (1990), 16 Journal of Alcohol, Drugs and Psychotropic Substances, 196-98.

47 Martín Sánchez, op. cit., 57.

48 Defensor del Pueblo, Informe anual 1991 y debates en las Cortes Generales. I. (1992) 206.

and Article 3.4 of the Ley General Penitenciaria, demand such action by the appropriate authorities. It is necessary to create a special housing programme for AIDS patients who are often homeless on prison discharge. This policy has already been started by the government of Cataluña.

Given that conjugal visits are allowed the majority of inmates have authorised sexual relationships. In a survey released in 1990 in the men's prison of Cuatro Caminos, Cataloña, about 50 per cent of the prisoners stated that they had unauthorised sexual or homosexual contacts inside prison. The majority stated that they had not used condoms although these are issued on a regular basis to prisoners.

The same survey indicated that 30 per cent of drug users shared needles in prison and 47.8 per cent did not share. Danger is increased because needles are sometimes hidden inside the rectum or the vagina. The price to hire a needle is around 300 or 400 pesetas each time.[49] Thirteen per cent disinfected their needles most of the time with bleach. Thirty point four per cent thought that their needles could have been infected upon use.[50] With such disturbing evidence in the public domain it is patently obvious that there is an urgent need to review the procedures which control and affect these risk practices which in turn affect the spread of HIV and ultimately AIDS. The tension, on the one hand, between discipline and control environment becomes clear in the matter of HIV. Condoms are available in prisons but now the issue of clean needles must be addressed.[51]

49 Moreno-Porta-Rovira, op. cit., 62.

50 Giménez Salinas, op. cit., 124-125.

51 Doctors are reluctant to support the distribution of sterile needles in prisons. D. Del Ojo Cordero, Aspectos médicos del S.I.D.A. en Instituciones Penitenciarias (1988), 73.

# AIDS IN PRISONS IN CANADA

RALF JÜRGENS
*McGill Centre for Medicine, Ethics and Law*
*McGill University,*
*Montréal*

## CANADA'S CORRECTIONAL SYSTEM

By virtue of Canada's constitution, jurisdiction for the criminal justice system is divided between federal, provincial and territorial governments.[1] Under the Constitution Act, 1867, the provincial legislatures have jurisdiction over 'prisons' under s. 92(6), while the federal Parliament has jurisdiction over 'penitentiaries' under s. 91(28). The Constitution does not supply definitions of prisons or penitentiaries.[2] The distinction among these different types of penal institutions is set out in section 731 of the Criminal Code of Canada, which prescribes that offenders sentenced to prison terms of two years or more must be sentenced to serve their terms in a federal penitentiary. The Correctional Service of Canada (CSC) provides these services under the auspices of the federal Ministry of the Solicitor General. Offenders receiving sentences of less than two years are sentenced to provincial institutions, that is prisons. After being convicted, however, federal prisoners are normally held in provincial institutions for a 15 day appeal period prior to being transferred.[3] Additionally, inmates may be transferred between jurisdictions under so-called exchange-of-service agreements which exist between the federal government and most provinces.[4] These agreements 'are negotiated for such purposes as transferring inmates across jurisdictions, accommodating parole suspensions, and providing for the delivery of parole supervision, community assessments, health, psychiatric and educational services'.[5] As a result of such exchanges, some double counting of inmates is possible.[6] In some provinces, municipal governments also share responsibility for the

1 Correctional Law Review, Correctional Philosophy (1986; working paper No. 1) 4.

2 P.W. Hogg, Constitutional Law of Canada (2nd ed. 1985), 434.

3 Corrections and Conditional Release Act, S.C. 1992, c. 20, s. 12.

4 Ibid., s. 16.

5 Canadian Centre for Justice Statistics, Adult Correctional Services in Canada 1990-91 (Minister of Industry, Science and Technology, 1991) 18.

6 Ibid.

delivery of custodial services. These services consist mainly of providing temporary lock-up and/or remand services.[7]

The provincial legislatures have jurisdiction over provincial prisons, but the federal government - through the Prison and Reformatories Act - is responsible for the basic legal framework governing offenders serving sentences for violating federal statutes. Release issues have also traditionally been viewed as an exercise of the criminal law power,[8] and therefore have been considered principally a matter of federal responsibility.[9]

In recent years, the development of community correctional programmes and services has been emphasized in light of the 'high costs and uncertain benefits of a custodial response to certain offender groups'.[10] Probation is the primary community-based sentencing alternative to incarceration, but other non-custodial correctional alternatives have evolved to varying degrees across Canada. The use of specialized programmes to respond to the specific needs of selected offenders such as women, natives or drinking/driving offenders, has also grown, as has the use of compensatory sentences.[11]

The complexity of Canada's correctional system has been widely criticized. The so-called 'two-year rule' has been described as 'both arbitrary and the source of duplications and overlap in federal and provincial responsibilities, inasmuch as both levels of government perform many of the same functions, albeit on different populations of offenders'.[12] Over the years, many task forces and committees have reviewed the rule,[13] but to date no change has been made to it. The split in jurisdiction also makes centralized collecting and recording of data difficult. The degree of centralization for the provision of adult correctional services within each province or territory, types of facilities, inmates housed, institutional and community programmes offered, and the degree of supervision vary across Canada. There also is a variety of different responses to HIV/AIDS in prisons in Canada. The federal government and each of the provinces and territories have adopted their own policies with regard to HIV/AIDS in prisons. Although these policies resemble each other in many respects, there often exist considerable differences in the way the problems arising from HIV/AIDS in the prison system are dealt with.

---

7 C. McKie, *Canada's Prison Population* (1987), Canadian Social Trends 2 at p. 5.

8 Parole is an institution that did not exist in 1867, so that the Constitution Act, 1867 is silent on the division of responsibility for it. The federal government has assumed responsibility for all prisoners sentenced for an offence against federal legislation, whether the prisoner is confined in a federal institution or a provincial institution.

9 Correctional Law Review, A Framework for the Correctional Law Review (1986; working paper No. 2), 3-4.

10 Op. cit., n. 5, p. 20.

11 Ibid., pp. 20-21.

12 Correctional Law Review, Federal-Provincial Issues in Corrections (1988; working paper No. 8), 3.

13 The last major federal-provincial review of the matter was in 1976-78, in the form of the federal-provincial Steering Committee on the Split in Jurisdiction in Corrections.

## PRISON POPULATION

In 1989-90, Canada's rate of adult imprisonment was 151 per 100,000 adult population,[14] and the rate of juvenile detention was 194 per 100,000 youth population.[15] With a combined adult and juvenile imprisonment rate of 111 per 100,000 total population, Canada ranked fifth in the world - after the United States (455 per 100,000), South Africa (311 per 100,000), Venezuela (177 per 100,000), and Hungary (117 per 100,000) - in a survey of imprisonment rates of selected countries conducted by the Washington-based research group, The Sentencing Project.[16]

On average, 24,470 inmates were serving a custodial sentence during 1990-91. Inmates in the 167 provincial and territorial facilities accounted for 13,181 (54 per cent) of the total count, while inmates in the 58 federal penitentiaries represented the remaining 11,289 (46 per cent). In addition, there were 4,711 inmates in provincial facilities who were remanded in custody awaiting some judicial action with respect to their cases, and 52 inmates on temporary detention. Overall, the average number of persons in federal penitentiaries and provincial prisons in Canada increased from 22,500 in 1980 to over 29,000 in 1990-91. Nevertheless, the average number of inmates in Canadian institutions, when expressed as a rate per 100,000 adults, is now lower than in the 1960s. The 1989-90 rate of 151 per 100,000 adult population compares to a rate of 173 in 1963.[17] The decline of incarceration rates from the levels attained in the 1960's is a result of the growth of non-custodial correctional services. Many persons convicted of criminal offences in Canada are handled through non-custodial programmes such as probation, parole, day-parole and mandatory supervision. In 1990-91, more than three times as many persons were supervised under these programmes as were actually in prison.

Women comprised only 3 per cent of the federal admissions in 1990-91, and approximately 8 per cent of total provincial sentenced admissions. While women are underrepresented in the prison population, aboriginal offenders accounted for more than 10 per cent of those admitted to federal penitentiaries and for approximately 19 per cent of all sentenced admissions to provincial institutions, and are thus vastly overrepresented.[18]

Sixty-one per cent of the on-register offenders in 1991 committed violent offences (homicide, other violent offences against individuals, and robbery), while approximately 30 per cent were convicted for property crimes, and 9 per cent for

---

14 Data on prison populations in Canada has been taken from the two publications, *Basic Facts about Corrections in Canada 1991* (Correctional Service Canada, 1991), and *Canadian Centre for Justice Statistics, Adult Correctional Services in Canada 1990-91*, op. cit., n. 5. Includes all adults in federal and provincial correctional facilities who are under sentence, remand or lock-up. Rate is per 100,000 adult population of 19.9 million, not of total population of 26.5 million.

15 Includes all juvenile of ages ranging from 12 to 17 years in provincial correctional facilities. Rate is per 100,000 juvenile population of 2.1 million, not of total population of 26.5 million.

16 M. Bauer, *Americans Behind Bars: One Year Later* (1992; Report of the Sentencing Project) 5; 'Imprisonment Rates' *The Toronto Globe and Mail*, 12 February 1992, A20.

17 Op. cit., n. 7, p. 2.

18 According to the 1986 census, aboriginal people accounted for 711,720 of the total population of 25,022,005 (less than three per cent).

offences against the Food and Drugs Act and the Narcotic Control Act. Violations against drug laws now account for 15 per cent of Warrant of Committal admissions to federal institutions, up from 9 per cent in 1986-87. In 1991, there were about 1,200 inmates serving time for drug offences in federal penitentiaries.[19]

The majority of drug offences are handled in the provincial system. Between 1985 and 1990, there were 16,541 sentenced admissions to provincial institutions for drug offences.[20] Most people sent to provincial institutions are there for short sentences. Eighty per cent of sentenced admissions are for sentences of 120 days or less. In 1990-91, the median sentence to be served in provincial institutions was 31 days.

## THE CORRECTIONAL SETTING

In general, penal institutions in Canada are operating at, or near, full capacity. In 1990-91, on average, federal institutions operated at 90 per cent of total rated capacity. However, 'certain institutions experienced peak periods during the year which may have resulted in periodic overcrowding problems'.[21] In the same year, provincial institutions operated at 97 per cent of operational capacity.[22] While it is the declared objective to house all inmates in single cells, often this is not possible, and some provincial prisons and federal penitentiaries are chronically overcrowded.

Private family visits are permitted in federal correctional institutions, and there are 78 private family visiting units within the perimeter of 35 institutions in Canada. Eligible inmates are permitted to visit with their families in a private homelike setting for up to three days at a time. The goal of the programme is the maintenance of family ties and the preparation of inmates for their return to life in the community outside the penitentiaries. Eligible family members include wives, husbands and common-law partners.[23] In 1990, the Federal Court of Appeal, in the case of The Commissioner of the Correctional Service of Canada v. Timothy Veysey,[24] held that common-law partners of the same sex could also apply to participate in the so-called 'Private Family Visiting Program'.

In most provincial systems there are no such visiting programmes.[25] However, inmates are eligible for temporary absences after one third of their sentence has been served.

---

19 L. Coates, *Coming to Grips with Substance Abuse in the Federal Prison System* (1991), 11(2), Canadian Centre for Substance Abuse News Action 6 at p. 6.

20 Ibid.

21 Op. cit., n. 5, p. 89.

22 Ibid., p. 58.

23 Pursuant to subsection 37(3) of the Penitentiary Act, R.S. 1985, c. P-5, the Commissioner of the Correctional Service of Canada, on 1 January 1987, issued Directive 770, *Visiting*, paragraphs 16-19 of which set out provisions respecting 'Private Family Visits'.

24 The Commissioner of the Correctional Service of Canada v. Timothy Veysey (1990), 43 Admin. L.R. 316.

25 Exceptions are Alberta, one Correctional Centre in British Columbia, and Saskatchewan. In Saskatchewan, 'in instances where an inmate is confirmed HIV/AIDS, conjugal visiting privileges are suspended until the Centre Director is satisfied that the inmate and spouse are adequately informed about

Sexual activity is still officially prohibited in Canada's prisons.[26] Thus, 'when prisoners are having sex they will be less likely to have safer sex; the extra time required is time in which they may be discovered and penalized.'[27] The Prisoners with AIDS/HIV Support Action Network (PASAN) recommended that consensual sex between prisoners should not be an institutional offence. According to PASAN, the argument that sex must be prohibited in order to maintain order in the prison is unsound:

Sexual activity continues to take place in prisons, despite being banned, and there is no loss of order and control. In fact, the need to be furtive while engaging in sexual activity is more a source of disorder than the sex itself.[28]

PASAN added that consensual sexual activity should be allowed not only because this will increase the effectiveness of HIV prevention, but also because it considers that prohibiting sexual activity between prisoners 'is a violation of human rights'.[29]

Federal corrections officials are considering an end to the ban on sex between prisoners, particularly in light of the decision to make condoms available to inmates in federal penitentiaries as of 1 January 1992. The Director-General of CSC's Health Care Services acknowledged the dichotomy between making condoms available to inmates and, at the same time, prohibiting sexual activity, and said that CSC is 'looking at changes'.[30]

## HIV SEROPREVALENCE

As of January 1993, Health and Welfare Canada had received reports of 7,282 cases of AIDS. These included 7,205 adults and 77 paediatric cases. A total of 4,685 deaths had been reported. In 78 per cent of adult cases, the mode of infection was attributed

---

the inmate's condition.' (Personal correspondence received from Larry Wilson, Director of Institutional Operations, Saskatchewan Justice, dated 31 August 1992).

26 Sodomy between consenting persons twenty-one years of age or older was decriminalized in Canada in 1969 (see Criminal Code, R.S.C. 1970, c. C-34, s. 158). On 1 January 1988 new sexual offences sections were brought into force. 'Buggery' was eliminated as an offence and 'anal intercourse' became legal between consenting persons aged 18 or over. A new system based on age and power between the partners was adopted in the defining of sexual offences (see Criminal Code, R.S.C. 1985, c. C-46, s. 159(2)). The age of consent for sexual acts other than anal intercourse, whether heterosexual or homosexual, was set at 14. As a result of these changes in the law, homosexual activity is now being treated in exactly the same way as heterosexual activity. Some have argued, however, that because homosexuals are more likely to engage in anal intercourse, the law discriminates against them by setting the age of consent for anal intercourse at 18, whereas it is 14 for any other sexual acts. For references, see R. Jürgens, *Equality and Gay Rights in the United States and in Canada* (Master's Thesis, Institute of Comparative Law, McGill University, 1990, 13).

27 'HIV/AIDS in Prison Systems: A Comprehensive Strategy', Brief from the Prisoners with AIDS/HIV Support Action Network (PASAN) to the Minister of Correctional Services and the Minister of Health (1992), at 14.

28 Ibid.

29 Ibid.

30 'Prisons may end ban on inmate sex' *The Toronto Globe and Mail*, 7 November 1991, at A1.

to homosexual or bisexual activity. Only in 150 cases (2 per cent) the risk factor was injection drug use; in 257 cases (3 per cent) both of the above risk factors were identified; in 8 per cent of the cases the risk factor was identified as heterosexual activity; in 4 per cent of cases infection was attributed to treatment with infected blood or blood products; and in the remaining 4 per cent no risk factor was identified.[31] Studies in 1988-1989 have estimated seroprevalence rates to be 4 to 10 per cent among injection drug user populations in Toronto and Montreal respectively;[32] more recently, in Montreal the seroprevalence in this population has been estimated to have exceeded 10 per cent and may be as high as 20 per cent.[33] It is estimated that 25,000 to 30,000 people in Canada are HIV positive.

The number of prisoners with HIV infection or AIDS in Canada is unknown, since there has thus far been no widespread testing of prisoners for HIV infection. To date, only two studies have been carried out in provincial institutions in Quebec to determine behavioural risk factors and levels of infection in inmate populations.[34] The first study was undertaken in a medium security prison for women in Montreal.[35] Participation in the study was anonymous and voluntary. Of 321 participants, 23 (7.2 per cent) were HIV positive and 160 (49.8 per cent) reported injection drug use outside prisons.[36] Of 130 participants, 108 (83.7 per cent) had loaned or borrowed needles and 56 (51.9 per cent) had done so with strangers. Thirteen (10.2 per cent) reported having shared needles with an HIV infected person.[37] Of 321 participants, 78 (24.4 per cent) indicated prostitution as their main source of income prior to incarceration and of these 82 per cent reported using injection drugs prior to incarceration. Ten of 60 (16.7 per cent) injection drug users who engaged in

---

31 Health and Welfare Canada, Surveillance Update: AIDS in Canada (January 1993).

32 'Curbing HIV spread among drug users still possible' *The Medical Post*, 30 April 1991, at 19.

33 *Épidémiologie du sida au Québec. La situation en octobre 1992*, 2 SIDA-PRESSE, November 1992, at 4.

34 At the time of writing, an HIV seroprevalence surveillance research project was being implemented at Joyceville Penitentiary. Another study, 'An Anonymous Unlinked Study of the Prevalence of HIV Infection by Screening Urine Samples Obtained from Persons Admitted to Ontario's Jails and Detention Centres', was proposed in 1992 by Dr Liviana Calzavara, Department of Preventive Medicine and Biostatistics, Faculty of Medicine, University of Toronto, and was underway at the time of writing. The objective of this study is to screen approximately 13,000 urine specimens collected from prisoners for other purposes. The specimens are routinely collected as part of medical care when these individuals are admitted to Ontario jails and detention centres. The study proposes to measure the prevalence of HIV infection among a sample of female and male adults and adolescents admitted during a period of two to six months (Correspondence received from Dr Calzavara, dated 14 September 1992). In April 1992, the British Columbia Corrections Branch conducted a short-term saliva testing project at the Surrey Pretrial Services Centre. Participation was voluntary. At the time of writing, a voluntary testing programme was being run at all regional correctional centres in the province.

Results from these studies will be available in the autumn of 1993.

35 C. Hankins *et al.*, *HIV-1 Infection in a Medium Security Prison for Women - Quebec* (1989), 15-33 Canada Diseases Weekly Report 168 at p. 168.

36 C. Hankins *et al.*, *Risk Factors for Human Immunodeficiency Infection Among Incarcerated Women* (1990) 13 (Suppl. B 59) Clin Invest. Med. Abstract 371.

37 Op. cit., n. 34, p. 169.

prostitution were HIV infected, compared with 11 of 100 injection drug users who did not engage in prostitution. All prostitutes who were not injection drug users were found to be HIV seronegative. Nonsterile injection drug use practices and unprotected sexual activity with an injection drug user were found to be the strongest risk factors for HIV infection.

The second study, of risk factors for HIV infection among incarcerated men, has been underway in two provincial correctional institutions in Quebec since January 1990. Of 588 participants, 21 (3.6 per cent) were HIV positive. Of 490 participants, 237 had a history of injection drug use before imprisonment and of these 18 (7.6 per cent) were HIV infected. Of the 253 participants with no history of injection drug use, only one (0.4 per cent) was HIV infected.[38]

The extent to which participants in these studies are representative of the total inmate population of the institutions is not known.[39] It has also been claimed that there are differences in seroprevalence between federal and provincial inmate populations and that it would be misleading to make links between the seroprevalence rates estimated from the Quebec studies and any expected rates at the federal level. In particular, it has been said that the first study consisted of an 'exclusively female inmate population in an area of Quebec, which ... is heavily overrepresented by prostitutes and drug addicts'.[40] However, and regardless of whether there are significant differences in seroprevalence between federal and provincial inmates, the Quebec studies suggest that the problem of HIV/AIDS in Canadian prisons, including federal penitentiaries and regardless of gender, may be more widespread than has previously been thought.

During the month of June 1993, 95 federal inmates among 13,110 were known to be infected with HIV.[41] This suggests an infection rate of one in every 138 inmates (0.72 per cent). However, it has been claimed that it is more likely that the number of individuals with HIV infection in federal penitentiaries is closer to one in 20 than to one in 200.[42] This would be consistent with the findings of the Parliamentary Ad Hoc Committee on AIDS. In a report issued in 1990, the Committee suggested that 'the actual number of inmates with HIV infection or AIDS must be so vastly different from the official statistics as to make these statistics a mockery.'[43] On the other hand, estimates that up to 15 per cent of the inmate population of federal penitentiaries may be infected are unproven.

The necessity of undertaking studies on the prevalence of HIV infection in prisons has been the subject of extensive debate in Canada. In 1990 the Parliamentary

---

38 C. Hankins *et al.*, 'HIV-1 Infection Among Incarcerared Men - Quebec' (1991) 17-43 *Canada Diseases Weekly Report* 233 at p. 233-4.

39 In the women's study, however, analysis revealed no difference between participants and eligible non-participants with respect to age, educational level, language and sentence-length.

40 Personal correspondence, dated 24 September 1991, received by Dr Hankins from Dr Roy, Director General, Health Care Services, Correctional Service Canada.

41 Correctional Service Canada, Health Care Services. HIV/AIDS Statistics, August 1993.

42 C. Hankins, *HIV Behind Bars: Where Do We Stand.* Paper presented at the 6th British Columbia AIDS Conference, Living with HIV/AIDS, 1-3 November 1992.

43 Parliamentary Ad Hoc Committee on AIDS, Confronting a Crisis: The Report of the Parliamentary Ad Hoc Committee on AIDS (1990), 46-47.

Ad Hoc Committee on AIDS recommended 'that the Department of National Health and Welfare, in cooperation with the Correctional Service of Canada, immediately set up a pilot study, using unlinked seroprevalence survey techniques, and with appropriate ethical safeguards, to assess the level of HIV infection in federal prisons.'[44] At the time, the Commissioner of CSC acknowledged and lamented the lack of information on which to base an extensive HIV/AIDS prison policy, saying that he 'did not have any hard information on the extent of HIV infection in the prisons.'[45] However, he also suggested that it would not be possible to gather such information and that any attempt to do so would raise legal and ethical questions. To this the Ad Hoc Committee responded that 'unlinked testing using left-over samples, which would bear no information identifying any particular inmate, would give us some reliable knowledge about the prevalence of HIV infection in the penal system' and that 'the same sort of testing using blood from incoming inmates, and from those being released, would give us a picture of how much infection was being incurred inside the prisons.'[46]

It has been argued that, if seroprevalence studies are not undertaken, 'no clear picture of the extent and seriousness of the HIV epidemic in federal prisons can be obtained' and that 'in the absence of this information, policy development, resource allocation, and the evaluation of effective interventions, both prison and community-based, are severely impeded.'[47] However, this view is not universally accepted. In April 1992, the Director General of CSC's Health Care Services, stated that 'at the present time HIV seroprevalence testing is not planned' and that 'the Correctional Service of Canada has concerns that the procedure might further stigmatize an already stigmatized population and, as well, raise contentious ethical considerations.'[48] Recently, PASAN stated that 'we do not need HIV seroprevalence studies to know that HIV/AIDS is threatening prisoners' lives.'[49] PASAN pointed out that 'the HIV/AIDS epidemic is known to be raging in prisons elsewhere'[50] and that therefore Canadian authorities should be aware that there is at least a possibility of an HIV/AIDS epidemic among Canadian prisoners. PASAN concluded that although 'there are some legitimate reasons for HIV testing ... in these times of economic restraint, HIV sero prevalence studies may not be the wisest use of severely limited funds.'[51] It added that 'thorough HIV testing of inmates would be a very time-consuming and expensive procedure, using money that would be better spent improving the care of and services to prisoners with HIV/AIDS.'[52]

---

44 Ibid., p. 52 (recommendation 39).

45 Ibid., p. 48.

46 Ibid.

47 C. Hankins, 'Brief to the Expert Committee on AIDS and Prisons' (24 October 1992) 1.

48 Personal correspondence received from Dr Jacques Roy, dated 1 April 1992. Nevertheless, at the time of writing a seroprevalence study was being undertaken at Joyceville Penitentiary.

49 Op. cit., n. 28, p. 34.

50 Ibid., p. 33.

51 Ibid., p. 24.

52 Ibid.

PREVALENCE OF DRUG USE

There is no reliable data on the prevalence of injection or other drug use in Canadian prisons. The only available data is on the prevalence of drug use by inmates prior to incarceration. A Computerized Lifestyle Screening Instrument developed by the Ministry of the Solicitor General and CSC in 1988 is being used to obtain information about the extent and nature of federal offenders' drug and alcohol use. Of 371 inmates tested in 1989/90, more than 10 per cent admitted using drugs every day in the six months prior to incarceration, 17 per cent had regular drinking binges, and 64 per cent said they had consumed alcohol or other drugs on the day of their crime.[53] Fifty-three point seven per cent of all federal inmates were classified as having a serious substance abuse problem.[54]

It has been said that drug use is more visible in the prisons than outside[55] and that 'inside an often overflowing incarceration system where there is little treatment, drugs help contain a situation that would otherwise explode.'[56] Riley pointed out:

Many of the inmates of federal penitentiaries and provincial jails as well as those on parole use drugs as a part of their lifestyle. Drugs relieve tension, boredom and hopelessness and it should be no surprise that they are popular among those caught up by the criminal justice system.[57]

Similarly, PASAN stated:

Those in our overcrowded correctional facilities often turn to substance use as a means to cope with the harsh reality of prison life. They end up being more concerned with their daily struggles than with health issues regarding HIV.[58]

Drugs enter prisons on a regular basis, and availability of drugs in prisons has significantly increased since the early 1970s, in part due to increased visiting rights in most prisons.[59] It has been estimated that only 5 per cent of all drugs entering Canadian prisons are apprehended by prison authorities.[60] Allegations that drug use in prisons is quietly tolerated by prison authorities were denied by a CSC spokesperson who maintained that 'looking the other way is something penitentiary staff do on very few occasions.'[61]

The Parliamentary Ad Hoc Committee heard evidence that 'up to 50 per cent of inmates may be involved in drug use.'[62] According to other estimates, two-thirds of

---

53 Op. cit., n. 20, p. 7.

54 D. Riley, *Drug Use in Prisons: A Harm Reduction Approach.* Paper presented at the 6th British Columbia Conference on AIDS, 1-3 November 1992, with reference to 'Findings from the National Alcohol and Other Drugs Survey' (1990) 2 (4), Forum on Corrections Research, 3-6.

55 'AIDS adds lethal element to widespread drug use in jails' *The Toronto Globe and Mail*, 5 November 1991, A2.

56 Ibid.

57 Op. cit., n. 56.

58 Op. cit., n. 28, p. 15.

59 Op. cit., n. 20, p. 7.

60 Ibid.

61 Op. cit., n. 57.

62 Op. cit., n. 44, p. 47.

all prisoners use drugs while in prisons.[63] The 1991 Task Force Report on the Reduction of Substance Abuse acknowledged that 'the problem of drugs in prisons, including their contribution to prison violence, is ... significant.'[64] The Report continues by saying that consequently 'a significant percentage of institutional security measures are devoted to drug detection and reducing illegal sales of drugs.'[65] Further, the Report states:

Prison violence often occurs to obtain drugs or to settle debts related to the sale of drugs. From 1981 to 1986, 49 persons were killed in Canadian penitentiaries; many of these crimes were a direct result of alcohol or drug use and trafficking in drugs. During 1985-1986 alone, 181 major violent incidents occurred, of which 106 (58 per cent) were believed to be related to drug abuse.[66]

Similarly, the CSC Contraband Control Study states that 'it is commonly accepted that many offenders have significant problems with alcohol or drug abuse that relate to their criminal behaviour,' and that 'drugs and alcohol can be identified as the most important contraband problem.'[67] The Study continues by saying:

The incidence of substance abuse among offenders means that:

(1) A significant number of offenders may continue to use substances during their incarceration which creates a heavy demand for drugs and alcohol within institutions; and

(2) Many, or most of these offenders will be at high risk for re-offending if their substance use/abuse problems are not dealt with effectively.[68]

With regard to injection drug use, a CSC spokesperson maintained that 'when drugs are used ... they are mostly the non-injectable ones ... .'[69] However, the Parliamentary Ad Hoc Committee heard evidence that 'needle sharing for injection drug use is common, and that needles and other implements are also used for tattooing purposes.'[70] An ex-prisoner estimated that 10 per cent of the inmates in the Guelph Correctional Centre share needles,[71] and a study on HIV transmission among injection drug users in Toronto found that 'over 80 per cent of the participating injection drug users had been in jail overnight or longer since beginning to inject drugs, with 25 per cent of those sharing injecting equipment while in custody.'[72]

While it is generally agreed that it is difficult to determine exactly how much injection drug use and needle sharing occurs in prisons, it is also agreed that, in Canada and elsewhere, injection drug use is prevalent in prisons, and that the scarcity

---

63 Op. cit., n. 57.

64 Task Force on the Reduction of Substance Abuse, Final Report (Supply and Services Canada 1991), 11.

65 Ibid.

66 Ibid.

67 Ibid., p. 19, with reference to CSC Contraband Control Study.

68 Ibid.

69 Op. cit., n. 57.

70 Op. cit., n. 44, p. 47.

71 Op.cit., n. 57, p. A1.

72 P. Milson, 'Evaluation of a Programme to Prevent HIV Transmission in Injection Drug Users in Toronto' (Toronto Board of Health, 1991).

of needles often leads to needle sharing. With regard to the Canadian situation, PASAN stated:

Despite high levels of injection drug use, the presence of syringes used to inject illegal drugs is severely limited. Only a handful of needles will circulate in a population of 400-600 people. Accordingly, once incarcerated, with no access to clean needles or bleach, yet ongoing access to injectable drugs, inmates using injection drugs must share needles even though they may not have shared on the outside. Needle sharing usually occurs in bathrooms, cells, and hidden areas. Home-made and unsafe sharps (needle substitutes) are fashioned out of hardened plastic and ball-point pens, often causing damage to veins, scarring, infections, and blood poisoning.[73]

## PREVALENCE OF SEXUAL ACTIVITY

There is no reliable data on the prevalence of sexual activity in Canadian prisons. The Parliamentary Ad Hoc Committee on AIDS stated that 'we know that there is sexual activity in prison'[74] and referred to several studies on the extent of sexual activity in prisons in the United States. These studies suggest that between 10 and 30 per cent of inmates engage in homosexual activity.[75] 'Homosexual activity among male prison inmates, including situational homosexuality, is a significant, widely-recognized behaviour pattern in prisons.'[76]

## POLICIES

A directive relating to the management of inmates with AIDS, ARC, or HIV infection in federal penitentiaries was issued by the Commissioner of CSC on 1 January 1988. Policy directives setting out standards and guidelines for dealing with HIV infection in the provincial and territorial prison systems have also been issued by all provinces and the Northwest Territories. Yukon will announce its policy in the near future.

A catalyst for the development of these policies was a number of complaints by inmates with HIV infection or AIDS alleging that they were receiving unequal treatment. For example, many of the early complaints to the Ontario Human Rights Commission filed on the subject of HIV/AIDS have alleged unequal treatment of inmates with HIV infection or AIDS in Ontario correctional facilities. The general allegation is that, as a result of testing positive for antibodies to HIV, individuals have been removed from the general inmate population and denied equal opportunity to eat, socialize and recreate with fellow inmates. The complaints have also alleged that inmates with HIV infection or AIDS have been subjected to humiliating treatment and demands, including being approached by corrections officers wearing gloves, and have

---

73 Op. cit., n. 28, p. 33.

74 Op. cit., n. 44, p. 47.

75 M.D. Decker *et al.*, 'Seroepidemiology of Hepatitis B in Tennessee Prisons' 150 J. Inf. Dis. 450; P. Nacci and T. Kane, 'Sex and Sexual Aggression in Federal Prisons' (1982), Federal Bureau of Prisons, Washington, 7-9.

76 L.A. Pagliaro and A.M. Pagliaro, 'Sentenced to Death? HIV Infection and AIDS in Prisons - Current and Future Concerns' (1992), *Canadian Journal of Criminology* 201 at p. 205.

been forced to scrub showers and phones after using them. In addition, many inmates have complained of being denied essential medical and dietary requirements.[77]

In 1989 the Ontario District Court, in R. v. Downey,[78] stated that detention centres in Toronto were generally failing to come to grips with this problem the problem of detaining people with HIV infection or AIDS, from two aspects: (a) providing facilities where such detainees may obtain adequate treatment; and (b) of educating staff and, in particular, guards as to not only the nature and extent of this disease ... but also what dangers, if any, it poses to the rest of the population of the detention centre and of the staff of the detention centre.

The Court had to decide whether to grant bail to an accused who had previously been denied it on the grounds that he had a long record of serious offences and was likely to commit further offences. One of the reasons advanced to support an order that the accused be released was that, five weeks after he was detained, he tested positive for antibodies to HIV. Additional tests indicated that he had developed disease associated with HIV infection. The Court found that the accused was not receiving adequate treatment for his disease. In particular, he was locked up virtually 24 hours a day, was the target of threats, and was not provided with an appropriate diet. The Court held that the accused had been subjected to cruel and unusual treatment, in violation of s. 12 of the Canadian Charter of Rights and Freedoms, which provides that everyone has the right not to be subjected to any cruel and unusual treatment or punishment. The Court ruled that the detention order be set aside and that the applicant be released on his own recognizance.

Following the adoption of a new policy on communicable diseases by the Ontario Ministry of Correctional Services in 1989, the Ontario Human Rights Commission expressed its hope that such discriminatory treatment of inmates with HIV infection or AIDS in Ontario would be eliminated and that 'through the spirit of this policy better trained staff and inmates will be less likely to respond to infected inmates with fear and anger. ...'[79] However, the Commission's database shows that in 1991-92 there were four new complaints in which prisoners with HIV infection or AIDS alleged that they were receiving unequal treatment because of their HIV status.[80]

In Quebec, the provincial human rights commission on two occasions explicitly recommended that the minister responsible for the provincial prison system act without delay to guarantee that all HIV infected inmates be treated in a manner appropriate to their physical condition. A policy on HIV/AIDS in prisons was adopted only on 1 April 1992. In the case of Sylvain A.[81] the complainant, an inmate in a Montreal institution, was transferred to the institution's health care unit after testing positive for HIV antibodies. He alleged that the transfer constituted inhumane treatment. He further alleged that detention of HIV infected inmates in the health care unit of the

---

77 Personal correspondence received from Bruce Drewett, Policy Analyst, Ontario Human Rights Commission, dated 28 March 1990.

78 R. v. Downey, Ontario Judgements: 1989 O.J. No. 436 (Ontario District Court).

79 Op. cit., n. 79.

80 Personal correspondence received from Calvin Bernard, Acting Director, Policy Unit, Ontario Human Rights Commission, dated 14 October 1992.

81 Re: 'Sylvain A.', File #8906005371-0001-0; COM-351-5.10 (Quebec H.R.C.).

institution violated their right to physical integrity and that the increased exposure to viruses and microbes in the unit represented a great risk for these inmates. The complainant also reported that the staff distanced themselves from HIV infected inmates and that they 'pointed them out with their fingers', thus disclosing their identity to everyone. Finally, the complainant maintained that he was refused the right to work and that he was accorded only one hour of 'daily outing', during which he was identified as HIV infected by fellow prisoners and staff. The Quebec Human Rights Commission held that the transfer to the institution's health care unit did not in itself constitute inhumane treatment, but that the complainant's right under s. 26 of the Quebec Charter of Rights and Freedoms to a 'distinct treatment' appropriate to his sex, age and physical and mental condition while in detention had been violated by unduly exposing him to the risk of contracting other diseases in the institution's health care unit. The Commission also held that results of eventual HIV tests had to remain confidential and that no exceptions should be made to this rule.

In the case of Pierre M.,[82] an inmate alleged that confidentiality had not been respected by the staff of the institution because his seropositivity was apparently known to everybody before he even arrived at the institution, that he had been isolated at the health care unit from the day of his arrival at the institution, and that this isolation had meant 'more difficult detention conditions' for him. In this case also, the Quebec Human Rights Commission concluded that the complainant had not received inhumane treatment, but that he had not received treatment appropriate to his physical condition.

While the policies on HIV/AIDS in prisons in Canada vary widely in content, they generally focus on the importance of educating both staff and inmates regarding communicable diseases in general, and HIV/AIDS in particular. They usually emphasize the importance of maintaining the confidentiality of the HIV status of inmates and recommend that HIV infected inmates be managed as ordinary members of the general prison population. Most of the policies point out that integration of inmates with HIV infection or AIDS with other inmates should be achieved wherever possible. Adoption of such policies is important, as they provide guidelines for treatment of inmates with HIV infection and, through information and education, they may reduce fears, ignorance and prejudice of both staff and prisoners and the abuses of rights which often result from them. However, such policies are not always followed. Also, some parts of the policies have been criticized. The following review of these policies identifies some of their key problems.

## TESTING AND CONFIDENTIALITY

No jurisdiction authorizes the involuntary testing of inmates for HIV infection, and such testing is deemed 'unwarranted'.[83] It is agreed that it would not be consistent with the provisions of the Canadian Charter of Rights and Freedoms. In this regard, the policy of Newfoundland and Labrador explicitly says:

---

82 Re: 'Pierre M.', File #8906005490-0001-0; COM-351-5.9 (Quebec H.R.C.).

83 Health and Welfare Canada, 'Human Immunodeficiency Virus Antibody Testing in Canada' (1989) 15, *Canada Diseases Weekly Report*, 37-43.

No person may be forced to submit to an HIV Antibody test. Such a test may only be administered by a medical professional if the patient provides informed consent. Any attempt to coerce an inmate to submit to the test in the absence of consent may not only be a violation of fundamental human rights under the Charter of Rights (the right to 'life, liberty and security of the person' and the right to be 'secure against unreasonable search or seizure') but may also be regarded as an offence under the Criminal Code.[84]

It was in the prison setting that the Charter was first used to declare invalid a pilot project of mandatory drug testing, and the principles of that decision would also be relevant to an HIV antibody testing programme.[85] In Re Dion and the Queen,[86] it was found that random demands for urine samples to detect drug use violated the inmate's rights to life, liberty and security under section 7 of the Charter. Similarly, in the case of Jackson v. Joyceville Penitentiary,[87] mandatory urine testing for drugs and alcohol in federal prisons was struck down by the Federal Court as a violation of sections 7 and 8 of the Charter.[88]

In practice, it seems that not many inmates seek to be tested while in prison. One reason for this might be that, while testing is undertaken only voluntarily and with informed consent, and pre- as well as post-test counselling are provided, prisoner's access to testing is limited. Testing is often carried out at the discretion of the institutional physician.

Another reason for prisoners' reluctance to be tested while in prison is widespread concern that test results will not remain confidential. The Parliamentary Ad Hoc Committee stated that the 'most likely reason for the low number of inmates identified as HIV positive in the federal prison system is the complete lack of confidence that most inmates appear to have in the confidentiality of prison health services' and that 'many inmates have undoubtedly waited until they were released to be tested.'[89] At a seminar on HIV/AIDS in Prisons at the 6th Annual British Columbia AIDS Conference, Michael Linhart, a prisoner with HIV infection in a federal institution, stated that 'many prisoners who have suspected they may be HIV positive have refused to be tested because they fear being isolated and ostracized.'[90]

---

84 Newfoundland and Labrador, Department of Justice, Adult Corrections Division, Policy Directive 16.40.06, section: Special Health Care Services - HIV/AIDS, revised 1 April 1992.

85 W.C. Bartlett, 'AIDS: Legal Issues of Federal Concern' (1988; Library of Parliament, backgrounder) 8.

86 Re Dion and the Queen (1986), 30 C.C.C. (3d) 108 (P.Q.S.C.).

87 (1990) 55 C.C.C. (3d) 50.

88 According to ss. 54-56 of the new Corrections and Conditional Release Act, CSC may carry out urinalysis when there are reasonable grounds to believe an offender has consumed drugs or alcohol; it is required for participation in a substance abuse program or activity involving community contact; or the offender is on conditional release with the condition that he or she abstain from alcohol or other drugs. Further, urinalysis may be carried out when it is part of a random check process by which every offender has an equal chance to be selected. The constitutional validity of this provision remains to be established.

89 Op. cit., n. 44, p. 53.

90 M. Linhart, *An HIV Positive Prisoner's View*. Paper presented at the 6th British Columbia AIDS Conference, Living with HIV/AIDS, Vancouver, 1-3 November 1992.

Linhart summarized the questions prisoners have when they are considering being tested for antibodies to HIV as follows:

(1) Would I be isolated and subjected to the same kind of inhumane treatment I had seen on W5 a news-documentary television programe?

(2) With a positive diagnosis would I be able to transfer to other institutions?

(3) How would I be received by other inmates if they knew I was positive? Would I be subjected to verbal or physical abuse, or both?

(4) What about medical treatment? Would I be provided with knowledgeable doctors and have access to new treatments and medications being developed?

(5) Was it really possible to keep my diagnosis confidential, or could I expect to hear from staff and inmates alike that they knew?

(6) What kind of support would I be provided with?

(7) What would happen to me if the virus was to become an immediate threat to my life?

(8) Why doesn't the Correctional Service ensure that prisoners know what they can expect if they test positive for the HIV virus?

(9) What will the Correctional Service do in the future to ensure that my needs will be met?

Canadian prison policies generally stress the importance of maintaining the confidentiality of the HIV status of inmates, and medical officials are usually appointed as the guardians of this information. But there does exist a wide range of exceptions to this principle, exceptions which permit disclosure of such information without the affected prisoner's consent. Each policy is different in this respect, but it is most common to find an exception to confidentiality based on a 'need to know' basis. This sometimes calls for staff who come into regular contact with an infected inmate to be informed (in more or less detail) of the inmate's condition. Some other policies mandate the disclosure of medical information when there is reason to believe that an inmate's conduct poses a danger to himself or to others. Health care staff may then provide information to other prison personnel without the inmate's consent.

The question of whether incarceration should diminish the rights of an inmate to maintain HIV/AIDS-related personal information confidential, was addressed in the report, AIDS and the Privacy Act by the Privacy Commissioner of Canada. The report established the general principle that confidentiality should be respected, but said that 'there may be a merit in a policy that allows disclosure where an infected inmate's conduct threatens others. ...'[91] While acknowledging that this would seriously compromise the privacy of infected inmates and might endanger their physical safety, breaching infected inmates' right to confidentiality was seen as 'one of only a limited number of actions available to protect other inmates'.[92] The other possibility mentioned in the report is to segregate an infected inmate who does not stop 'risky conduct', without disclosing the grounds for segregation to other inmates. It was recommended that before an inmate's infected status is made known to other inmates, ... he should be asked whether he prefers to be segregated from other prisoners (while keeping his HIV infection confidential) or whether he wishes to remain in the general

---

91 The Privacy Commissioner of Canada, AIDS and the Privacy Act (1989), 40.
92 Ibid.

population (which will then be told of his status and warned to avoid risky behaviour with him).[93]

To ensure the confidentiality of test results and to encourage prisoners to be tested in prison, it has been recommended that prisoners have access to anonymous testing, and that additional measures be implemented to secure the confidentiality within correctional facilities of all HIV related information. For example, testing could be carried out by outside health services such as community clinics. PASAN argued that inmates would be 'more likely to trust a counsellor from a community-based agency, with whom they would not have to worry about a breach of confidentiality', and that 'a "safe" testing environment would likely lead to more inmates choosing to be tested and would therefore allow inmates to avail themselves of information, counselling, and treatment to delay the onset of HIV related illnesses.'[94]

Prison staff have often opposed measures to increase the confidentiality of test results, claiming that they 'need to know' the identity of prisoners testing positive for antibodies to HIV in order to be able to better protect themselves against transmission. This claim seems irreconcilable with demands for better protection of confidentiality of inmates' personal medical information. However, while the prisoners' interest in maintaining their test results confidential and the interest of staff in protecting themselves from exposure to HIV are often perceived to conflict, they are in reality compatible. Most measures that can be undertaken to prevent exposure to and infection with HIV have to be undertaken regardless of whether an inmate or staff member is or is not known, to staff, wardens, or inmates, to be infected with HIV. In order to best protect themselves, prison staff need to apply precautions universally. Arguments that 'extra precautions' could be taken with known HIV positive inmates are misguided because the concept of universal precautions requires that the same precautions be taken for every inmate, whether or not the inmate is known to be seropositive. Were staff to be routinely informed about prisoners known to be HIV infected, it would create a false sense of security; without all prisoners being tested repeatedly, staff would know of only a few of the infected prisoners. As PASAN has stated:

It is an illusion to think that staff and inmates would be protected from AIDS by knowing every inmate's HIV status. In fact, it would be practically impossible to be certain of everyone's status, because the results of the HIV antibody test are not always 100 per cent accurate. Tests must be repeated after a period of approximately six months, during which time the individual must not have participated in any high risk activities ... The test measures the presence of antibodies to HIV, not the presence of the virus itself. People who have recently been infected (within the past six months) may not have developed antibodies to the virus yet, and thus may test negative. There can be false negative and false positive results to the test. Because of this, public health campaigns argue that we can only assume that everyone, including staff, could be HIV positive. The proper use of universal precautions when dealing with anyone's potentially infectious bodily fluids is the only way to meet the concern of work place safety effectively.[95]

---

93 Ibid.
94 Op. cit., n. 28, p. 24.
95 Ibid.

PASAN therefore recommended that 'HIV related information in the possession of medical providers should be released to prison authorities only under extraordinary circumstances and only with the consent of the prisoner.'[96] Permitting 'outside' workers to offer counselling and anonymous testing in prisons might actually increase prison security since 'staff would feel protected by an informed population who begin to change their behaviour voluntarily.'[97]

HOUSING

As a general rule, most policies direct that attempts must be made to house infected inmates among the general prison population. The standard exceptions fall under three headings: segregation is deemed acceptable if (1) an inmate's behaviour threatens transmission of HIV; (2) the reactions of other inmates require that an infected prisoner be put into protective custody, or (3) an inmate's medical condition warrants it.

In practice, inmates with HIV infection or AIDS have sometimes been segregated on the basis of their being infected. For example, the British Columbia Civil Liberties Association received a complaint by an inmate in a British Columbia remand centre who told prison officials that he might be HIV positive:

He was placed in 24 hour lock-up for 16 days despite two negative HIV tests, was allowed visits only when separated by a plastic window from visitors, was accompanied by guards in rubber gloves when out of his cell, and friends claim they were denied visits 'because he has AIDS'.[98]

It has been alleged that prisoners with HIV infection or AIDS have been isolated from the rest of the population in provincial remand centres as late as 1989.[99] While there are sporadic reports of such isolations, the true prevalence of unwarranted isolation of prisoners with HIV or AIDS in Canadian correctional facilities is unknown. While PASAN stated that 'the isolation of HIV positive prisoners has been an all-too-frequent reality, if not official policy, of both provincial and federal prisons,'[100] the statistics provided by CSC on the location of known offenders with HIV infection or AIDS in federal institutions demonstrate that cases of segregation, disciplinary dissociation or protective custody of inmates with HIV infection or AIDS are rare. For example, in October 1992 a total of 59 inmates known to have HIV infection and three inmates with AIDS were incarcerated in federal institutions. Of the 59 inmates with HIV infection, 55 were housed in the general population, two in health care centres, one in disciplinary dissociation, and one in protective custody. Of the three inmates with AIDS, two were housed in the general population and one in a health care centre. From January to October 1992 there were never more than five

---

96 Ibid., p. 22 (recommendation 23).

97 Ibid.

98 The British Columbia Civil Liberties Association, AIDS Discrimination in Canada. A Study of the Scope and Extent of Unfair Discrimination in Canada against Persons with AIDS, and Those Known or Feared to be HIV Positive (1989), 21.

99 Op. cit., n. 92.

100 Op. cit., n. 28, p. 23.

inmates with HIV infection in federal institutions who were not located in the general population.

A decision by the Ontario Court of Justice has reaffirmed that segregation of inmates with HIV infection is justified only in exceptional cases. In the case of Ratte v. Kingston Penitentiary,[101] Mr Ratte, an inmate with HIV infection who had been put in solitary confinement, applied to be returned to the general prison population. The Court dismissed the application. While it recognized that segregation or isolation of inmates because of their positive HIV status is generally unjustified, the Court held that Mr Ratte was in isolation not because he was infected but because he was potentially dangerous to the good order and discipline of the institution. According to correctional staff, he had once 'attempted to incite the range to riot' and on three occasions he threatened to kill, bite or stab staff members. In other words, the Court held that isolation might be warranted not because of the inmate's HIV infection but because of behaviour that could expose others to HIV.

EDUCATION ON HIV/AIDS

Education of prisoners on HIV/AIDS is particularly important since prisoners are often 'the people previously missed by traditional and mainstream education and prevention ... because they are usually out of school and may have low levels of literacy. ...'[102] Educational programmes about HIV/AIDS for both inmates and staff have been established in most Canadian prisons. The prison policies do not usually describe these programmes; it is therefore unclear whether or not they are mandatory, who will implement them, and through what medium the information will be disseminated. Specifics concerning content are also minimal, although some policies do state that information must be relayed about the nature of the disease, how it is transmitted, and how transmission may be prevented. Although most policies envisage education as an ongoing process, except for some indications concerning the structures of the orientation process no information is provided regarding the fora in which it will be carried out.

In the federal prison system, an ongoing educational programme for staff and inmates was initiated prior to 1985 when the first case of AIDS was identified within the federal system. According to the Director General of CSC's Health Care Services, 'the type, quality and quantity of educational material that has been made available has steadily improved as new information about AIDS and HIV has become available.'[103] Educational and preventive activities include the showing of a video about HIV/AIDS on entry into the system, availability of brochures and pamphlets about HIV/AIDS, counselling upon request, group discussions with an institutional physician, and seminars.

The information programmes concerning HIV/AIDS provided to inmates and staff have been criticized as ineffective. In particular, it has been said that 'they are not likely to be effective in changing behaviour, and that they are not mandatory or

---

101 Ratte v. Kingston Penitentiary, Ontario Judgments: 1991 O.J. No. 1745 (Ontario Court of Justice - General Division).

102 Op. cit., n. 28, p. 34-35.

103 Op. cit., n. 49.

even pressed upon the inmates, although the prison setting would allow for this.[104] It has also been pointed out that 'information probably will not be of much use if inmates do not have the means to act on it.'[105] Inmates themselves have said that education sessions are 'simply frustrating' when they get information about how to protect themselves but the means to do so are not made available to them.[106] Zoltan Lugosi, an ex-prisoner, pointed out that, 'while there is a need for films to educate prison workers, general populations of all prisons need explicit HIV/AIDS education presented by recognized community educators,'[107] and that, since 'prisoners distrust prison authorities and are unlikely to discuss proscribed activities, peer groups and programs are the best approach.'[108] PASAN has recommended that HIV/AIDS education: (1) be made compulsory for all inmates and all staff; (2) be comprehensive; (3) 'recognize and respond to the needs of prisoners with disabilities, from different ethnic and linguistic backgrounds, with varying language skills, and of different races, sexes, and sexual orientations'; (4) be provided through group HIV/AIDS educational sessions, and also be made available to inmates individually upon their entering and exiting the correctional facility; and (5) be provided by external, community-based HIV/AIDS and health organizations.[109] Similar recommendations can be found in the AIDS education needs assessment study undertaken by the John Howard Society of Metropolitan Toronto, which examined the level of HIV/AIDS awareness and knowledge in two provincial institutions in Ontario:

Given the inmates' preference to receiving education from non-Ministry officials, it is strongly recommended that training and education be provided by health/AIDS individuals and organizations external to the Ministry of Correctional Services. Continuous consultation with these organizations and community groups is critical to ensure that the program and information remains current, is unbiased, accurate, discouraging AIDS-phobic attitudes and false beliefs. The design, implementation and delivery of an AIDS educational program should be done by external health and/or AIDS experts and professionals. ... The Ministry should recognize and access the expertise and educational skills concerning HIV/AIDS which are available outside the field of corrections.[110]

The study revealed that the surveyed offenders 'were keen on receiving HIV/AIDS education while incarcerated, and strongly supported initiatives to develop such a program in prison.'[111] A second study undertaken by the John Howard Society examined inmates' knowledge, attitudes and behaviours concerning HIV/AIDS. In particular, the study examined inmates' attitudes toward HIV infected inmates, toward correctional staff and community groups, and toward HIV testing. Further, identified risk-producing behaviour prior to incarceration was explored. Surveyed inmates had a

---

104 Op. cit., n. 44, p. 49.

105 Ibid.

106 Ibid.

107 Z. Lugosi, 'Some Policies Can Not Wait' (1991) 3 *Journal of Prisoners on Prisons* 81 at p. 86.

108 Ibid.

109 Op. cit., n. 28, pp. 11-13.

110 A. Riesch Toepell, 'AIDS Education Needs Assessment' (1992; John Howard Society of Metropolitan Toronto) 56.

111 Ibid., p. IV.

high level of awareness concerning HIV and AIDS. However, the study also revealed many gaps in inmates' knowledge that were due primarily to myths and misconceptions. Further, many inmates expressed 'strong AIDS-phobic and homophobic attitudes,' felt threatened if fellow inmates infected with HIV were in their units or ranges, and suggested separate living arrangements in the institution for infected offenders. With regard to risk-producing behaviour in which inmates had engaged prior to imprisonment, the study results have been summarized as follows:

Generally, prisoners only used condoms with sexual partners they did not know well, and stopped practising safer sex after an average of one month. Inmates who injected intravenous drugs tended to share their equipment, mostly with their sexual partners, and commonly cleaned the shared equipment. Prisoners with tattoos were generally unaware of the risks involved with HIV transmission when sharing tattoo guns, needles and/or inks.[112]

The study concluded that 'an education program should target the gaps in prisoners' knowledge, emphasize risk-reduction intervention for life in prison and outside prison, and encourage healthy attitude changes which will ultimately decrease their phobic-laden opinions'.[113]

In some prisons, HIV/AIDS educational and support services are already provided by community-based AIDS organizations. For example, the Kingston AIDS Project's Prison Outreach Program, funded by the federal government, provides HIV/AIDS education, support, one-to-one counselling, and advocacy to prisoners with HIV infection or AIDS. Peer education and support groups made up of inmates and sponsored by the Kingston AIDS Project operate in two correctional facilities. In Dorchester Penitentiary, a federal institution in New Brunswick, a support group for prisoners with HIV infection or AIDS has been established with the help of the local community group SIDA/AIDS Moncton. Monthly meetings are held at the institution in an effort to disseminate information about infectious diseases, information material has been distributed on the ranges, and seminars on HIV/AIDS have been held for inmates and for staff.

Former CSC Commissioner Ole Ingstrup has stated that 'the Correctional Service puts a high value on the information and support the various community AIDS groups ... can provide for offenders with HIV',[114] and that it encourages community groups 'to come in and participate in education sessions.'[115] Further, he has stated:

It is our feeling that the inmates may be more likely to believe warnings that come from groups independent of the Correctional Service of Canada. We therefore count to a large extent on these external groups for help.[116]

It is hoped that the recognition of the valuable work of community groups will translate into increased funding of existing prison activities, and encourage other groups to become involved in HIV/AIDS education and support in prisons.

---

112 A. Riesch Toepell, 'Prisoners and AIDS - Knowledge, Attitude and Behaviour. A Research Study of Inmates in the Toronto Region' (1992; John Howard Society of Metropolitan Toronto) III-IV.

113 Ibid.

114 Personal correspondence received by Gerald Benoit, Dorchester Penitentiary, from Ole Ingstrup, Commissioner of the Correctional Service of Canada, dated 21 October 1991.

115 Op. cit., n. 44, p. 52.

116 Ibid.

## PROTECTIVE MEASURES FOR STAFF

Policies generally go into great detail concerning the protective measures to be taken by staff to avoid contracting HIV/AIDS. They dictate that staff be supplied with the necessary protective equipment, and contain instructions concerning the proper methods for handling blood and other body fluids and for engaging in searches of inmates. All policies stress that every inmate should be treated as a potential carrier of HIV and that the precautions should accordingly be applied universally.

In Walton v. Treasury Board (Correctional Services Canada),[117] the applicant, a correctional officer, refused to work with 'certain inmates suspected of suffering from AIDS or Hepatitis B' on the ground that working with these inmates constituted a 'danger' to his health. The claim was dismissed by a safety officer who concluded that no danger existed. At the applicant's request, the decision was referred to the Public Service Staff Relation Board. The Board partly denied and partly affirmed the safety officer's decision. With respect to the applicant's fear of AIDS, the Board held that there was no evidence that contacts of the kind feared by the applicant, i.e. having faeces, urine, or semen thrown at him, or being spat upon or bitten by an HIV infected inmate, were capable of leading to transmission of infection. However, the evidence indicated that hepatitis B could be transmitted through 'casual contact'. The Board concluded that hepatitis B, but not AIDS, constituted a danger to correctional officers. The employer was directed to offer correctional officers vaccination against Hepatitis B and to counsel all correctional officers on the danger of contracting the disease.

## PREVENTIVE MEASURES FOR PRISONERS

In an attempt to prevent transmission of HIV in the prison setting, the National Advisory Committee on AIDS,[118] the Royal Society of Canada,[119] and the Parliamentary Ad Hoc Committee on AIDS[120] each recommended that condoms be made available to inmates of Canadian prisons. However, in most Canadian prisons it was not until 1992 that condoms became available. Two reasons were usually given for the long-standing policy against condom distribution. First, concern was voiced that condoms would be used for smuggling and storage of contraband, and that the maintenance of security and order in the institutions would be endangered. Second, it was argued that providing condoms to offenders would be perceived as implementing contradictory policies, since sexual activity in prison is prohibited.

---

117 Walton v. Treasury Board (Correctional Services Canada) (1987), 16 C.C.E.L. 190 (P.S.S.R.B.).

118 National Advisory Committee on AIDS: Statement Concerning Correctional Settings. This statement was prepared by the Working Group on HIV Infection and Injection Drug Use of the National Advisory Committee on AIDS, and approved by the Committee on 14 December 1989. The statement is published as an Appendix in Confronting a Crisis: The Report of the Parliamentary Ad Hoc Committee on AIDS, op. cit., n. 44.

119 Royal Society of Canada, AIDS: A Perspective for Canadians. Summary Report and Recommendations (1988; Royal Society of Canada) 17 (recommendation 27).

120 Op. cit., n. 44, pp. 46-54 (recommendation 38).

In federal penitentiaries, condoms were made available on 1 January 1992. Each penitentiary has established its own system for making them available. These range from distributing condoms to every inmate and leaving supplies of them in living units in some institutions, to restricting distribution of them to prison health care services. Dental dams are also being made available to female inmates.

Some provinces, including Alberta, British Columbia and Quebec, also started distributing condoms in 1992. In the Northwest Territories and in Yukon, condoms have been made available to prisoners for several years. According to information received in the autumn of 1992, Manitoba was considering the issue, and in Ontario an announcement that condoms would be made available to prisoners was expected soon. In Saskatchewan, condoms are made available to an inmate only when he or she is approved for conjugal visits and requests condoms. In Newfoundland, Nova Scotia, Prince Edward Islands, and New Brunswick condoms are not made available. These provinces argue that since the average length of stay in provincial institutions is only 30 days, prisoners are less likely to engage in sexual relations and that condom distribution is therefore not necessary. However, it is not the duration of incarceration which should determine condom availability but sexual activity of inmates within prisons.

In federal penitentiaries, as in the provincial systems where condoms have been made available, 'finding the best distribution channels and encouraging condom use remain problems, even when the principle of availability is accepted'.[121]

The provision of bleach and of clean needles is not mentioned in any of the policies. However, bleach is made available to inmates as a general cleansing agent in some institutions, for example in British Columbia, the Yukon, Nova Scotia, and the Newfoundland and Labrador Youth Corrections. Bleach is not officially available to inmates in federal penitentiaries. However, some inmates may have covert access to bleach in laundries or kitchens.

Since it is unrealistic to believe that injection drug use and tattooing in prisons will stop, reducing the risk of contracting infections through these activities has to be an immediate priority. One solution would be to make bleach officially available to prisoners. This has been widely recommended in Canada. However, simply providing access to bleach is insufficient - a 'band-aid' approach - unless accompanied by increased efforts to educate prisoners about the potential harms from needle sharing and drug use, and to make treatment more accessible to prisoners who need it. Another possible solution, although very controversial, would be to make clean needles and tattooing equipment available in prisons. Some injection drug users have stated that the only time they ever shared needles was during imprisonment and that they would not otherwise share needles.[122] In 1991, the Minister of National Health and Welfare suggested that clean needles or bleach to clean needles be made available to inmates in federal penitentiaries. However, at the time, the Solicitor General of Canada rejected this suggestion. Providing sterile needles or even bleach in prisons is often rejected because it would appear, 'in an environment designed to uphold the law,

---

121 T.W. Harding and G. Schaller, 'HIV/AIDS Policy for Prisons or for Prisoners?' in *AIDS in the World*, ed. J. Mann et al. (1992), 761 at p. 767.
122 Op. cit., n. 74.

to condone illegal drug use: a contradiction in terms.'[123] There is also concern for the security of fellow prisoners and staff because it is feared that needles could be used as weapons. The executive secretary-treasurer of the Union of Solicitor-General Employees said:

A needle is a weapon. I'd hate to even think about some prisoner coming up and stabbing me, or injecting me, with his blood if it's infected. ... Whether it the needle is rusty or new hardly matters. The whole idea is ridiculous. It would be the same as giving bank robbers normal bullets so they won't use dum-dums. People talking about this aren't in the real world.[124]

On the other side, prisoners'-rights activists have rejected the contention that clean needles pose a security risk, saying that 'a prisoner wishing to use violence against a guard or another prisoner will likely utilize other already available methods, such as pencils, pens, razors, utensils, toothbrushes, etc.'[125] Making clean injection equipment available 'would probably reduce the risk by eliminating dangerous, handmade syringes that have to be hidden within the prison.'[126] Furthermore, 'if the issuing of needles was more open and protected, there would be less concern about violence and security.'[127]

In Canada and internationally, making clean drug injecting equipment available in prisons has been recommended by many individuals, groups and organizations. For example, the Canadian Association of Elizabeth Fry Societies passed a resolution at the 1991 annual general meeting supporting free needle exchange inside and outside the criminal justice system. PASAN recommended that 'a confidential needle exchange program should be implemented' in prisons.[128] It suggested that needle exchange programmes 'should be modelled after existing outside exchange programs while simultaneously protecting prisoners from harassment from prison staff and fellow prisoners'.[129] According to PASAN, needles should be exchanged through the health service in a confidential one-for-one manner and prisoners should not be accountable to non-medical staff when obtaining needles. At the same time, PASAN rejected the provision of a needle exchange machine in prisons since such machines 'can be faulty and are easily vandalized' and because using them 'poses problems for prisoners who wish to maintain their confidentiality'.[130] PASAN further suggested that 'a public relations campaign should be initiated to combat anticipated resistance by staff or the public to a needle exchange program'.[131] PASAN stated:

Needle exchange programmes on the 'outside' are becoming more common. Experience has shown us that the few opponents they encounter in the community can be overcome through consultation and education. Harm reduction is the framework in

---

123 M. Kirby, 'AIDS in Prisons in Australia' (1991) 59/4 *Medico-Legal Journal* 252 at p. 263.
124 'Guards abhors needles for inmates' *The Toronto Globe and Mail*, 5 November 1991, p. A7.
125 Op. cit., n. 28, p. 16.
126 Ibid.
127 Ibid.
128 Ibid., p. 15 (recommendation 8).
129 Ibid., p. 16.
130 Ibid.
131 Ibid., pp. 16-17 (recommendation 10).

which we promote needle exchanges to the outside community. A similar strategy should be pursued in supporting a prison exchange programme.

Information regarding drug use in the prisons and the health risks it involves should be made public. The success of needle exchanges in halting the transmission of HIV should also be conveyed. It should be noted that keeping a prisoner free of HIV and AIDS is a massive cost saving.[132]

Importantly, PASAN claimed that 'bleach provision to prisoners (in isolation from other programs around injection drug use, such as needle exchange) is not highly successful because prisoners who are injecting drugs usually feel the time and activity it takes to clean a syringe or home-made sharp could be time in which guards would detect the activity.'[133] There is therefore concern that inmates would not take the extra time to clean their injection equipment and would thus continue to share dirty needles.

However, making needles and syringes available in prisons raises many contentious and potentially divisive issues and creates fear among both inmates and staff. It is not clear whether the model developed for needle exchanges outside prisons could be adapted to prisons. Whereas the impact of needle distribution or exchange on levels of injection drug use outside prisons appears to be negligible, its impact in prisons is unknown. Security issues also have to be examined, although there is no inherent reason to believe that the needles that would be made available would be more dangerous than those already present in institutions. While it will be inevitable to make needles and syringes available in prisons, it is probably not feasible to make them available at this time. The reason for this is not that making them available might be unacceptable to prison authorities, staff, inmates or the pubic, but that how to make them available in a safe and confidential manner is not known. Research is therefore urgently needed on this issue.

## MEDICAL CARE

CSC claims that the quality of care in federal correctional institutions is on par with the rest of the country.[134] In 1988, CSC's Health Care Branch adopted national standards for health care 'to ensure that offenders receive up-to-date care throughout their sentences, care which is comparable to that available in the community.'[135] These standards 'must be considered when programs are being developed and delivered,'[136] and include, among others:[137]

Standard 101:

Informed consent of a mentally competent offender shall be obtained before commencing a treatment programme and such an offender shall have the right to refuse treatment.

Standard 110:

---

132 Ibid., p. 17.
133 Ibid., p. 33.
134 'Health Care Services' *Let's Talk*, June 1992, p. 8.
135 Ibid.
136 Correctional Service Canada, Standards for Health Care (1989), 4.
137 Ibid., pp. 5-25.

Any research which involves offenders as subjects, shall be approved by a research review committee. This committee shall ensure that all research meets the highest ethical standards and has proper design and supervision. Offender participation shall be contingent upon voluntary and informed written consent.

Standard 201:
The Correctional Service of Canada shall ensure the provision of a range of health services for offenders including mental health and general health care. Services shall be available at a primary, intermediate and intensive or tertiary service level.
Criteria
(1) Primary level of services shall be provided on an ambulatory basis to offenders who remain in general population.
(2) Intermediate level of service shall be a specialized programme delivered in a dedicated living space within a regular institutional setting.
(3) Intensive/tertiary level of service refers to in-patient beds in a facility designated under mental health legislation or to in-patient beds in a general hospital.

Standard 203:
Offenders shall have access to health services on a 24-hour basis.
Criteria
(1) Clustering of all services, where proximity of institutions allows for cost effective use of it, shall be implemented.
(2) Where 24-hour nursing coverage is not provided on-site, staff with basic first aid and cardio-pulmonary resuscitation (CPR) training will be on duty.
(3) Nursing services shall be provided 24 hours per day in institutions where in-patients are cared for (Intermediate level).

Standard 208:
Referrals to outside agencies for consultation, treatment and surgery shall be for essential services. Essential services can be categorized as emergency, urgent or non-urgent.
Criteria
(1) Emergency: a case where delay will endanger the life of the offender.
(2) Urgent: the condition is likely to deteriorate to an emergency or it is interfering with the offender's ability to carry out his or her activities of daily living.
(3) Non-urgent: the condition is not affecting the offender's activities of daily living now, but may in the future.

Standard 301:
Assessment of all offenders' health status shall be completed on admission.
The Correctional and Conditional Release Act also emphasizes health, safety and personal dignity. Further, it prohibits any treatment that is cruel or degrading and seeks to ensure that standards comply with United Nations treaties and the Canadian Charter of Rights and Freedoms. The relevant provisions of the Act read as follows:
86.(1) The Service shall provide every inmate with

(a) essential health care; and

(b) reasonable access to non-essential mental health care that will contribute to the inmate's rehabilitation and successful reintegration into the community.

(2) The provision of health care under subsection (1) shall conform to professionally accepted standards.

87. The Service shall take into consideration an offender's state of health and health care needs:

(a) in all decisions affecting the offender, including decisions relating to placement, transfer, administrative segregation and disciplinary matters; and

(b) in the preparation of the offender for release and the supervision of the offender.

With regard to treatment, s. 88 of the Act provides that offenders must give their informed consent to any treatment, have the right to refuse treatment, and may participate in research projects, but only if they give informed consent to do so and if an independent committee has reviewed the case and approved the project.

In accordance with these provisions and the above standards, every inmate entering the federal prison system goes through a thorough health assessment. This includes screening for tuberculosis. Inmates are also offered hepatitis-B vaccination.

Provincial prison policies on HIV/AIDS are generally silent on the topic of medical care. Only Ontario's and Newfoundland's policies comment that prisoners have the right to receive adequate medical care. Alberta's policy specifically provides that HIV positive offenders with opportunistic infections should be registered with and under clinical supervision of the local STD clinic or infectious diseases unit of a hospital. No policy refers to the provision of drug treatment programmes or to access to experimental HIV/AIDS therapies.

Prisoners with HIV infection have sometimes complained that they have not received adequate medical care:

The prisoners with HIV/AIDS know that, without the specialized medical attention which they will not receive in a Canadian prison, they are facing terrible suffering.[138]

PASAN has recommended that 'prisoners with HIV/AIDS must be guaranteed access to medical and dental workers of their choice', and that 'they must have access to experienced and expert HIV primary care physicians.'[139] Further, it has been suggested that a comprehensive plan for the medical and psychosocial care of prisoners with HIV infection should be developed and that prison populations be included in research on new treatments of HIV infection and AIDS.

While these suggestions and recommendations address some of the immediate needs of infected prisoners, the underlying problem remains: namely, prisoners' distrust with regard to prison health care services. In Canada, as in most other countries, prison health services are an integral part of, and those who provide them are responsible to, the prison system. They are often perceived by prisoners to lack independence and confidentiality. Micheal Linhart, a prisoner with HIV infection, stated:

---

138 Op. cit., n. 109, p. 85.

139 Op. cit., n. 28, p. 5.

Any prisoner who has served a few years in a prison will tell you that health care is a primary concern among prisoners. We need to feel that we are being provided with competent and knowledgeable medical services. Often in prescribing medications to prisoners, doctors seem to follow a set of administrative procedures and policies outlining the types of medications given to prisoners. I know of many cases where doctors were about to prescribe a medication for a prisoner only to be told by the nurse in attendance that inmates are not allowed to have that drug in this institution. To myself, and many other prisoners, this seems to indicate that institutional policy is dictating to the doctor the type of medical attention they may render.[140]

In at least one provincial institution in Quebec, health care is provided by an outside community clinic. Demands to apply such a model are increasingly made in many countries and at the international level. In an article which recently appeared in *Le Monde Diplomatique*, it was stated that HIV/AIDS would force prison administrations to transfer the costly and over-burdened prison health care services to the community.[141]

In Canada, the Parliamentary Ad Hoc Committee on AIDS recommended that the advantages of prison health care services being provided by outside agencies should be further studied.[142]

One issue related to medical care is that of drug use and its treatment. A Correctional Service Canada Task Force on Substance Abuse recently completed a two year study to design a national substance abuse programme strategy for the next five years. Studies included research on drug offenders, existing treatment programmes and the need for community after-care services. The review of more than 170 substance abuse programmes showed there was need to revise and upgrade drug treatment services for prisoners. Correctional Service Canada is now in the process of implementing programmes based on these recommendations.[143]

DISCUSSION

Initially, responding to the problem of HIV/AIDS in Canadian prisons was slow. Only small steps were made to develop policies and to provide educational programmes for staff and prisoners. As a result, many questioned whether the prison systems in Canada were taking the issue seriously. For example, the Ad Hoc Committee on AIDS stated:

'In some ways the issue of programs to prevent HIV transmission in prisons is relatively simple. The need for such programs would appear to be clear, and the measures that need to be taken are agreed upon by all the medical authorities. The prison population is literally a captive population, and prison authorities are in a position to institute whatever programs are regarded as essential for the protection of the health of inmates. Yet, on the federal level at least, they refuse; and they refuse

---

140 Op. cit., n. 92.
141 'Ce que le sida peut apprendre', *Le Monde Diplomatique*, February 1993, p. 27.
142 Op. cit., n. 44, p. 54 (recommendation 41).
143 Op. cit., n. 20, p. 8.

for reasons that only another prison administrator can presumably understand, because they are all grounded on 'correctional experience.'[144]

Concern was expressed that 'the fear of AIDS in our institutions would seriously affect the welfare of prisoners through purposeful or accidental discrimination of inmates who were HIV positive or who had AIDS.'[145] In particular, it was feared that prisoners with HIV infection or AIDS would be isolated, that their rehabilitation programming would be reduced or denied, and that all prisoners would be subjected to mandatory HIV antibody testing. In addition, neither condoms nor clean needles or syringes, or bleach with which to cleanse injection equipment, were available in prisons, and education programmes for prisoners as well as for staff appeared inadequate or insufficient. Some of these concerns turned out to be unfounded - for example, from the beginning, testing for HIV antibodies has been undertaken only voluntarily and with informed consent, and prisoners with HIV infection or AIDS have usually been housed in the general prison population. There still is concern about the quality and effectiveness of educational programmes, and about the refusal to make bleach or clean needles and syringes available to prisoners. This recently prompted PASAN to say that, 'after more than 10 years of the AIDS crisis, there has yet to be an adequate governmental response to the effects of the crisis in prisons', and that 'because of this neglect, inmates are being infected with HIV during their incarceration and prisoners with HIV/AIDS are suffering from worsening health and are needlessly dying.'[146]

The common reply to early criticism of government inaction was that medical recommendations had to be balanced with correctional concerns. Many of the complex problems HIV/AIDS raises in prisons derive from the perceived conflict between public health and law enforcement. Correction is a public safety (law enforcement) rather than a public health activity.[147] Prison life is not organized on the basis of care, but of coercion. Coercion occurs where measures are compulsory rather than voluntary. Outside the prison setting, it has long been recognized that coercive interventions are counter-productive in controlling HIV transmission and its consequences; that effective HIV/AIDS interventions need to be based on respect for persons and their rights and dignity; and that personal responsibility has to be encouraged. Prevention of disease and the provision of medical care in prisons, however, require reconciling or balancing a medical model of prevention, diagnosis, care and treatment with the correctional requirements of custody, control, and punishment.[148] The punitiveness inherent in the prison system, and security concerns, have often been seen as obstacles to effective prevention of HIV/AIDS in prisons. In response to this, there is a persuasive argument that, because HIV has such devastating consequences, contradictions resulting from making condoms and bleach or clean needles available in prisons when both sexual activity and drug use are prohibited,

---

144 Op. cit., n. 44, p. 46.

145 Submission to ECAP received from James M. MacLatchie, Executive Director, The John Howard Society of Canada, dated 5 October 1992.

146 Op. cit., n. 28, p. 9.

147 T.F. Brewer, 'HIV in Prisons - The Pragmatic Approach' (1991), 5 AIDS 897.

148 N. Neveloff Dubler *et al.*, 'Management of HIV Infection in New York State Prisons' (1990), 21 Columbia Human Rights Law Review 363 at p. 365.

should be tolerated.[149] Furthermore, since offenders are imprisoned as punishment and not for punishment, governments and prison administrators have the duty to face up to the risks of the spread of HIV infection.[150]

The promotion of health in prisons does not necessarily entail lessening of the safety and the security of prisons; what have often been perceived as conflicting interests between prisoners on one side and staff and correctional authorities on the other, are compatible interests. Indeed, promotion of health in the prison population and the education of both prisoners and staff may be the best ways to create safety and security.[151] In particular, there may be no real conflict between the needs of prisoners and the needs of prison staff with respect to HIV/AIDS.[152] The establishment of a dialogue between prisoners and staff, and between community groups and the prison system, is important, because any measure undertaken to prevent transmission of HIV in prisons must be acceptable to prisoners, to staff, to correctional authorities, and to the public. If such a dialogue were established, the concerns and fears of prisoners, as well as of staff for their safety and of prison authorities for the maintenance of safety and order in the correctional environment, could be addressed and made understandable to the parties involved.

In Canada, this dialogue was started at the 6th Annual British Columbia AIDS Conference. At a session dedicated to HIV/AIDS in prisons, representatives of CSC and the British Columbia Corrections Branch, as well as a prisoner with HIV infection, a representative of a community group involved in needle and syringe exchange, and people working in prisons or with an interest in the issues, presented the issues raised by HIV/AIDS in prisons. Instead of offering only 'easy solutions', the presentations and the ensuing debate centred on what can and should be done to make changes possible and acceptable. This session was organized by the Expert Advisory Committe on AIDS ('ECAP'). This Committee was created by the Solicitor General of Canada on 15 June 1992. The Committee's goal is to assist the federal government in promoting and protecting the health of inmates and of staff, and preventing transmission of HIV and other infectious agents in federal correctional institutions. The Committee has visited many institutions, received submissions from a variety of interested parties, and surveyed inmates' and staff's attitudes, opinions and suggestions about how to resolve some of the issues raised in this article.[153]

In conclusion, while it is true that much remains to be done in Canada to resolve the many issues raised by HIV/AIDS and drug use in the prison system, there are encouraging signs that the issue of HIV/AIDS is being taken seriously by correctional authorities:

---

149 Ibid.

150 Ibid.

151 Op. cit., n. 28, p. 3.

152 Ibid.

153 HIV/AIDS and Prisons: A Working Paper of the Expert Committee on AIDS and Prisons was released in June 1993. The Working Paper has been prepared for the Committee by the author of this article, and some of its chapters have been adapted from this article. However, the Working Paper addresses many of the issues addressed in this article in much greater detail. A final report of the Committee will be available in the autumn of 1993.

Policies that discourage segregation of HIV positive individuals, policies which provide condoms to prisoners to prevent HIV transmission, and policies which facilitate the implementation of educational interventions for both inmates and guards are all in the right direction.[154]

Canada has a unique opportunity to act to reduce the harm from HIV/AIDS in prisons. Rates of infection are still relatively low in prisons, particularly when compared with those of many other industrialized countries. Needle exchanges have been established in all major Canadian cities at a time when rates of infection among injection drug users were still relatively low. They have been successful in reducing the spread of HIV infection among injection drug users, and in providing them with education and in facilitating access to numerous support services. Since injection drug users constitute by far the largest group of infected inmates, the work of needle exchanges has probably been the major contribution to prevention of the spread of HIV infection in prisons. Needle exchanges, including the education, counselling, access to treatment and advocacy they provide, deserve to receive recognition for this, and the support, both financial and political, that they need to continue their work. Further, it should be acknowledged that interventions which can reduce both the incidence of HIV infection in prisons and the harms deriving from this infection are not, and cannot, be limited to the prison setting. Many prisoners spend years of their lives getting in and out of prisons. Prevention and support services are essential to protect prisoners' health inside and outside prisons; and prisoners should be able to use such services both in prisons and outside.

Finally, some of the underlying issues also need to be addressed. It should at least be questioned whether it is necessary and advisable to send to prison many of the people who are convicted of using drugs, thereby shifting the responsibility of dealing with drug use and the harms deriving from it from society to the prison system. One consequence of this policy is that prisons have to deal with an increasing number of HIV infected injection drug users. It has been pointed out that:

Canada has the dubious honour of having the highest number of drug arrests per capita of any nation other than the US; with respect to drug legislation and enforcement it has recently been described as having 'a bite worse than its bark'.[155]

Of the participants in the seroprevalence study in the women's prison in Montreal, nearly 50 per cent reported injection drug use prior to incarceration.[156] Another study, of injection drug users, found that 81 per cent of participants had been imprisoned in the past.[157]

One can foresee that the re-evaluation of drug laws and enforcement practices will become increasingly urgent, and indeed necessary.[158]

---

154 Op. cit., n. 43.

155 Riley, *op. cit.*, n. 56, citing from R. MacCoun *et al.*, 'What Harms do Harm Reduction Strategies Reduce? A Cross-National Study of Heroin Addiction' (1992), paper presented at the Third International Conference on the Reduction of Drug Related Harm, Melbourne, March 1992.

156 Op. cit., n. 36.

157 Op. cit., n. 74.

158 The views presented in this paper are the author's personal views, and not the views of the organizations he is working for.

The author wishes to thank Norbert Gilmore for his helpful comments and his criticism.

# AIDS IN PRISONS IN THE USA

THEODORE M. HAMMETT, LYNNE HARROLD, ANDREA NEWLYN
AND SAIRA MOINI
*Abt Associates Inc.,*
*Cambridge, Mass.*

HIV infection and AIDS remain extremely difficult and complex public health problems in the United States of America and also worldwide. In the first 11 years of AIDS (1981-1992), almost 250,000 cases were reported to the US Centers for Disease Control and Prevention (CDC). Over 47,000 of these cases (19 per cent) were reported during 1992. Although the epidemic appears to be abating slightly among gay men in the United States, it is still accelerating among injecting drug users (IDUs) and their sexual partners. Injecting drug users are of primary concern when we consider prisons and jails. Data collected by Abt Associates Inc. for the US Department of Justice and the Centers for Disease Control and Prevention reveal that, as of November 1992-March 1993, a total of 11,565 cases of AIDS had been reported among inmates in the federal prison system, all 50 state departments of correction, and a sample of large city and county jail systems. This figure represented 5 per cent of all adult cases reported to the CDC through December 1992. HIV/AIDS is a major policy and management issue for correctional administrators in the United States. Prisons and jails are a focus of public concern about HIV disease. This is due to perceptions that these institutions hold high concentrations of individuals at risk for HIV infection as a result of prior injecting drug use and that inmates frequently engage in behaviours associated with transmission of HIV particularly homosexual activity and needle sharing. There is also continuing concern among correctional officers and other staff about occupational HIV infection, although such fears have abated since peaking in the period 1987-1988.

In May 1987, a CDC report that three health care workers had been infected with HIV apparently through surface exposures sparked concern for a time about the possibility of 'casual' transmission. However, all three cases in fact involved either blood-to-blood or blood-to-mucous membrane contact which had previously been established as routes of transmission. Additionally, as the number of cases of HIV infection and AIDS increases among prisoners, the cost of medical care escalates. This has become a problem of serious proportions for many already financially pressed correctional systems.

Finally, the resurgence of tuberculosis, which is closely related to HIV infection, and particularly the frightening appearance in several prison systems of multi-drug resistant tuberculosis, has raised new issues regarding infection control and health care costs.

## CORRECTIONAL SYSTEMS IN THE UNITED STATES

As of the end of 1991, there were over 800,000 men and women in prisons in the United States and probably close to 500,000 more in jails. The American system of government comprises multiple levels of authority, three of which are of primary interest in examining correctional issues: federal, state, and city/county. Correctional systems at each level of government make their own policy pursuant, of course, to statutory and regulatory requirements and constitutional and other legal mandates, as interpreted by the courts. As a result, one finds a broad diversity of correctional policy and practice on many issues.

The Federal Bureau of Prisons, the national government's prison system, operates institutions all over the country. These institutions house persons convicted of violating federal laws. As of 1990, there were 65,000 federal prisoners, the majority of whom had been convicted of drug law violations, bank robbery, and various types of fraud and 'white collar' crimes. Most violent, property, and drug-related crime is prosecuted under state law. All 50 states maintain their own correctional systems, which vary tremendously in size. California now has more than 100,000 prisoners while North Dakota has less than 500. City and county jails hold persons charged with state violations who, if convicted, will be sent to state prisons, as well as persons who have been convicted of minor street crimes and other offences.

Until quite recently, the federal prison population looked quite different from the inmate population of state prisons and city/county jails. The federal prison population was dominated by white-collar offenders, while state and county prisoners were primarily street criminals. However, the upsurge in drug offences and drug prosecutions beginning in the 1980s has landed many more street drug offenders in federal prisons, so the demographic and socio-economic profiles of correctional populations at the different levels of government have grown more similar.

Overcrowding is an extremely serious problem in US prisons and jails. The public call for tougher sentencing has resulted in burgeoning prison populations, but the public's willingness to pay for new facilities to house these offenders has not kept pace with higher incarceration rates and longer sentences. The combined federal and state prison population grew from 329,000 in 1980 to 823,000 in 1991 - an increase of 150 per cent. As of the end of 1991, 36 state prison systems were operating at or above capacity (rates over capacity ranged from 16 per cent to 31 per cent). The Federal Bureau of Prisons was operating at 46 per cent over capacity. Inmate programmes, health care and psychosocial services - never adequate in the best of times - all suffer even more when institutions are overcrowded. Overcrowding also exacerbates tensions among inmates and between inmates and staff. Notably, as well, overcrowding makes supervision and control more difficult, thus increasing opportunities for high risk behaviours to occur.

Inmate populations in the United States have, for many years, contained large numbers of substance abusers. This proportion became even larger in the 1980s as drug use and drug enforcement intensified. The US Department of Justice's Drug Use Forecasting (DUF) programme tests arrestees in 24 major American cities for evidence of recent drug use. Of course, not all arrestees go to prison. However, it is probably safe to assume that the arrestee population and prisoner population are similar. DUF statistics from the second quarter of 1991 reveal that the percentage of male arrestees who tested positive to any illicit drug (opiates, cocaine, marijuana, amphetamines, or PCP) ranged from 39 per cent in Indianapolis (Indiana) to 79 per cent in Manhattan (New York City). The range for female booked arrestees was similar, although the positions of the cities were somewhat different: from 39 per cent in San Antonio (Texas) to 78 per cent in Cleveland (Ohio). Cocaine (which includes 'crack') was the most prevalently used drug among arrestees. Opiate use was less prevalent but still significant in some cities. Clearly, there are large numbers of persons with histories of illicit drug use in inmate populations and, in many correctional systems, drug users constitute solid majorities of all prisoners.

The indicators of crowding, drug use, and budgetary constraints, among other things, suggest the problems afflicting American correctional systems. As these problems worsen, and resources allocated to address them fall farther and farther behind need, correctional facilities increasingly become simply warehouses whose primary function is to 'keep the lid on' and move people in and out. All hope of rehabilitation is lost, and the correctional environment becomes an incubator of further criminal behaviour rather than a force to reduce crime. HIV/AIDS is really only a piece of a larger picture of a system stretched to the absolute limit.

## HIV INFECTION AND AIDS IN AMERICAN PRISONS AND JAILS

The Data in the 1992 survey conducted by Abt Associates Inc. for the US Department of Justice and the Centers for Disease Control and Prevention (individual responses prepared between November 1992 and March 1993) revealed a cumulative total of 11,565 inmate AIDS cases since initial reporting of the disease in 1981. Of these, 8,525 cases were among inmates in 49 state and federal correctional systems. In addition, 31 large city and county jail systems reported a cumulative total of 3,040 cases of AIDS among inmates. As for current cases, the 1992 survey revealed 3,035 among state and federal inmates in 45 systems and 395 among city and county inmates in 25 large jail systems. Due to incomplete, inconsistent and under reporting, these should be considered low-end estimates. The survey was completed by correctional administrators who may have an interest in under reporting the problem. Prisoner advocacy groups and correctional 'watchdog' organizations, such as the Correctional Association of New York, feel strongly that there are many more cases of HIV disease in prisons than are reported by correctional officials. No cases of occupationally acquired HIV infection or AIDS have been documented among US correctional staff, although one such case has been reported in Australia.

Cumulative total inmate AIDS cases in the United States have increased by over 1,400 per cent since the first Abt/NIJ survey was completed in 1985 and 66 per cent since the sixth survey in 1990. As shown in Table I, (overpage), between 1990 and 1992-1993, - the increase in total US correctional cases (66 per cent) slightly exceeded the increase in cases in the population at large (64 per cent). Nineteen ninety-two survey data regarding demographics and exposure categories of AIDS cases are incomplete. However, studies performed by individual correctional systems suggest that demographic and risk factor patterns among prisoners with HIV infection and AIDS have remained stable. Inmate cases are primarily male, blacks and Hispanics are over-represented relative to the outside population, and injecting drug use is the predominant exposure category.

TABLE 1

CUMULATIVE TOTAL AIDS CASES AMONG CORRECTIONAL INMATES
AND THE POPULATION AT LARGE, US
1985 - 1992/1993

| | Correctional Cases[a] | | Cases in Total US Population[b] | |
|---|---|---|---|---|
| | Number of Cases | Per cent Increase from Preceding Survey[c] | Number of Cases | Per cent Increase from Preceding Survey[d] |
| November 1985 | 766 | N/A | 14,519 | N/A |
| October 1986 | 1,232 | 61 per cent | 26,002 | 79 per cent |
| October 1987 | 1,964 | 59 per cent | 41,770 | 61 per cent |
| October 1988[e] | 3,136 | 60 per cent | 73,621 | 76 per cent |
| October 1989[f] | 5,411 | 72 per cent | 110,333 | 50 per cent |
| October 1990[g] | 6,985 | 29 per cent | 152,231 | 38 per cent |
| November 1992 March 1993[h] | 11,565 | 66 per cent | 249,199 | 64 per cent |

a    The figures in this and other tables represent inmate AIDS cases in the federal prison system, all 50 state prison systems, and a *sample* of 28-37 city and county jail systems (depending on the year of the NIJ Survey).

b    Adult/adolescent cases only. Paediatric cases excluded.

c    In most cases, the column presents the difference between the number of cases in the given year and the number in the period from October 1990 through November 1992-March 1993.

d    As with the correctional cases, the per cent reflects the change from the preceding survey. In most cases, this is a one-year interval. However, the per cent increase for November 1992 through March 1993 reflects a two-year interval.

e    Figures for 1988 include 28 city/county jail systems.

f    Figures for 1989 include 32 city/county jail systems.

g    Figures for 1990 include 27 city/county jail systems.

h    Figures for 1992/1993 include 31 city/county systems.

Sources: CDC, *AIDS Weekly Surveillance Reports - US,* November 4, 1985, October 5, 1986, October 5, 1987, October 3, 1988; CDC, HIV/AIDS Surveillance Report,

November 1990, February 1993 (cases reported through 1992); NIJ/CDC Questionnaire Responses.

The regional distribution of cumulative total AIDS cases remains uneven, in both state and city/county systems, although less so than when the survey was first conducted in 1985. Among state systems, the Middle Atlantic states (especially New York and New Jersey) contributed 50 per cent of total cases. Among city/county jail systems, the Pacific region had 42 per cent of total AIDS cases and the Middle Atlantic region had 54 per cent of total cases. AIDS incidence rates are predictably higher in the correctional setting than in the population at large because of the higher concentration in inmate populations of individuals with histories of high risk behaviour. The annual incidence rate of AIDS for the entire US population was 18 cases per 100,000 population in 1992, while the aggregate incidence rate for State/Federal correctional systems was 362 cases per 100,000. However, there was an extremely wide range of incidence rates across correctional systems. This wide range reflects the uneven distribution of cases across systems. The aggregate AIDS incidence rate in city/county jail systems responding to the 1992 survey was 297 cases per 100,000. Here, too, there was a wide range of rates across systems. The figures for city/county jail systems are problematic, however, due to extremely high turnover in these populations.

HIV seroprevalence rates among inmates in most correctional systems are still probably lower than 1 per cent, according to available data from mass screening programmes and blind epidemiologic studies. Most high prevalence states have not undertaken mass mandatory HIV antibody screening of prisoners, but some of these jurisdictions have undertaken epidemiologic studies. Higher seroprevalence rates, mostly between 2 and 8 per cent, are found in correctional systems covering jurisdictions with larger numbers of AIDS cases in the outside population. These include California, Texas, Florida, Maryland, and Illinois. A blinded study of incoming male New York State prisoners in 1992 found an HIV seroprevalence rate of 12 per cent. A similar study found an even higher rate of 20 per cent among female prison entrants in New York State. In general, HIV seroprevalence rates are often higher among female prisoners than among male prisoners. This is probably because larger proportions of female than of male prisoners have histories of injection drug use.

Although substantial debate continues, relatively little hard data exist on the extent of HIV transmission within correctional institutions. Logic and common sense indicate, however, that even in the best-managed correctional facilities, at least some transmission of HIV is occurring among inmates. A number of facts suggest this probability. There have been outbreaks of syphilis and other sexually transmitted diseases in prison populations. Although the prevalence of sexual activity among inmates may vary widely across jurisdictions, it is undeniable that such activity occurs to some degree in virtually all prisons and jails. A study of New York City jail inmates found that 10 per cent of rectal gonococcal infections diagnosed during a two month period had been acquired after the patient entered the facility. Several other studies have found that sizable proportions of prison inmates have had homosexual contact while incarcerated. Of particular concern is the extent to which inmate sexual activity is coerced. Estimates vary widely: a Federal Bureau of Prisons report suggested that only about 1 per cent of inmates were victims of aggressive sexual acts while prisoner advocates and other observers contend that the real figure is much higher. Prison sexuality is complex, with lines between consensual and coerced activity hard to draw with precision. Some suggest that truly consensual sex cannot occur in a prison setting.

Parenteral (blood-to-blood) transmission may occur through needle sharing and tattooing. Both practices are known to occur in prisons although their prevalence is uncertain and probably varies across jurisdictions. Data from several jurisdictions (the Federal Bureau of Prisons, Maryland, Nevada, and Illinois in particular) suggest low rates of HIV transmission among inmates. Most recently, a CDC- funded blind study of male prison inmates in Illinois found that, in a sample of 2,390 male prisoners who tested HIV negative at intake, there were seven confirmed seroconversions after one year's incarceration, for a projected annual transmission rate of 0.3 per cent. This represents a low, but non-trivial, rate of transmission. The available data, in short, confirm that HIV transmission is occurring in correctional facilities, but belie the widespread perception that prisons and jails are large-scale 'breeding grounds' for HIV/AIDS.

## HIV RELATED POLICIES IN CORRECTIONAL FACILITIES

While the crisis atmosphere of 1987-1988 surrounding HIV/AIDS in American prisons and jails seems to have dissipated somewhat, the disease remains a serious issue for correctional administrators. However, concern among correctional systems has shifted significantly from short-term 'crisis' matters such as fear of casual transmission to 'long-haul' issues such as housing, programming, and medical care for prisoners with HIV disease.

Resolving these issues is often complicated by political, legal, and cost considerations. The degree to which correctional systems have addressed these complex and difficult issues with effectiveness and compassion is a matter of dispute. In the Spring of 1991, the National Commission on AIDS released a report which was sharply critical of the correctional response to HIV/AIDS in virtually all policy areas. The Commission stated that 'the situation today for many prisoners living with HIV disease is nothing if not "cruel and unusual."'... Too many correctional facilities subject inmates to a series of unnecessary, arbitrary indignities which fundamentally affect their basic human rights.' This assessment contains a good deal of truth. Conditions in many correctional facilities are horrendous, for HIV infected as well as non HIV infected prisoners. In some systems, administrators have failed to apply available resources effectively to optimize conditions. However, in many other systems, administrators, health care staff, and correctional officers have worked tirelessly to make the best of a bad situation. Although much remains to be done, some significant improvements have been made. The major policy areas in the correctional response to HIV are education and training; HIV testing and counselling; confidentiality and disclosure of inmates' HIV status; medical services; psycho-social services; housing and correctional programming; and precautionary and preventive measures. Trends and issues in these areas are summarized in the following sections.

## EDUCATION AND TRAINING

Education and training programmes still represent the cornerstone of efforts to prevent transmission of HIV infection and to reduce discrimination against people with HIV in prisons and jails, as well as in the population at large. Regrettably, there is evidence that substantial misinformation regarding the means of HIV transmission remains among correctional inmates. A 1990 study of Pennsylvania prison inmates revealed, for example, that 46 per cent believed they could become infected from eating food prepared by an HIV infected person, 44 per cent believed that transmission could occur through coughing or sneezing, and more than two-thirds said that mosquitoes and other insects transmit the virus.

According to 1992 survey data, virtually all correctional systems were offering or developing face-to-face AIDS training or educational materials for staff and inmates. There remains some unevenness in the provision of AIDS education. Two-thirds of prison and jail systems were providing face-to-face AIDS education to staff at all of their institutions, down from 85 per cent in 1990. Only about half of prison systems (57 per cent, down from 80 per cent in 1990) and jail systems (55 per cent, almost identical to the 56 per cent in 1990), were providing face-to-face training to inmates at all institutions. There continues to be a serious shortage of programmes and materials for Spanish-speaking prisoners and those with special needs, such as the hearing or visually impaired. Sixty-five per cent of responding correctional systems had at least some mandatory AIDS training for staff, while less than half (44 per cent) of the prison and jail systems had at least some mandatory education for inmates. The percentages were higher for state/federal than for city/county systems. The discrepancy regarding inmate education is probably a result of logistical problems posed by high inmate turnover in city/county jail systems. Ironically, because the high turnover may increase the risk of transmission both within and outside institutions, some form of mandatory education for every jail inmate, possibly as part of orientation or medical screening, is particularly important.

HIV/AIDS education has two basic objectives: to foster behaviour change, thus reducing HIV transmission, and to allay concerns regarding casual transmission of the virus. Inducing changes in firmly entrenched social, sexual and addictive behaviours poses serious challenges for AIDS educators and policymakers. Research is beginning to show clearly that simply providing information is insufficient. Behaviour change requires ongoing empowerment, support and reinforcement. However, the effort is worthwhile, since AIDS education has been effective in significantly changing behaviour among injecting drug users and gay men in the community. The use of peer trainers along with knowledgeable and approachable professionals will help to build credibility, a critical element in the success of AIDS training. Peer education and support programmes may be particularly useful in fostering and maintaining risk reduction among inmates. However, less than 25 per cent of state/federal systems and only 15 per cent of city/county systems have instituted such programmes.

As knowledge about HIV education increases, educational strategies become more sophisticated. Some correctional systems are moving to develop and implement more comprehensive educational strategies which may involve counselling, HIV antibody testing, ongoing support groups, drug treatment opportunities and other components. Several examples exist of consortia of community organizations that are successfully working with correctional administrations to bring such programmes to inmates. Because of the large numbers of injecting drug users and other drug abusers in prison, drug treatment programmes are a particularly important component of a comprehensive correctional response to AIDS. The 1992 survey found that only 29 per cent of inmates with histories of injection drug use were enrolled in residential drug treatment or ambulatory counselling, presumably far below the percentage of prisoners in need of such services. Some prison systems have established excellent treatment programmes but their capacity is far below need in the population.

## HIV TESTING AND COUNSELLING

Although recent European clinical data have brought controversy about the efficacy of early medical intervention, there has certainly been increasing emphasis on early identification of HIV infection. In the world outside correctional institutions, testing is generally viewed as an integral part of medical treatment. In correctional facilities, however, testing is still considered by some to be an infection control tool. But many correctional systems are now offering voluntary or on-request testing. This trend is at least in part responsive to the movement toward early therapeutic intervention. Mass screening (the mandatory testing of all inmates, all new inmates, or all releasees in the absence of clinical indications) continues to be a controversial testing policy. There was a strong trend toward mandatory mass screening in correctional facilities between 1986 and 1987 but this has since levelled off. As of November 1992-March 1993, 17 State systems and the Federal Bureau of Prisons (but no city/county systems) had mass screening policies. There had been no change in the list since 1990. The majority of jurisdictions currently conducting mass screening are small states with few inmate AIDS cases. Several state systems have discontinued policies of mandatory mass screening. Reasons have included funding shortages and the realization that mass screening was creating more problems than it was intended to solve. Because of earlier findings regarding medical intervention for asymptomatic HIV infected inmates, increasing emphasis has been placed on voluntary/on-request testing to all inmates. As of November 1992-March 1993, 53 per cent of state/federal systems and 87 per cent of responding city/county jail systems had testing policies based on a voluntary/on-request model. There is evidence that voluntary testing of inmates serves the needs of both inmates and correctional systems. Several carefully controlled studies show that voluntary testing programmes can capture a significant percentage of injecting drug users and seropositive inmates.

Appropriate and sensitive pre- and post-test counselling are also critical. According to the 1992 survey, three quarters of prison and jail systems provide individualized post-test counselling available to inmates who test HIV positive. It is particularly important that counselling sessions be seen as occasions for education and that post-test counselling be provided on an individual basis for those who have both positive and negative results.

## CONFIDENTIALITY AND DISCLOSURE OF INMATES' HIV STATUS

Policy-making regarding the confidentiality and disclosure/notification of an inmate's HIV status remains a controversial and difficult issue for correctional systems. Many states have laws protecting the confidentiality or anonymity of individuals tested for HIV antibody. While almost all prison and jail systems notify the inmate and attending physician or health care worker of an inmate's test results, only a small fraction of systems had official policies of notifying correctional officers. However, it is apparent from lawsuits filed by inmates that news of a particular inmate's HIV status travels rapidly through an institution. Breaches of confidentiality are alleged to occur frequently. Continued staff education on the low-risk nature of most staff-inmate contacts and training on following universal infection control precautions is necessary to ease staff concerns about transmission which prompt demands for widespread disclosure of inmates' HIV status. Such disclosures may, in fact, lull correctional officers into a false sense of security, leading them to believe that all infected prisoners have been identified. False negatives do occur on the antibody tests and, because of the sometimes long 'window' period between infection and appearance of antibodies, no testing programme can guarantee the identification of all HIV infected prisoners. Since disclosure has potentially serious consequences, it is essential that correctional systems adapt and enforce clear policies on the issue.

## MEDICAL SERVICES

Costs of medical care have escalated dramatically in recent years and represent a major budget item for correctional systems. In many correctional systems, the increasing numbers of prisoners with HIV disease and now tuberculosis have rendered medical care costs an even more severe financial strain. In these constrained circumstances, correctional systems are, and will continue to be, under pressure to contain medical care costs. However, cost containment should not come at the expense of reducing standards of care for HIV infected prisoners.

There have been significant advances in medical treatment of HIV infected persons. These therapeutic advances have prompted optimism that in many patients HIV infection may be manageable as a chronic disease and that life expectancy for AIDS patients may increase. Virtually all prison and jail systems reported providing zidovudine to inmates. However, not all correctional systems were providing the drug to all HIV infected inmates with CD4 (T4 cell) counts below 500 (the US government standard). Because zidovudine is an expensive drug, it may represent a serious budgetary strain for many jurisdictions.

Many of the improvements in treatment depend upon early identification and ongoing monitoring of HIV infected persons. For this reason, it is important that all correctional systems offer HIV antibody counselling and testing to all inmates on request, and regular CD4 monitoring for HIV positive prisoners. With a few exceptions prisoners have not had access to clinical trials of new HIV therapies or to any experimental drugs. This has been due, in part, to the stringent federal regulations regarding participation of prisoners in medical or behavioural research. These regulations were promulgated to end what had been a long train of often shocking abuse of prisoners in research studies.

## PSYCHOSOCIAL SERVICES

The close link between psychological and physiological health in HIV infected persons is increasingly well established. Therefore, it is critical that they be provided with a range of supportive services. Correctional and public health officials, as well as AIDS advocacy groups, have established programmes of supportive services for HIV infected prisoners in several jurisdictions. Inmates in a few systems have initiated innovative peer support services. Inmates with HIV infection and AIDS who are about to be released into the community also require important services. First, they need intensive counselling on their responsibility to notify their sexual partners of their medical status and to avoid any behaviour that may transmit infections to others. Second, pre-release planning should include notifying and referring inmates to all government benefit programmes for which they may be eligible - such as Medicaid and Supplemental Security Income (SSI). Of course, pre-releasees should also be referred to appropriate sources of hospice care, hospitalization, outpatient care, counselling, and other support services in the community.

## HOUSING AND CORRECTIONAL PROGRAMMING

There has been a clear trend in housing policy away from blanket segregation of HIV infected prisoners toward presumptive 'mainstreaming' or case-by-case determination of housing - that is, maintaining all categories of HIV infected prisoners in the general population in the absence of some particular medical, security or behavioural reason for separate housing. By 1992-1993, only five state/Federal systems were segregating (or housing separately) all AIDS patients and only two state prison systems (Alabama and Mississippi) were segregating all known asymptomatic HIV infected prisoners. Since 1990, two states have moved away from total segregation policies. Colorado now mainstreams HIV infected prisoners but all remain within one institution. As part of the settlement of a lawsuit, California established a pilot programme for selected male HIV infected prisoners in which they remained in a separate housing unit but went into the general population for programmes. Since then, California has moved still further towards mainstreaming both male and female inmates with HIV infection.

As of 1992-1993, 88 per cent of state/federal prison systems and 97 per cent of responding city/county jail systems were making housing decisions for HIV infected prisoners based on presumptive mainstreaming or case-by-case determination. The trends in housing policy for HIV infected inmates reflect a combination of factors. Both presumptive general population housing and case-by-case decision making policies are more in accordance with offender classification schemes, which may be overridden when systems decide to base housing decisions solely on HIV status. Other factors include a less fearful and more compassionate attitude on the part of inmates and staff towards individuals with HIV disease, increased costs of hospitalizing inmates, and class action lawsuits filed by segregated inmates. Segregated prisoners generally have only severely restricted, if any, access to institutional programming and recreational activities. However, most HIV infected persons, and even many with AIDS diagnoses, are able to lead perfectly normal lives for long periods. It can be very damaging psychologically to be isolated from one's peers. Less restrictive housing also follows the realization among correctional systems that, due to the increasing numbers of inmates with HIV disease, segregation/separation may be impractical and unfeasible, as well as unjustly discriminatory.

## PRECAUTIONARY AND PREVENTIVE MEASURES

Correctional systems continue to face the challenge of protecting their staff and inmates from HIV infection without raising suspicions or exacerbating fears through extreme precautionary measures. To address the issue, correctional agencies have instituted a wide range of precautionary measures to control the spread of AIDS within institutions.

While most systems have instituted infection control measures to help staff and inmates protect themselves, only five have taken the much more controversial step of making condoms available to inmates in institutions. Virtually all correctional systems have established some infection control policies in response to the HIV epidemic. In 1989, the US Centers for Disease Control released guidelines for the prevention of HIV transmission to health care and public safety workers, including correctional officers. These guidelines encourage institutions to tailor their infection control procedures to their unique needs, within the framework of 'universal precautions' - i.e., treating all persons as if they are infected.

Precautionary measures should always be commensurate with the risk involved. Obviously, correctional personnel cannot predict with certainty when they will encounter blood or body fluids in the course of their duties. Many situations involve the potential for such contact. Staff members must exercise their professional judgement in using gloves, CPR masks, infectious waste receptacles or other protective devices. Precautionary measures addressing very rare or casual modes of contact, even if implemented in a good faith effort to reduce the fears of staff and inmates, may ultimately increase those fears by encouraging the view that HIV infection is transmitted by unusual or casual contact. Such a conflict between educational messages and practical measures may not only increase fear within the institution, but also foster suspicion of the correctional system for, in effect, saying one thing about the transmission of HIV but doing something else. Hence, correctional systems should be extremely cautious in adopting precautionary measures beyond those recommended by CDC. An example of such a policy commonly in effect in correctional facilities is to bar HIV infected prisoners from work assignments in food service.

The issue of condom availability in correctional institutions continues to evoke argument. Only six US correctional systems - those in the states of Vermont and Mississippi, the District of Columbia, and the cities of New York, Philadelphia, and San Francisco - make condoms available to inmates while in the institutions. In these systems, condoms are dispensed either through medical staff (with counselling) or at institutional canteens. Most correctional officials continue to believe that making condoms available, in effect, condones conduct that is prohibited by correctional regulations and, perhaps, by state law as well. By contrast, the few systems that make condoms available have essentially acknowledged that sexual activity occurs in correctional facilities despite its prohibition and determined that the importance of preventing HIV transmission outweighs any appearance of 'condoning' proscribed activity. These systems emphasize that they are not condoning the conduct, but rather taking what they believe to be a reasonable step to help inmates protect themselves against a deadly disease.

No American correctional systems make bleach or clean needles available to prisoners, and it is highly unlikely that any systems will establish such policies in the future. However, educational programmes for inmates in some systems include information about cleaning injection material, and household bleach and other cleaning agents are present in the institutions. Correctional staff have noticed that these agents tend to disappear with some frequency.

## LEGAL ISSUES

Since 1985, AIDS-related issues have produced substantial litigation involving correctional inmates and staff. Most cases have been filed in United States District Courts, although some have been filed in state and county courts as well. Several major cases are moving toward decision or settlement. Recent developments include the first successful challenges to correctional systems' policies on segregation, medical care and AIDS education. Most of these cases ended in settlements providing for significant changes in the correctional system's policies. Few of these dispositions resulted from court decisions. Indeed, courts have almost invariably upheld the policies of correctional systems - whether those policies provided for mandatory or voluntary testing, segregation or mainstreaming of HIV infected prisoners. Courts seem to take the implicit position that correctional systems are best positioned to make policy and should have the flexibility to do that, within very broadly defined constitutional limits.

The main types of cases brought by inmates have involved challenges to mandatory HIV antibody testing and to segregation and conditions of confinement for persons with HIV infection or AIDS. Lawsuits also include allegations of inadequate medical care for persons with AIDS, breaches of confidentiality, and inadequate AIDS education. In Walker v. Sumner, the US Ninth Circuit Court of Appeals denied the state correctional department's request for summary judgement, ruling instead that the Nevada system had provided no evidence that its mandatory testing policy served a legitimate penological interest (the precedential standard).

On the other hand, in a decision substantially affirmed by the US Circuit Court of Appeals, a US District Court upheld the state's policy of mandatory testing and segregation in Harris v. Thigpen, a case brought by Alabama inmates. The plaintiffs also alleged that the medical care provided to prisoners with HIV infection and AIDS was inadequate. The District Court held that the state's policies represented reasonable measures taken in pursuit of a legitimate penological interest and that the right of uninfected prisoners to be protected from potential exposure to HIV infected prisoners outweighed the claims of the latter group to be free from discrimination on the basis of their HIV status. The Circuit Court of Appeals essentially upheld the lower court's rejection of plaintiffs' challenge to the testing and segregation policies. However, the Appeals Court remanded for rehearing the plaintiffs' claim that the Federal Rehabilitation Act barred their blanket exclusion from programmes. The rehearing on this issue, as well as an appeal of the overall decision to the US Supreme Court, are currently pending. A California case, Gates v. Deukmejian, challenged the state's policy of segregating all HIV infected prisoners in a locked unit at a correctional medical facility. As noted above, the settlement of this case provided for a one-year pilot project in which 20-30 HIV infected inmates lived in a separate but not closed unit of the institution and participated with general population inmates in all programmes and activities. Following successful implementation of the pilot programme, the California correctional system has moved to expand access to programmes and, ultimately, mainstream housing for prisoners with HIV.

Settlements in Connecticut cases resulted in the termination of the state's policy of permanently segregating all prisoners with AIDS diagnoses, and initiation of sweeping improvements in medical and psychosocial services for prisoners with HIV disease and in HIV education for prisoners and staff. A major lawsuit challenging the quality of care provided to New York State inmates with HIV remains pending. Several cases seeking expanded testing, disclosure of results, and restrictions on HIV seropositive prisoners are also pending.

Many correctional systems are justifiably concerned about their potential liability should HIV infections occur among inmates while incarcerated and among staff while on the job. Such cases would face serious proof problems given the difficulty in linking infection with a particular episode. However, the most important actions correctional systems can take to minimize potential liability and maximize safety in their institutions are to intensify efforts to prevent sexual victimization of inmates and provide all inmates and staff with clear and complete education and training on how to avoid becoming infected with HIV.

CONCLUSION

AIDS continues to pose complex and difficult problems for correctional systems, their inmates and staff. The only certainty is that these problems will not go away. With accumulating experience and information, many correctional systems are developing fairer and more reasonable policy responses to AIDS. But this remains an evolutionary process. Correctional administrators and policymakers need up-to-date information on policy options and programmatic experience to continue the refinement and improvement of their HIV/AIDS policies. Ultimately, the humanity of a nation's response to HIV must be judged by how it treats its most despised and outcast citizens. Prisoners provide a good test case. As of this writing, we must conclude that the jury is still out.